Library Displays Handbook

Mark Schaeffer

The H. W. Wilson Company

NEW YORK

1991

Library of Congress Cataloging-in-Publication Data
Schaeffer, Mark.
  Library displays handbook / Mark Schaeffer.
    p. cm.
  Includes bibliographical references.
  ISBN 0–8242–0801–3
  1. Library exhibits—Handbooks, manuals, etc. 2. Public relations—Libraries—Handbooks, manuals, etc. I. Title.
  Z717.S3 1990 1991
  021.7—dc20   90–49442
                                                         CIP

**Editorial development and production by
Visual Education Corporation, Princeton, N.J.**

Printed in the United States of America

Contents

Acknowledgments

I have had the help of many people in writing and illustrating this book, and I would like to thank them here.

Members of the 1989 and 1990 John Cotton Dana Library Public Relations Award Committee of the American Library Association offered valuable advice throughout the book's development. Their comments, plus those of many other librarians I spoke to, helped define the content and tone of the book.

My friends at Visual Education Corporation edited, designed, and produced the book for The H. W. Wilson Company. They demonstrated extraordinary patience, flexibility, and creativity in handling this far-from-routine project.

In producing the displays that appear in chapters 6 through 9, I had enormous help from Fred Slater and Amanda Taylor. The photographs are by Valrie Massey. Several of the line drawings in chapter 4 (notably the cartoon faces, bodies, and hands) were executed by Amanda Taylor.

Finally, this book would not have been possible without the help of my wife and collaborator, Debra Goldentyer. She spent many hours doing research, gathering hard-to-find information and supplies, proof-reading manuscripts, and offering suggestions. The appendixes, in particular, owe much to Debra's efforts.

Mark Schaeffer

The members of the 1989 and 1990 John Cotton Dana Library Public Relations Award Committee are:

Pyddney Jones (Chairperson)
Kentucky Department for
Libraries and Archives

Charles Beard
Ingram Library
West Georgia College

Blane Dessy
Alabama Public Library Service

Floyd Dickman
State Library of Ohio

Michael Haeuser
Gustavus Adolphus College

Carol Heller
White Plains (New York) Public
Library

Marian Karpisek
Salt Lake City School District
District Media Center

John McGinnis
Cerritos (California) Community
College

Evelyn Olivier
University of Texas Health
Science Center at San Antonio

Sandra Scherber
Cromaine Library
Hartland, MI

Marilyn Shuman
Arlington Heights (Illinois)
Memorial Library

Jeanne Thorsen
King County (Washington)
Library System

Nancy Woodall
Fairfax (Virginia) County
Public Library Administration

Preface

Congratulations! If you are reading this preface, you have already taken the first steps toward effective library public relations—you have decided that PR is important to your library, and you are looking for resources that will help you improve the physical design of your library's PR program.

As members of the John Cotton Dana Library Public Relations Award Committee, we believe that an effective public relations program is vital to the success of any library—public, school, academic, or special. People today are busier than they have ever been. They are faced with an overwhelming array of activities at home, at school, and at the office, all of which compete for their limited time and money. Without a dynamic, ongoing, effectively designed public relations program to promote our services and products, libraries will simply get lost in the shuffle. Worse yet, if people don't know why we are important, the library will also be forgotten when it comes time to make funding decisions. We cannot allow this to happen. An active library public relations program that truly supports our valuable services and products is our first line of defense against budget cuts.

The John Cotton Dana Library Public Relations Award Committee is a committee of the Library Administration and Management Association of the American Library Association. Each year the committee members judge a national library public relations contest which is jointly sponsored by The H. W. Wilson Company and the ALA. Over 100 libraries from across the country submit entries, including scrapbooks, videocassettes, and other materials documenting their public relations efforts. Awards are given in two categories. The John Cotton Dana Award is for a total annual library PR program that is ongoing, sustained, and well rounded, and promotes the complete range of library services utilizing all recognized promotional outlets. It can be awarded annually to only one institution in each of the four categories of libraries—public, school, academic, and special. Each year the judges also give a number of Special Awards which recognize a discrete aspect of library public relations, promoting a program that is directed toward a specific goal and is limited in time and scope.

In looking over the entries from year to year, one fact has become very obvious: the need for libraries to present a professional-looking public relations program. Although few libraries have professional art and design experts on staff, given the proper tools, and a few tricks of the trade, anyone, even librarians in the smallest libraries, can produce high-quality material to support the institution's activities.

This book covers a vital component of library PR, visual displays, including exhibits, signs, bulletin boards, and posters. It gives practical, down-to-earth advice on developing displays and is written in clear, easy-to-understand language. It is also comprehensive and up to date. Part one gives detailed information on the techniques and materials you will need, even down to specifics such as the best type of felt marker to use in different situations. Part two gives suggestions for applying the techniques discussed in part one and provides hints for producing five different types of displays. Beginners will find many of the techniques simple to learn and easy to implement. Those with experience in developing library displays will also find a wealth of information in the new ideas and products that are featured.

Good luck in applying the knowledge you gain from this book. We on the John Cotton Dana Library Public Relations Award Committee are in public relations because we think it is both important and fun. We believe that as you become more adept in this area, you too will realize how exciting library public relations can be. You will find that your PR program opens new opportunities for you to serve your library public. Not only will you be proud of your efforts, but your patrons will be more aware of your library and the many exciting things you have to offer. Ultimately, library PR should result in both more and better-informed users of the library—and that's what the library business is all about.

Pyddney Jones, Chairperson,
and the John Cotton Dana
Library Public Relations Award
Committee

Part One: *SKILLS*

CHAPTER 1

The Power of Displays

As a librarian, you play an active role in promoting library use, and today libraries' public relations campaigns take many forms: newsletters, press releases, special events, fund raisers, even political lobbying. Among the most visible elements, however, is a renewed emphasis on visual displays such as signs, posters, and exhibits. Such displays, of course, have always been a part of the library environment (especially in elementary school libraries and in the children's section of public libraries). Since the 1960s, however, librarians have begun to realize that the sophisticated marketing techniques used on television and in the print media could be used to boost library awareness. Bold and creative displays in windows and glass cases would draw passers-by into the library. Once inside, library users could be comforted, encouraged, instructed, and entertained by inexpensive displays on walls, bulletin boards, and table tops.

There is evidence that promotion by libraries pays off. In Berkeley, California, for example, voters recently passed Proposition H—an initiative that restored library funding to its preausterity level. Around the country, growing concern about illiteracy, innumeracy, and declining educational standards has prompted communities to pledge greater support not only to their public schools but also to libraries. Advertising and public relations—including the design and production of displays—have become permanent parts of a librarian's job description.

Especially when the public is more aware of—and grateful for—its libraries, there are some compelling reasons why librarians should concern themselves with library displays:

1. *Aesthetics.* Nearly every library has built-in display spaces that should not be left empty: bulletin boards, picture windows, exhibit cases, blank walls. As long as you have to fill these spaces, it pays to do so as attractively and effectively as possible.

2. *Economics.* By attracting new library users (and encouraging current users), good displays can help to increase your library's circulation. Rising circulation figures can be a powerful argument for increased funding.

3. *Efficiency.* If library users aren't supplied with certain basic information (for example, how to find the reference section, how to use the microfilm reader), they must ask a librarian for help. Answering such basic questions by means of signs or posters will free staff time for other tasks.

4. *Enthusiasm.* Most librarians love books and appreciate the other resources of a library. It may be of concern to them that many patrons are unaware of the resources available to them. By using creative displays, the librarian can share her knowledge with library users in a direct and appealing way.

Displays are certainly not the only way to satisfy these four needs. Printed handbooks, for example, can help to increase efficiency, and periodic book talks are a good way to share enthusiasm. Visual images, however, have a special appeal that should not be neglected. When used effectively, library displays can be a very powerful tool.

THE POWER OF VISUAL APPEAL

The first five minutes a newcomer spends in your library are crucial. Within that time, a potential library user will develop a decisive first impression. If the library seems like a cold, forbidding, or confusing place, he or she will not stay very long. In contrast, if the library feels friendly and hospitable, the visitor will most likely linger and browse.

Your library has certain clear advantages over a commercial establishment, such as a shopping-mall bookstore, when it comes to attracting customers. Unlike the designers of commercial displays, who must establish a series of broad visual themes that will appeal to people all over the country, you can gear your library's image to the specific community in which you operate. Familiarity with the interests and concerns of the people you wish to attract allows you to appeal to those interests through library displays.

You also have the advantage of quality. Compared to the chain bookstores, which stock only the most popular titles, your library—even if it is small—undoubtedly has a collection of some depth and diversity. Not all of the books on your shelves may be physically attractive, but they are, for the most part, good books: classics, current books that promise to withstand the test of time, forgotten gems, off-the-beaten-track books that deserve (but have not found) a popular audience, well-thumbed reference works that most individuals have neither the money nor the inclination to buy for themselves. As any advertising expert will tell you, the first step in convincing the public that you have a better product is *to have a better product*. Once you've identified the strong points of your collection, you can use sophisticated display techniques to exploit those strong points.

CREATING DISPLAYS

The term *library displays* can be a loose one; it covers anything from a row of books on a tabletop to an elaborate, multimedia presentation. This book will use *display* a bit more narrowly, to mean a creative arrangement of visual elements designed to convey a specific message. This definition is meant to focus on the kinds of displays that encourage library users to respond thoughtfully and positively to their surroundings: signs, bulletin boards, posters, and exhibits. These kinds of displays nearly always incorporate text of some sort, and they often include illustrations or objects as well. They can be used to instruct, entertain, publicize events, draw attention to certain resources in a library, or simply create an inviting atmosphere.

Some libraries are able to hire professionals to design and produce displays. In most libraries, however, the task falls to librarians or to other members of the library staff who very well may lack the training and experience to create effective displays. Despite the almost universal need for displays in public and academic libraries, art and design techniques are rarely part of a librarian's professional skills.

There are, however, easy shortcuts that allow virtually anyone to turn out quite presentable lettering and illustrations. Some of these techniques—such as tracing or gridding—are as old as art itself. Many others, however, are fresh, new, and exciting. Technological devices that have come of age in the past ten years—personal computers, laser and ink-jet printers, high-quality photocopiers—have greatly narrowed the gap between what "talented" and "untalented" people can achieve. A trained eye and a steady hand are no longer necessary to produce attractive and sophisticated graphics.

ABOUT THIS BOOK

This book seeks to combine the best of both types of earlier books on library displays—handbooks and idea books—into one volume. It is divided into three parts: skills, ideas, and appendixes.

Part one, "Skills," is intended primarily for reference. It comprises five chapters: this introductory chapter and four chapters on design, lettering, illustration, and construction that give detailed descriptions of the techniques and equipment you will need to create professional-looking displays. With the exception of chapter 2, "Design," which takes the form of a single tutorial, the material in each chapter is arranged alphabetically. You may want to read these chapters in sequence the first time, but the alphabetical arrangement will allow you to look up specific techniques easily in the future.

You may not be able to use all of the techniques described in the skills section. Although most of the techniques are usable immediately by complete beginners, a few may require a small amount of skill, experience, or practice. You may have to rule out others because they require equipment to which you don't have access or supplies that are beyond your budget. If you are unable to make use of a particular technique for any reason, don't fret. You are certain to find alternative techniques in the same chapter that will serve your purposes just as well. Start with the techniques that are practical for you now; the others may become practical later.

Part two, "Ideas," offers detailed suggestions for applying the techniques described in part one. Its first four chapters are on signs, posters and wall displays, bulletin boards, and exhibits and give step-by-step, fully illustrated directions for producing eleven different displays. These display ideas may be used as is or may be adapted to your own needs. (For the most part, the themes of the suggested displays are general enough to be suitable for all kinds of libraries. Chapter 8, "Bulletin Boards," however, offers separate examples for school and public libraries, since bulletin boards tend to serve different purposes in the two institutions.)

Once you have experimented with the illustrated display ideas, you should be ready to try designing your own displays. Chapter 10, "On Your Own," offers helpful suggestions for doing so, along with practical tips for generating themes, gathering supplies, and storing display elements.

The last section of the book, "Appendixes," contains lists of additional information. Appendix A lists sources for the materials and equipment referred to throughout the book. Appendix B lists sources for computer software that you may find useful. Appendix C offers suggestions for further reading, including general books on library displays and books on specific, related subjects (for example, calligraphy and origami). Appendix D lists hundreds of holidays, anniversaries and other annual events that may help you develop ideas for displays. Appendix E contains generic templates for several common types of displays.

In short, this book has been designed to be as flexible as possible. Librarians of all backgrounds, in any kind of library—large or small, school or public, well-funded or on a shoestring budget—should find it useful. In fact, even nonlibrarians may find it useful. Although the sample displays in the ideas section are geared specifically to libraries, the techniques in the skills section may be used by anyone—teachers, store owners, party planners—who has the need to produce decorative signs or exhibits.

CHAPTER 2

Design

The creation of a display always involves two stages: design and production. *Design* is the process of forming a plan—a sketch, a set of instructions, or both—for a proposed product. Design usually involves a good deal of trial and error. *Production* is the process of implementing that plan—using tools and materials to construct the final product. If the design stage is handled well, production should involve little or no trial and error.

In much of the professional world, design and production are thought of as quite separate operations, even to the point of being handled by two different sets of people. In architecture, for example, an engineer constructs buildings according to an architect's designs. In visual art, however, there is a popular conception that the design stage doesn't exist—or that it is so intertwined with the production process as to be indistinguishable from it. Perhaps this is because we have seen so many movies and read so many accounts of painters as "free spirits": Van Gogh, in a fit of mad inspiration, slaps paint onto the empty canvas with his palette knife; Picasso, the impish child, fills a space with animated doodles and then obliterates them, relentlessly reworking until the result pleases him.

In fact, even the most free-spirited artists tend to plan their compositions carefully, and commercial artists—those who turn out the illustrations we see on posters and in magazines—are among the most detail-oriented planners of all. Nevertheless, the romantic image of "art as improvisation" persists. No doubt it is this image that allows normally prudent people—people who would never think of baking bread without a recipe or giving a speech without written notes—to make a sign simply by writing with a felt-tip marker on cardboard, without even bothering to pencil in the letters first. Hoping to save time, these people end up wasting both time and materials.

Some people, of course, have a natural instinct for design. Even without formal training, they can invent a pleasing design and sketch it easily with a minimum of fuss. Some can even fix an image in their minds and begin the production process immediately, assembling a finished display that matches their mental image. If you are one of these people, you may want to skip this chapter and go on to chapters 3, 4, and 5, which concentrate on production techniques.

If, however, you are one of the many people to whom the design process is intimidating or incomprehensible, you will find this chapter quite useful. It explains the mechanics of planning and sketching out display ideas. It also offers a number of guidelines to help you to improve the attractiveness and effectiveness of your displays.

TWO KINDS OF QUESTIONS

At its core, the design process is a series of decisions—a series of questions that must be answered. Some of these questions are practical; others are aesthetic. Examples of practical questions might be: "How big should I make this poster? Should it be freestanding or wall mounted? What materials should I use to make it?" Questions like these tend to have straightforward answers that depend on specific circumstances, such as the amount of room available to display the poster and the amount of money in the library's budget.

Aesthetic questions are more difficult to answer. Some examples might be: "What colors should I use in this poster? Which type style should I use? Should the poster include decorative elements? Should it be serious or entertaining in tone?" Questions of this sort can be dealt with only through judgment and experience; they have no objectively correct answers. (They may, of course, have *incorrect* answers. It is clearly wrong, for example, to use a whimsical typeface and pastel colors for a sign that says EMERGENCY EXIT.)

You might expect to be able to make all the practical decisions first, and to put off aesthetic decisions until later. In reality, however, practical and aesthetic considerations are inextricably interwoven. Suppose, for example, that you were designing a simple EMERGENCY EXIT sign. You might first determine the maximum proportions of the sign (a practical decision). You might then decide to use red block letters on a white background (an aesthetic decision). Because you do not feel capable of drawing such letters yourself, you decide to use vinyl stick-on letters (a practical decision). However, your local art supply store carries such letters only in black or white, so you decide to use white letters (a practical decision) on a red background (an aesthetic decision). Then, because a red background is more obtrusive than a white background, you decide to make the sign a bit smaller (another aesthetic decision).

These compromises between practical and aesthetic considerations are the heart of the design process. In order to make such compromises comfortably, however, you need to be as confident of your judgment in aesthetic matters as you are in practical matters. Such confidence comes mostly with experience; your expertise will almost certainly grow as you begin to plan more sophisticated displays. In the meantime, you can increase your level of confidence by becoming more familiar with the way professional designers think about design.

THE ELEMENTS OF DESIGN

Learning about design is similar to learning a second language. Every spoken language has parts of speech—nouns, verbs, adjectives, and so on—that carry meaning. Every spoken language also has rules of syntax and style that determine how those parts of speech can be combined most effectively.

The "language" of design has a similar structure. Instead of parts of speech, it has elements of design: line, shape, space, color, and texture. Instead of a formal syntax, it has principles of design—such as balance, emphasis, simplicity, variety, and unity—that allow the design elements to work together compatibly. (Different authorities offer different combinations of design elements and principles. The very basic lists used here are sufficient for introductory purposes, but they are not necessarily exhaustive.)

The first step in learning the language of design is to acquaint yourself with the five design elements—line, shape, space, color, and texture—and to see how they relate to the typical components of library displays.

Line

Lines represent order. They give the eye explicit directions about where to look and how to interpret what it sees. Lines can group related objects together and divide unrelated objects. They can call attention to the important features of a display and draw attention away from less significant features.

The lines used in displays may be divided into two basic types: visible and invisible. Visible lines are lines that are meant to be seen. They may be thick or thin; straight, jagged, or curved; continuous or broken. When used purely for decoration, visible lines can convey moods and feelings. Horizontal and vertical lines connote stability; diagonal lines connote informality or unpredictability; curved lines give a sense of fun; jagged lines give a sense of excitement or crisis.

Most often, however, visible lines serve functional rather than purely decorative purposes. (See figures 2.1 and 2.2). One common function of visible lines is that of a border or boundary. Used in this way, lines can draw attention to important objects or pieces of information (see figure 2.1). Even when a border encloses an entire sign or poster,

Figure 2.1 Border

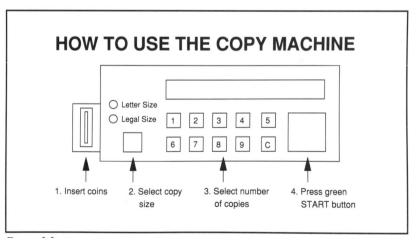

Figure 2.2 Arrows

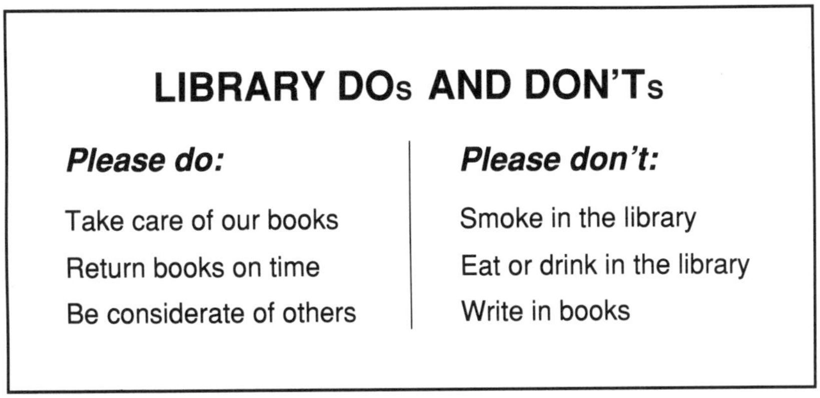

LIBRARY DOs AND DON'Ts

Please do:

Take care of our books

Return books on time

Be considerate of others

Please don't:

Smoke in the library

Eat or drink in the library

Write in books

Figure 2.3 Line divider

Figure 2.4 Slanted text

its purpose is the same: to draw the eye away from the surrounding environment and focus it on whatever is within the frame.

Visible lines may also be used as links, connecting two objects or two pieces of information to show that they are related. An arrow, which is essentially a specialized form of line, adds directionality to the link (see figure 2.2).

Ironically, visible lines are also commonly used as dividers. In a chart, lines may be used to separate headings from data or to separate one column of information from another. More generally, lines are used to divide different kinds of related information: text and illustrations; generalities and details; questions and answers. (See figure 2.3.)

Like arrows, objects that do not fit the traditional definition of a line may still function as lines in a design context. A line of text, for example, may serve some of the same decorative or functional purposes as other visible lines: for example, it may express a mood (see figure 2.4) while it conveys a literal meaning. Similarly, a long, narrow drawing (or a row of drawings) may function as a visible line; this technique is often applied to decorative borders (see figure 2.5). Border patterns associated with historical periods or cultures may be used to particular effect. Note that the border in figure 2.5 picks up a pattern used in the display.

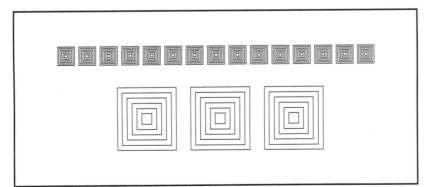

Figure 2.5 Decorative border

Figure 2.6 Disordered arrangement

Figure 2.7 Ordered arrangement

Invisible lines, like their visible counterparts, help to bring order to a display. Although they cannot be directly perceived by the eye, they can be grasped from the relationship of one object to another. For example, the objects in figure 2.6 seem to be randomly arranged; it is not clear which are the most important objects or in what order they are supposed to be looked at. In figure 2.7, however, the objects have been rearranged into areas divided by invisible lines, and, as a result, the figure is much easier to look at.

Invisible lines, like visible lines, can be used as borders or as dividers. In the poster in figure 2.8, for example, the alignment of each column at the left edge gives the impression of dividing lines between the columns. Similarly, the alignment of text at a fixed distance from the top, bottom, and sides of the poster gives the impression of a border surrounding the text.

Whether visible or invisible, lines are never restricted to the two-dimensional realm of markings on paper. A length of yarn suspended in a display case, as in plate 14, is a legitimate example of a visible line. Similarly, solid objects arranged in rows, as in plate 15, may be thought of as separated by invisible lines.

Shape

A shape is any enclosed area, whether filled in or outlined. Shapes range from simple geometrical figures (for example, rectangles, triangles, and circles) to elaborate configurations. Whatever form they take, shapes represent substance. They are the visual core of any design.

FRIENDS OF THE
BROOK COUNTY LIBRARY

ACQUISITIONS COMMITTEE	FUND-RAISING COMMITTEE	PROGRAM COMMITTEE
Michael Chen	Tim Barry	Rebecca Gross
Peter Dempsey	Leslie Buchanan	Christopher Lu
Mabel Derry	Sarah Buchholtz	Thomas Mundorff
George P. Gulliver	Debbie Linn	Norm Nordstrom
Meryl L. Katz	Robert Pace	Clark Rochester
Joseph Lucia	Jose Remy	

Figure 2.8 Columns

Figure 2.9 Text as boundary

Every display includes at least one shape: its own outline formed by the physical edges of the display. (The vast majority of displays, of course, are rectangular.) Most displays include other shapes as well, some of which may be three-dimensional (for example, cubes, spheres, and cylinders). Among the most common components of library exhibits are books, which also qualify as shapes from a design point of view.

The distinction between lines and shapes is not always clear cut. Look at the curved line of text in figure 2.9, for example. Should it be considered a line or a shape? On the one hand, it encloses an important piece of text (the word BESTS) and draws attention to it, as a line does. On the other hand, it creates a very definite oval shape that the other design elements depend on. Which is it, then?

The answer, of course, is both. Seen in the context of the word BESTS, it is a line. Seen in the context of the overall design, it is a shape. The difference is simply a matter of scale—a matter of looking at the forest versus looking at the trees.

The issue of scale comes up frequently in design. You already saw one example in figure 2.5. Seen up close, the decorative border is clearly made up of shapes—but from a distance, the shapes function as a line. For another example, look again at the word BESTS in figure 2.9. You will see that it is made up of five different shapes—letters of the alphabet that have been modified to work together visually. Yet, taken as a whole, these five shapes form a single oval—a shape echoed by the outlined oval that surrounds it. The point of these examples is that you, as a designer, will have to be aware of several levels at once. Quite often, the components of your display will have to be designed individually. Then you will have to step back and look at the design of the whole display to determine how those components can be arranged into a unified whole.

**DOW
JONES
IS NOW ON
TWO TERMINALS**

**See the reference librarian for
information on using the Dow
Jones News Retrieval Service**

Figure 2.10   Triangle and rectangle

When you look at a display from a distance, you may see shapes that occur by pure chance. In figure 2.10, for example, the lines of text come very close to forming a triangle and a rectangle. Enhancing and clarifying these shapes (by rearranging words or even changing the text) can add strength to a design.

Space

Lines and shapes exist within the space provided by the confines of a display. Therefore, space becomes as vital a design element as lines and shapes. In a well-designed display, there is no such thing as "wasted" or "unused" space.

Space represents freedom, both literally and figuratively. From a purely practical point of view, the eye needs a certain amount of free space in order to read text comfortably. A crowded sign such as that in figure 2.11 is not only unattractive; it is also close to useless, because reading it requires so much effort that it will probably be ignored. Figure 2.12 shows the same sign revised to be more legible, with wider margins and a reasonable amount of space between lines.

Space serves more than just a practical function, however. Exposing ample amounts of free space can actually make a display seem more inviting and appealing. In fact, the design of this book leaves white space on nearly every page for that very reason. You may have noticed especially large areas of free space at the beginning of each chapter. This is an old designer's trick to draw the reader into the chapter—to make it seem enticing rather than forbidding.

Space can play a similar role in library displays. For example, compare the poster in figure 2.13 to the one in figure 2.14. In figure 2.14, the uppercase letters have been changed to lowercase in order to allow more "air" within the block of text. The text lines have also been moved left to create a larger, unbroken area of free space on the right. Finally,

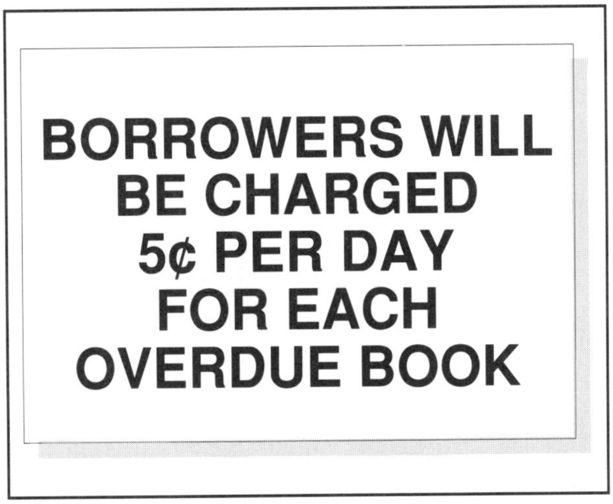

BORROWERS WILL
BE CHARGED
5¢ PER DAY
FOR EACH
OVERDUE BOOK

Figure 2.11 Crowded sign

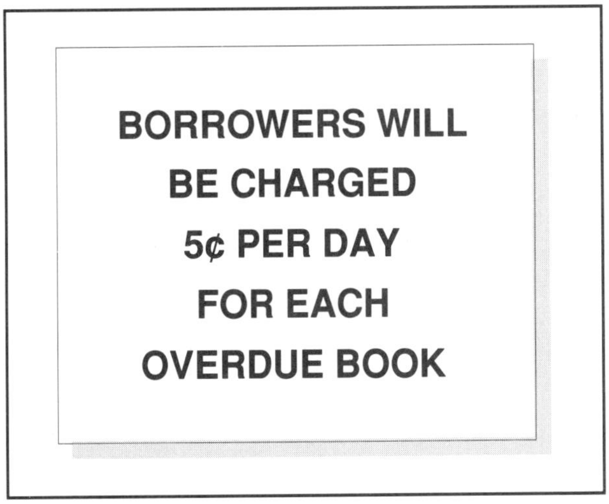

BORROWERS WILL
BE CHARGED
5¢ PER DAY
FOR EACH
OVERDUE BOOK

Figure 2.12 Sign with space added

the border has been removed from the illustration to achieve an increased sense of freedom. Which poster looks more inviting?

EXPLORE
THE LITERATURE
OF FRANCE

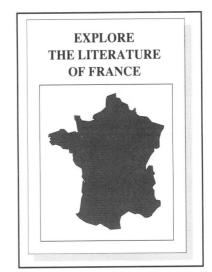

Figure 2.13 Crowded poster

Color

Color represents emotion. While it is possible to construct a colorless (that is, black-and-white) display, such a display would appear to lack heart and soul. From a practical point of view, it might also be overlooked by its intended audience. Color—especially bright color—allows objects to stand out from their surroundings.

There are a few technical terms that you will need to be familiar with if you want to use color intelligently in design. (This discussion will apply only to colors that can be mixed physically—by means of paint, ink, or dye, for example.)

The three colors from which all other colors are made—red, blue, and yellow—are called *primary colors*. Each primary color may be combined with an equal amount of another primary color to produce a *secondary color*. The three secondary colors are orange, a combination of red and yellow; green, a combination of yellow and blue; and violet, a combination of blue and red. (The color brown, a combination of all three primary colors, is not technically a secondary color.)

When the primary colors are arranged in a circle, with their shared secondary colors between them, the result is known as a *color wheel* (see plate 1). Colors that are directly opposite each other on the color wheel are called *complementary colors*. Three basic pairs of complementary colors are red and green, blue and orange, and yellow and violet. Of course, the color wheel has room for many more than six colors—an infinite number, in fact, since the primary colors can be mixed in any ratio. Nevertheless, all of these colors have complements. Plate 2 shows, for example, that the color blue-green, consisting of 75 percent blue and 25 percent yellow, has as its complement a color called red-orange, consisting of 75 percent red and 25 percent yellow.

Explore
the Literature
of France

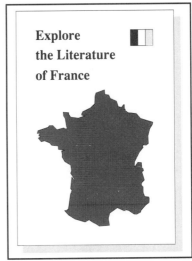

Figure 2.14 Poster with space added

Any color may be lightened or darkened by adding white or black to it. A color to which white has been added is called a *tint;* a color to which black has been added is called a *shade.* Some tints and shades have names of their own—the combination of red and white, for example, is known as pink.

A designer's choice of color combinations can greatly influence the character of a display. For example, juxtaposing two complementary colors creates a sense of excitement and action. (Think of where you have seen complementary colors used together: Christmas decorations are usually green and red; many communities paint their police vehicles blue and orange; comic-book wizards are often robed in violet and yellow.) In contrast, juxtaposing different shades or tints of the same color imparts a sense of calm. (Most Valentine's Day cards use red and pink; hospital rooms and classrooms were, for many years, typically painted in two shades of blue or two shades of green.)

Normally, the most pleasing color schemes are those that combine *families* of colors—colors that are near each other on the color wheel. For example, red, orange, and yellow (often known as the "warm" colors) work well together, as do green, blue, and violet (often known as the "cool" colors). Brown, which includes all three primary colors, works well with nearly any color combination.

As the warm and cool labels suggest, colors often carry connotations and associations linked to their uses in the real world. Red, for example, suggests danger and passion (blood); blue suggests tranquility (sky); green suggests nature (leaves); yellow suggests prosperity (sun, grain, gold). These connotations are not ironclad—red can be a perfectly peaceful color, for example, with suggestions of sunsets and glowing embers—but they can often be counted on to contribute additional emotional layers to a display.

Texture

Texture represents immediacy. There is an old saying that "seeing is believing," but the more common truth of human experience is that touching is believing—in a world of illusion, the way to know whether something is real is to reach out and touch it. Touch is one of our most acute senses, and, especially in childhood, our experience of an object depends largely on how it feels against our skin.

Textures, like colors, carry strong associations. The coarse surface of burlap or muslin makes us think of farms or sea voyages; the puffiness of cotton balls or yarn brings to mind clouds or kittens; the glossy finish of a photograph reminds us of fashion magazines or lacquered wood. The associative power of texture is so strong, in fact, that most people no longer have to touch an object in order to experience its physical character. Simply seeing a piece of velvet, for example, allows us to feel its supple richness as vividly as if we were touching it.

This sort of "visual texture" is an important element in library displays. Most displays cannot (or should not) be touched by the people who view them, but they should be designed as if they were meant to be touched. Including even a single highly textured item—a feather, a strip of cloth, a balloon—can draw attention to a display and give it a visceral impact that it might otherwise have lacked.

Clearly, the five elements of design provide an extensive vocabulary for a designer to work with. Line, shape, space, color, and texture, when handled with sensitivity, can bring order, substance, freedom, emotion, and immediacy to a display. In their own way, they communicate as powerfully and effectively as the written words whose meaning they reinforce.

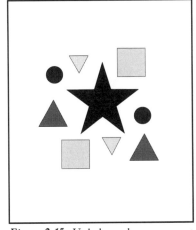

Figure 2.15 Unbalanced arrangement

THE PRINCIPLES OF DESIGN

Comparing the principles of design to the principles of English syntax (like comparing the elements of design to parts of speech) is helpful, but not entirely apt. Syntax, for the most part, sets up rigid requirements and clearly distinguishes right from wrong. In contrast, the principles of design tend to be loose guidelines rather than hard-and-fast rules. Having acknowledged that distinction, however, you can usually trust the principles of design to guide you toward good displays rather than bad ones.

Like most good guidelines, the principles of design—balance, emphasis, simplicity, variety, and unity—are grounded in common sense. They will probably seem quite obvious to you when you read about them—and that, in fact, is one measure of their value. The principles of design are explicit statements of ideas that you, on some unconscious level, already know to be true. Because nearly everyone else shares your unconscious acceptance of these ideas, your displays (if they follow the principles) will feel comfortable and seem "right" to the people who view them.

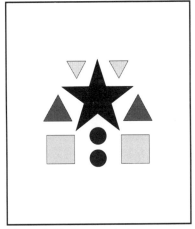

Figure 2.16 Symmetrical arrangement

Balance

The principle of balance requires that the visual "weight" of a display be evenly distributed. A good analogy might be the passengers on a small boat, who must distribute their weight evenly in order to keep the boat from capsizing. Unfortunately, the visual weights of display elements are harder to measure than the physical weights of boaters. Lines and shapes cannot be weighed on a bathroom scale, and most displays will not actually tip over if their components are badly arranged. Still, the effects of visual weight are very easy to see. Compare figure 2.15, whose elements are out of balance, to figure 2.16, whose elements are balanced. The balanced version is much more comfortable to look at.

Figure 2.16 uses a type of balance called *symmetry*, in which the left half of the design is effectively a mirror image of the right. Symmetry is the easiest form of balance to achieve (in part because it is measurable), and it is commonly used for simple signs and posters. Symmetry has two drawbacks, however: it can be boring if it is overused, and it is sometimes inefficient in its use of space. The demands of symmetry often require that a component be placed in a certain spot (to balance another component), rather than in a different part of the display where it might make more sense.

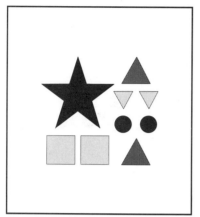

Figure 2.17 Asymmetrical arrangement

Figure 2.17 illustrates another type of balance, called *asymmetry*. Asymmetrical designs offer much more freedom than symmetrical designs—their elements can be placed just about anywhere, so long as they balance each other visually. The key to asymmetry is the notion of visual weight, which, as noted earlier, cannot be measured objectively. In general, objects that are big, bright, or bold have more visual weight than objects that are small, dull, or pale. In figure 2.17, for example, the star has the greatest visual weight not only because it is large, but because its flat black color is bolder than the other objects' shades of gray.

If you are uncomfortable with the concept of visual weight, you may be hesitant to design asymmetrical displays. The best way to overcome that hesitation is to try to quantify the visual weight of each object in the display. Using a scale of one to ten, ask yourself (for example), "How bright is this object?" Once you have assigned values for brightness, boldness, and bigness, average the three values and call this number the object's "weight." You can then arrange the objects mathematically, so the total weight of the objects on the left side of the display equals the total weight of the objects on the right side. (If any object straddles the center line, its weight will have to be apportioned properly to each side.)

This technique may seem arbitrary or even silly, but you probably won't have to use it very often. Once you become accustomed to dealing with visual weight, you will be able to make such judgments intuitively, without having to resort to mathematical calculations. Eventually, you may be able to arrange objects so that they "feel" balanced, without having to stop and figure out why.

Emphasis

The principle of emphasis requires that some elements of a design stand out from the rest. When a display follows this principle, viewers can tell at a glance which components of the display are the most important. For example, the sign in figure 2.18 is well balanced, but it lacks emphasis. Figure 2.19 shows how the same sign looks when its most important elements are given more weight.

PAPERBACK SWAP RACK:
TAKE ONE BOOK FREE
FOR EVERY BOOK
YOU CONTRIBUTE

Figure 2.18 Sign with no emphasis

PAPERBACK SWAP RACK
Take one book *free*
for every book
you contribute

Figure 2.19 Sign with emphasis

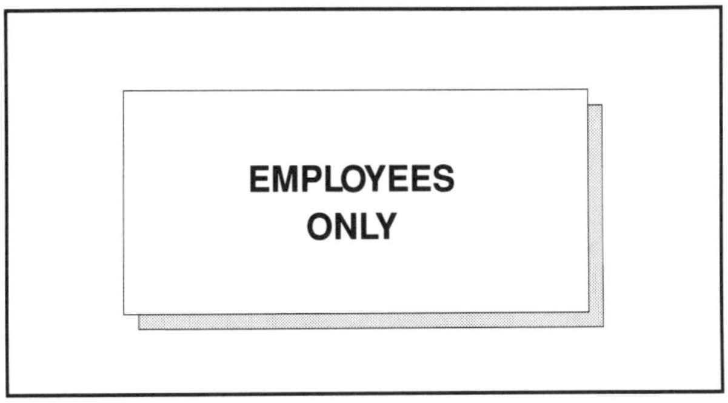

Figure 2.20 Sign with too much space

Figure 2.21 Sign with proper amount of space

You can emphasize a display element by using the techniques mentioned in the earlier discussion of visual weight: you can make it bigger, brighter, or bolder. There are, however, other ways of emphasizing an item: you can put a border around it; you can highlight it in a different color; you can point to it with other elements (such as arrows). If it is a line of text, you can use a different type style or a different version of the same type style (for example, **bold** or *italic*).

Emphasis is important even in very simple signs that consist only of a word or two. Keep in mind that space is an element of design, and that it carries its own visual weight. Unless the words on a sign are properly emphasized (which means, under most circumstances, that they must be adequately large and bold), they may be overpowered by the space that surrounds them. Figures 2.20 and 2.21 show a sign without, and then with, appropriate emphasis.

Simplicity

Every display is designed to carry out a function or to serve a purpose. The principle of simplicity holds that a design should accomplish its purpose as directly as possible, and that any design element not necessary for that purpose should be eliminated. (This idea is an important tenet of disciplines such as writing and science as well as of design.)

The idea of simplicity is easy to misinterpret. Contrary to what you might think, it does not require every display to consist of plain block letters on white cardboard. Such a display would obviously be boring, and it would therefore fail to carry out one of its most important purposes—to attract the attention of viewers and to add to the library's visual appeal.

Therefore, designers must often make quite subtle decisions. Adding an illustration, for example, is a fine way to dress up an all-text display. But would adding two illustrations make the display any more attractive than adding just one? If the answer is no, then the principle of simplicity requires that the second illustration be omitted.

The need for simplicity influences even the most basic designs. For example, the sign in figure 2.22 is certainly simple; it includes the minimum necessary amount of text. As it stands, however, it is too simple. It violates the principle of emphasis, which requires that important elements be distinguished from less important elements.

> **NEW HOURS OF OPERATION**
>
> MON-THURS   8:00 A.M. – 9:30 P.M.
> FRIDAY   8:00 A.M. – 5:00 P.M.
> SATURDAY   10:00 A.M. – 5:00 P.M.
> SUNDAY   CLOSED

Figure 2.22 Sign with no variety

In figure 2.23, the sign has gone too far in the other direction. It includes too many unneeded variations in the size, style, and color of the text. (It is not necessary, for example, to underline, italicize, and enlarge a word in order to call attention to it; one of the three techniques is certainly adequate.)

Finally, figure 2.24 shows an effective design with appropriate levels of simplicity and emphasis. It is clearly more attractive than either of its two predecessors.

Variety

The principle of variety states that every design should include the greatest possible variety of shapes, sizes, type styles, colors, textures, and so on. If you feel that this principle is in direct contradiction with the principle of simplicity, you are right. It is because of such contradictions that the principles of design are said to be guidelines rather than rules.

The principle of variety is certainly important—without it, the world would be filled with monotonous designs. For all practical purposes, a designer should not need more than two or three different type styles and a few colors of paint. Nevertheless, an innate desire for variety has led designers to invent thousands of each, with no end in sight. The popularity of circuses, patchwork quilts, and Christmas trees further

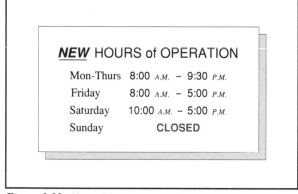

Figure 2.23 Sign with too much variety

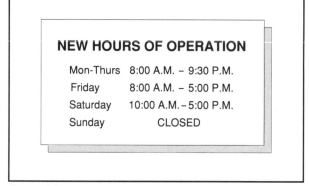

Figure 2.24 Well balanced sign

attests to the joy people feel when they can combine hundreds of incompatible elements into one extravagant whole.

How, then, can we reconcile the appeal of simplicity with the joy of variety? The solution, once again, is intuition. Neither simplicity nor variety, after all, can be measured—there is no objective way to tell whether a design is "as simple as possible" or "as varied as possible." The best that you, or any designer, can do is to strike a comfortable balance between the two opposing forces—a balance that feels right to you.

The sign in figure 2.24 is an example of a compromise that most people would agree is reasonable. Perhaps your ideal compromise would look somewhat different. If so, trust your judgment. So long as you are aware that there are limits—that a sign can be too simple (as in figure 2.22) or too varied (as in figure 2.23)—you will have no trouble staying within those limits when you create your own designs.

Unity

The principle of unity might also be called *consistency* or *harmony*. It requires all the elements of a design to work effectively toward a common goal. A unified design is a successful design—it looks attractive and "feels right."

Unity is, in a sense, the supreme principle, embodying every other principle and convention of good design. If you create a design that is visually balanced, if you emphasize the important elements, if you choose colors that look good together, if your type styles and illustrations are appropriate to your theme, and if you strike a reasonable compromise between simplicity and variety, then the result is likely to be a unified design.

Unity is not an impossible dream; it is not a goal attainable only by experts. A design can be unified without being perfect. Your first attempts at designing library displays may not meet the standards of professional designers, but they may still be unified. Even if each element of a design is a little "off," the quirks may blend together or compensate for each other in a way that achieves unity. Like so many other aspects of design, unity is in the eye of the beholder. If you can look at a design and say to yourself, "I am not sure why, but it *works*," you have given that design the highest possible compliment.

PRACTICAL STEPS FOR CREATING DESIGNS

Unless you possess exceptional talent, a unified design will rarely spring from your imagination in final, polished form. Even the most experienced professional designers often spend hours sketching, scribbling, and revising before they achieve a result that pleases them. Unfortunately, this "incubation" period—a time of risk-taking, frustration, and uncertainty—intimidates many beginners.

If the idea of designing worries you, the only reasonable solution is to jump right in and do it. Do it now, today, while this chapter is still fresh in your mind and your level of interest outweighs your level of apprehension. Do not give yourself a chance to learn the procrastinator's habits.

The following discussion of design techniques assumes that you have already decided on a purpose or theme for your display, and that you already have specific wording in mind. If that is not true, but you want to practice anyway, choose a simple project for which you do not have to invent any text—for example, a REFERENCE DESK sign or a list of holidays on which the library will be closed. The exercise here is only to create a design; you do not necessarily have to turn the result into a full-fledged display.

Step 1   The first step in creating a design is to measure the space you need to fill. If you are planning a three-dimensional exhibit or a bulletin board display, measure the dimensions of the display case or the bulletin board. If you are planning a poster or a sign, measure the amount of wall space you intend to have it occupy. (You can always modify the dimensions later.)

Step 2   Gather together three simple tools: a pencil (with eraser), a ruler, and a pad of graph paper. (Lined notebook paper can substitute for graph paper in a pinch.) Using the pencil and ruler, draw an outline of the display on the graph paper. The outline should be drawn to scale—that is, the dimensions of the outline should correspond to the measurements you took in step 1. Use whatever scale seems easy, practical, and appropriate. You may want to have one square on the graph paper equal 1 inch of display space, or you may want to have 8 squares equal a foot. Once you have decided on a scale, write it in the corner of the paper for future reference.

If you are designing a three-dimensional exhibit, your outline should represent a front view (that is, the dimensions of the front window of the display case). If you are unusually meticulous, you may later want to sketch a top view and a side view. In most cases, however, those additional drawings will not be necessary.

Step 3   Some components of a display are variable in size—lettering, for instance, can be made as large or as small as it needs to be. Other components, however, are fixed in size. For example, unless you have access to a darkroom, you cannot change the dimensions of a photograph that you want to use in a display. The dimensions of books and fine art reproductions are similarly fixed.

If you plan to include any fixed-size objects in your display, outline them on another sheet of graph paper and cut the patterns out. (Of course, the cutouts must conform to the scale you set in step 2. If you are using a scale in which 1 square equals 1 inch, your cutout model of an 8-by-10-inch photograph would measure 8 squares by 10 squares.)

Once you have made these cutouts, you can place them within the border you drew in step 2. By moving them around to different positions, you can see where they fit best. (Note that many people use this same technique to decide how to arrange their furniture.)

Step 4 Add the variable-sized components—lettering, illustrations, borders, and so on—by sketching them in very lightly with your pencil. You do not have to draw them in detail; just indicate their size and shape as roughly as possible.

This is the stage where the principles of design begin to play a major role. You will have to make dozens of decisions: How big should I make these letters? Should I include any illustrations? If so, how many and what kind? How much free space should I leave? Should this display be symmetrical or asymmetrical?

The best way to answer these kinds of questions is through trial and error. Sketch the design as you think you might like it; then, if it needs improvement, erase some of the elements and sketch them in again. If too much erasing and redrawing makes your sheet of paper unusable, copy (or trace) your outline onto another sheet and start again. If you have access to a copying machine, you can easily make multiple copies of your outline. (Some machines cannot copy the light-blue grid lines of graph paper. In that case, stack some sheets of clean graph paper in the paper tray and photocopy the original outline onto them.)

It may take you some time to develop a design that you are satisfied with. Once you have reached that stage, however, you can darken the pencil lines on your sketch—and, if you like, add some additional details—to get a better idea of how the finished product will look. At this point, you should trace the cutouts of the fixed-size objects onto your sketch and darken those as well.

Step 5 So far, by manipulating lines and shapes, you have come up with a fairly complete representation of your design. Nevertheless, many decisions remain to be made—chiefly those involving color, texture, type style, and materials. Gather samples of the materials you plan to use—paints, markers, fabrics, and so on—and hold them next to each other, to see how the colors and textures look together. You should also obtain samples of various typefaces and choose the one you feel is most appropriate for each block of text.

With the actual materials in hand, you may decide to use colors or textures different from those you had originally envisioned. You may also decide to go back and revise your design in order to accommodate the colors or materials you have selected. Once you have made your final choices, label each item on your sketch with appropriate information about color, style, and material so that you will not forget them.

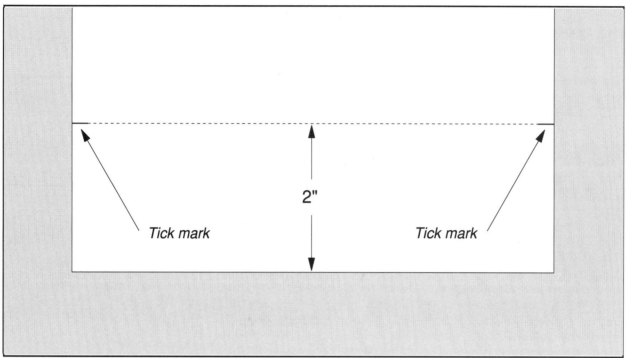

Figure 2.25 Tick marks

Step 6   Make sure your design is practical. For example, your design may call for rub-on letters that are 3/4 inch high, but the type style you want is available only in a maximum size of 2/3 inch. Or perhaps the particular type of paper you planned to use has risen in price since you last used it and is now beyond your budget. If you find that any aspect of your design will not work for practical reasons, go back to your sketch and revise it. A change in one element may require changes in other elements.

The time to investigate practical details is now, not later. At this point, you can easily revise your design with a few strokes of a pencil. If you wait until you begin production, you may end up having to throw away hours of hard work when you encounter an unexpected obstacle.

Step 7   (This is actually the first stage of production, but it is included here for better continuity with the following chapters.) Using a ruler or tape measure and very light pencil marks, copy your sketch onto the actual surface that you plan to use for the display.

As you outline each component, expand it to its full size using the scale you established earlier. (For example, if you have used a scale in which 8 boxes equal 1 foot, and the letters on your sketch are 1 box high, the letters you draw on the backing should be 1 1/2 inches high.) Your pencil marks do not have to show any details; they simply have to indicate the proper position of each element.

In order to draw straight lines, make tick marks along the edges of the backing and then connect them. (See figure 2.25.) For example, suppose the baseline for your lettering is going to be 2 inches from the bottom of the display. Using your ruler, make a mark 2 inches from the bottom on the left edge of the display; then make a mark 2 inches from the bottom on the right edge. When you use a straightedge and a pencil to connect the marks, the resulting line will be perfectly horizontal. This technique may seem tedious, but it is the only way to achieve complete accuracy with simple tools. The result is definitely worth the effort—there is no worse sign of amateurism in a display than lines that run uphill or downhill.

Another technique whose results are worth the effort is to pencil in every single letter that will appear on the display. This, too, is a tedious task, but it ensures against the problem illustrated in the well-known PLAN AHEAD cartoon (figure 2.26).

You are now prepared to use the production techniques described in chapters 3, 4, and 5. Once the production process is finished, you can erase all remaining pencil marks and guidelines.

Even after this long discussion of the theoretical and practical aspects of design, you may remain hesitant to try your hand as a display designer. If that is so, try working with the displays described in chapters 6 through 9. These displays have been predesigned for you, and there are step-by-step instructions for producing each one. Once you see how each of these displays accomplishes its purpose, you may feel more comfortable with the idea of designing your own.

Figure 2.26 Plan ahead

CHAPTER 3

Lettering

Lettering is an essential part of every display in your library. Some displays, such as signs or simple posters, may consist almost entirely of lettering. Even the most elaborate displays, whose visual power derives from eye-catching illustrations or three-dimensional objects, nearly always rely on lettering to convey their messages. You can probably learn to produce serviceable block lettering with very little practice, even if your handwriting is close to illegible. If not, you can always fall back on a variety of mechanical devices— such as templates, lettering machines, or computers—for help.

Legibility, however, is not enough. To be truly effective, lettering must be as attractive and expressive as possible. The style, size, and color of a lettered phrase deliver nearly as great a message as the phrase itself. The lettering techniques you will find later in this chapter will help you achieve both goals—legibility and attractiveness—with a minimum of effort. First, however, you will need to become familiar with a number of terms that designers use when they talk about lettering.

STYLES

There are hundreds of different styles of lettering, each with its own distinctive personality. Styles of type used in printing are known as *typefaces.* Styles of hand-drawn lettering are usually known as *alphabets.* In many cases (as when talking about stick-on or stencil lettering), the two terms may be used interchangeably.

In recent years, the designers and users of some desktop publishing programs have begun to use the word *font* to mean typeface. Traditionally, however, these words have quite different meanings. A *font* is a set of letters, numbers, and symbols in a specific size and style. The word *typeface* refers only to the style. If you have ever used a typewriter with a removable print element (for example, a ball or a daisy wheel), you will easily understand the difference. Imagine that you have two print elements for the same typewriter: one 10-pitch Courier, one 12-pitch Courier. Each print element constitutes a different font, but both represent the same typeface.

Typefaces are generally divided into two categories based on whether or not they include decorative lines called *serifs.* (Sample serifs are pointed out for you in figure 3.1.) Typefaces that include serifs are called *serif faces;* those that do not are called *sans serif faces.* Serif faces are usually seen as traditional and conservative, while sans serif faces are considered more contemporary and less formal.

The quintessential examples of a serif and a sans serif typeface are Times Roman and Helvetica, shown in figure 3.1. (In fact, they are the

Figure 3.1 Sans serif and serif letters

Old-Style:	
Bookman	T
Garamond	T
Century Old Style	T
Modern:	
Century Schoolbook	T
Palatino	T
Times Roman	T

Figure 3.2 Old-style and modern typefaces

only typefaces supplied with many computer graphics programs—other faces are available as optional add-ons, but these two are considered essential. Be aware that, for copyright reasons, computerized versions of these faces are sometimes identified by alternative names such as Dutch and Swiss, or Tymes and Helv.) The range of available typefaces, however, extends far beyond Helvetica and Times Roman. Serif faces, in particular, are almost endless in their variety—a number of classic faces developed over a century ago are still in use today, and newer faces (such as Palatino and Korinna) have achieved widespread acceptance in a relatively short period of time.

Serif faces are usually classified either as old-style or modern. (Figure 3.2 shows samples of several popular old-style and modern typefaces.) The distinction is based on a number of characteristics, most of which are not apparent to the untrained eye. For example, the vertical serifs on an old-style T tend to bow outward at an obtuse angle and are joined to the crossbar by curved brackets called fillets. The serifs on a modern T are perpendicular to the crossbar, and fillets are either vestigial or absent altogether.

Designers also like to distinguish between *display faces* and *text faces*. A display face is showy, dynamic, offbeat, or decorative; it is intended to catch the eye. A display face may be used for headlines or short phrases, but it is distracting and difficult to read if used in small sizes or multiple lines. Figure 3.3 shows examples of common display faces.

In contrast, a text face (also known as a book face) is meant to convey information clearly and easily, without calling attention to itself. It lends itself well to sentences and paragraphs. In small sizes, a text face can be used for magazine articles and books; in large sizes, it can be used for headings.

Most text faces—and some display faces—come in four varieties: roman, bold, italic, and bold italic. (Roman is used for standard text; the other three variations are generally reserved for emphasis.) Some typefaces have other variations as well, such as compressed, extended, light, and black (a bolder version of bold). Together, all of the variations of

Broadway
Brush Script
Cooper Black
Hobo
Murray Hill
Old English
Old Town

Figure 3.3 Display typefaces

Helvetica

Helvetica Bold

Helvetica Italic

Helvetica Bold Italic

Helvetica Narrow

Helvetica Narrow Bold

Helvetica Narrow Italic

Helvetica Narrow Bold Italic

Figure 3.4 Variations in the Helvetica family

a single typeface are known as a *family*. Figure 3.4, for example, shows some of the members of the Helvetica family.

SIZES

Because lettering encompasses so many different traditions and technologies—printing, typewriting, sign painting, graphic arts, and electronics—it makes use of a number of different measuring systems. Different kinds of lettering are measured in different units, some more precise than others.

The simplest unit, called *pitch*, is equivalent to characters per inch. It is a measure of width, not of height, and it applies only to fixed-width (also called *monospaced*) typefaces. In a fixed-width typeface, every letter is designed to take up an equal amount of space on a line—a lowercase *m*, for example, takes up no more space than a lowercase *i*. Typewriters, for which monospaced typefaces were originally designed, typically use either a 10-pitch or a 12-pitch font.

The typefaces traditionally used by typesetters and printers are not monospaced, but proportionately spaced—that is, some characters take up more room than others. Proportionately spaced fonts are measured in units called *points*, of which there are about 72 to an inch. Points are generally used to measure height rather than width: the point size of a font is roughly equivalent to the distance from its lowest descender to its highest ascender. (A *descender* is the part of a lowercase letter that extends below the baseline, such as the "tail" of a *y*. An *ascender* is the part of a lowercase letter that reaches above the tops of other letters, such as the "hook" of an *f*.) See figure 3.5 for an illustration of how point sizes are measured.

The amount of space between lines of text is called *leading*, after the lead strips historically used by printers to separate rows of metal type. Leading, like character heights, is generally expressed in points. A 10-point font, for example, might be set with 3-point leading, 1-point leading, or no leading at all. Traditionally, designers have specified line spacing by adding together the point sizes of the font and of the leading. For example, a 6-point font with 1-point leading would be described as 6 on 7.

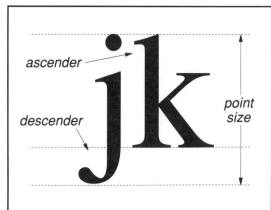

Figure 3.5 How point size is measured

The heights of hand-drawn letters are usually measured in inches or centimeters rather than points. Commercial lettering aids, such as stencils or stick-on letters, are measured in inches by some manufacturers and in points by others. If a measurement is given in inches, it most often refers to the height of a font's uppercase letters. If it is given in points, it refers to the distance from the lowest descender to the highest ascender of the font's lowercase letters.

TOOLS AND TECHNIQUES

The following lettering tools and techniques are arranged alphabetically for easy reference. Note that there is some overlap between techniques for lettering and those for illustration. Some techniques will be described only briefly, with a cross reference to a fuller explanation in the next chapter.

Calligraphy

Calligraphy, literally "beautiful writing," has come to refer to an ornamental style of penmanship accomplished with flat-nibbed pens and liquid ink. Although calligraphy comes naturally to some people, it most often requires a significant amount of study and practice. Calligraphy looks elegant and attractive when done well, but it can be extremely unappealing (and virtually illegible) when done by an untrained hand. If you are interested in calligraphy, you might consider taking a course in your spare time. (Such courses are often offered by community adult education programs.) If you do not want to invest the necessary time and energy, you probably shouldn't plan to include calligraphic elements in your displays.

Clip-Art Alphabets

Clip art is simple, copyright-free, commercially distributed artwork that can be clipped from a book and incorporated into displays. (For a fuller explanation, see *Clip Art* in chapter 4.) You can find a variety of decorative alphabets in clip-art books.

Using a clip-art alphabet requires very little skill, but the work can be slow and tedious. For this reason, you probably will want to use clip-art letters only for small jobs such as headlines.

Although a clip-art alphabet may be cut directly from the page, most people prefer to make a copy and cut that up instead. (That way, the original alphabet remains intact for future use.) Most clip-art alphabets include only one of each character; therefore, if your headline text uses any letter more than once, you will have to make multiple copies.

For recommended copying techniques, see *Photocopying* and *PMTs* in this chapter. (A PMT is a photomechanical transfer—a high-quality, high-contrast, photographic reproduction.)

The simplest way to use a clip-art alphabet is to cut the letters you need from your photocopy or PMT, arrange them on a piece of paper or cardboard, and glue them down. Unfortunately, the result of this proce-

Figure 3.6 Drawing baseline across clip-art alphabet

Figure 3.7 Cutting out clip-art letters

dure is not particularly attractive: the cut lines surrounding each letter are quite visible, especially if the letters are not perfectly glued. For this reason, you will probably want to make another photocopy or PMT of the finished headline and incorporate the copy into your final display.

The following is a suggested series of steps for producing the word LOOK with a clip-art alphabet.

1. With a light-blue pencil (see *Nonrepro Blue* in this chapter), draw baselines across each row of letters in the clip-art alphabet (figure 3.6). Use the same pencil to draw a guideline on a strip of white paper.

2. Cut the necessary letters neatly from the page (figure 3.7). The two *O*'s must be cut from different copies of the same alphabet. Save the remaining uncut letters for future projects.

3. Arrange the cut letters on your paper strip. Align the blue baseline of each letter with the blue guideline you drew earlier (figure 3.8). When you are satisfied with the arrangement of the letters, glue them down. (For hints on letterspacing, see *Spacing* in this chapter. For suggestions on gluing, see *Fastening/Mounting* in chapter 5.)

4. Make a photocopy or PMT of the result, enlarging or reducing as required.

If you have a light box (see *Light Box* in this chapter), you do not need to draw lines along the bottom of each row of letters. Simply draw a baseline on your paper strip and place it on an illuminated light box. When you position your clip-art letters on the backing sheet, the baseline will be visible through the paper that the letters are printed on.

If you do not have access to a real clip-art alphabet, you can make your own with letters cut from magazine advertisements or headlines.

Figure 3.8 Aligning baseline of each letter with guideline

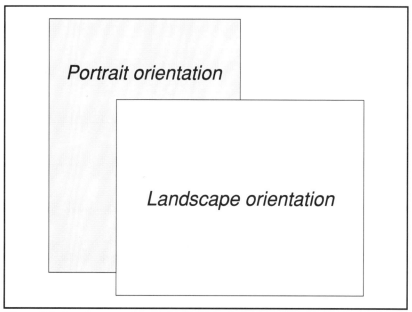

Figure 3.9 Landscape and portrait orientation

(Letters cut from magazines will reproduce much more satisfactorily than those cut from newspapers.)

For the nonartist, clip-art alphabets are an excellent source of professional-looking lettering in many different sizes and styles. Their chief drawback is that they are so complicated to use: all of that duplicating, cutting, and gluing can be time-consuming. Another significant drawback is that the designers of clip-art alphabets tend to concentrate on showy or ornate display faces. If you need a relatively modest typeface, you may have to look elsewhere.

Computer-Generated Banners

Banners are the most rudimentary form of computer-generated lettering. A typical banner consists of letters that are 5 or 6 inches high, printed in landscape orientation on a long strip of continuous-feed paper. (*Landscape orientation*, sometimes called sideways printing, is one of two standard directions for printing on a rectangular sheet of paper. See figure 3.9 to compare landscape with *portrait orientation*.)

Even the most inexpensive computer equipment can be used to generate banners. Unlike sophisticated graphics programs, most banner-printing software can be run on bare-bones computers (such as an IBM PCjr or an Apple II) with minimal memory and a single floppy drive. Furthermore, a banner is one of the rare applications for which a $200 dot-matrix printer is more suitable than a $2,000 laser printer. (Nearly all laser printers are designed to print on single, precut sheets of paper rather than on the perforated, fanfold paper that banners require.) Many computer stores and office supply stores sell assortments of colored computer paper that allow banners to be printed on eye-catching backgrounds. If your printer accepts colored ribbons, you can print a banner in one color on a background of another color.

The simplest banner-making programs simply ask you to type in the text that you want to appear on the banner; the computer then prints the banner in a fixed size and typeface. More elaborate programs allow you to choose from a number of typefaces or to incorporate symbols (such as hearts, stars, or pointing fingers) into the banner's design.

Sophisticated programs may also allow you to print banners in graphics mode rather than in character mode. In graphics mode, the letters on the banner are constructed from dark, solid boxes or dots. In character mode, the letters are made up of alphabetic characters such as *X*'s or asterisks. Banners printed in graphics mode are bolder, sharper, and more legible than those printed in character mode, but they also take longer to print—as much as ten times longer, in some cases. Also, many printers (such as daisy-wheel printers and some inexpensive dot-matrix printers) are incapable of printing in graphics mode.

Banner-making programs generally cost no more than $35. They can often be obtained free—or nearly free—on computer bulletin boards or through other shareware distribution channels. (See Appendix B for details.) If you have no computer, you may be able to get an inexpensive, custom-made banner from a local service bureau. (See *Service Bureaus* in this chapter.)

Printing a banner is one of the simplest, quickest, and least expensive ways to send an attention-getting message. It does have some serious drawbacks, however. Computer-generated banners come in only one shape (long and narrow) and in a limited range of colors. More to the point, even the best banner-making programs do not produce very attractive lettering. In many situations, computer-generated banners may seem trite or tacky. The best uses for banners are as temporary signs for special events (for example, WELCOME PARENTS) or as headings for displays pertaining to computer technology. Otherwise, banners are best thought of as a shortcut for last-minute displays, when you do not have the time to prepare anything more elaborate.

Computer-Generated Lettering

There are several ways to generate display-quality text from a computer. The method that will work best for you depends, for the most part, on the printer you have at your disposal. Three kinds of printers are in general use today: daisy-wheel, dot-matrix, and laser.

Daisy-Wheel Printers   A daisy-wheel printer is, for practical purposes, simply an automated typewriter. The improved print quality of dot-matrix printers and the reduced cost of laser printers have made daisy-wheel printers much less popular than they were ten years ago. Nevertheless, many of these reliable workhorses are still in use.

The largest characters a daisy-wheel printer can print are those that will fit on the "petals" of its wheel—a maximum of about 12 points (0.16 inch) high. Therefore, daisy-wheel printers are relatively useless for signs. They can, however, be used to produce small components for posters, bulletin boards, and exhibits—items such as map legends, identification labels, and explanatory notes. If you have a variety of print wheels, you can select the font that best suits your application.

Virtually any computer, and any word-processing program, can drive a daisy-wheel printer. If there are proportional fonts available for your printer, you may want to use a sophisticated word-processing program (such as Microsoft Word or WordPerfect) that can handle proportional spacing. With a proportionally spaced print wheel and the right software, many daisy-wheel printers can turn out handsome text with a typeset look.

A few models of daisy-wheel printers are capable of printing in graphics mode, making use of the period on the daisy wheel to build complex drawings dot by dot. However, using daisy-wheel printers in this fashion is slow, uneconomical, and quite punishing to the daisy wheel. It is not recommended.

Dot-Matrix Printers   Dot-matrix printers print by striking an array of pins in various combinations against an inked ribbon. The pins (sometimes called *wires*) are mounted on a moving print head, which travels back and forth across the page just as a daisy wheel does. The original dot-matrix printers had only nine pins, and the characters they printed were primitive, but the printers caught on because they were so much smaller, cheaper, quieter, and faster than daisy-wheel printers.

Since that time, a new generation of "letter-quality" dot-matrix printers has come into use. Some of these still have only nine pins, but they have been designed to pass the print head over a character several times, shifting the pins' arrangement slightly each time. The characters that result are very well formed, but the multiple passes required to print each line can make these printers uncomfortably slow. For this reason, twenty-four-pin dot-matrix printers, which can print letter-quality characters in one pass, have become increasingly popular.

If you have a letter-quality printer, no matter what the number of pins, you can use it to print the same small items that you can print with daisy-wheel printers. You may be restricted to one typeface—the one built into the printer—but you can usually choose among two or three different type sizes. Some printers have several different typefaces built in. Still others accept font cartridges that contain electronically encoded descriptions of a variety of typefaces. In most cases, however, the height of your characters is limited to about 12 points, just as on a daisy-wheel printer. (Among the exceptions are Epson's LQ-series printers, which can print double-height fonts with two passes of the print head.)

The true advantage of dot-matrix over daisy-wheel printers is that they offer a way around the style and size restrictions. By using graphics mode rather than character mode, you can make a dot-matrix printer print almost anything. In character mode, a printer uses built-in information (or information from a font cartridge) to tell it how to form each letter, number, or symbol. When your computer sends a code for the letter *A* to your printer, for example, the printer instantly fires its pins in the right combination to print an *A*. Character mode is easy and fast, but a printer in character mode can only print what it "knows" how to print.

In contrast, a dot-matrix printer in graphics mode is a slow, helpless machine. It surrenders control entirely to the computer, which tells the printer how and when to fire each pin during each pass of the print head. If a computer contains a digitized image of the *Mona Lisa* and can tell the printer which pins to fire to reconstruct the painting, the printer will print the *Mona Lisa*. Similarly, if a computer contains an image of the letter *A* in 72-point Palatino, a dot-matrix printer can print it. The printer has no idea that it is printing an *A* (as it does in character mode), but it prints it nonetheless.

In order to take advantage of graphics mode, you generally have to use a graphics program (rather than a word-processing program) on your computer. Most word-processing programs work only in character mode: if you want to print the word CAT, the computer will send the letters *C*, *A*, and *T* to your printer (along with some codes telling the printer which of its internal fonts to use). If you print the word CAT from a graphics program, however, the computer will convert each letter to a series of tiny dots called a *bitmap*. (What the bitmap represents—that is, what typeface and size the printed letters will be—is up to you.) After doing that conversion, the computer will send the printer dot-by-dot instructions for printing the word the way you want it.

A variety of graphics programs are available, with widely differing capabilities for printing text. Low-end signmaking programs (such as Broderbund's popular Print Shop) generally offer a selection of unsophisticated display faces with a clearly "computerized" look to them. High-end business presentation programs (such as Aldus Freehand or Software Publishing's Harvard Graphics) may offer fewer built-in typefaces—sometimes just Times Roman and Helvetica—but other faces may be added at extra cost, and the lettering produced by these programs invariably has a high-quality, professional appearance.

There are several advantages to using graphics software and a dot-matrix printer to produce display lettering. The chief advantage is flexibility: most graphics programs contain information about a wide variety of typefaces, and can use that information to construct a font of just about any size. A secondary advantage is that the process is entirely automated: you do not have to draw or arrange the letters and the computer takes care of spacing and alignment automatically. (You can, of course, override the automatic settings and make adjustments manually.) A third advantage, especially important in a library environment, is low cost: a good letter-quality dot-matrix printer can be had for under $300, and low-end graphics software often costs less than $100.

At the same time, there are a number of disadvantages that must be taken into account. Although a dot-matrix printer may be inexpensive, the computer hardware required to run high-end graphics software is not. (For best results, your computer should have a lot of memory and a hard disk.) Furthermore, no dot-matrix printer will ever give you top-quality lettering, no matter how well it is guided by your computer. Because dot-matrix printers print line by line, their graphic output tends to be somewhat streaky, and the edges of letters sometimes have a slightly ragged look. If your printer uses cloth ribbons (as most do), the lettering they print will be dark gray rather than sharp black. (Some dot-matrix printers allow you to use carbon film ribbons, which do print true black, but these may be an expensive luxury. Unlike cloth ribbons, film ribbons are not reusable, and one ribbon can easily be exhausted after just a few pages of graphics.)

A final disadvantage is that printing in graphics mode can be excruciatingly slow. Because your computer must convert your text to dot-by-dot instructions and the printer must follow these instructions one by one, it may take as long as an hour to print a single page. See figure 3.10 for an example of text printed in graphics mode on a dot-matrix printer.

Laser Printers   A laser printer is the ideal tool for producing display-quality text and graphics. Because it constructs an image electronically (by means of a laser beam) rather than mechanically (for example, by means of a print head shuttling back and forth across a page), it can deliver a finished page with amazing speed, even at a resolution of 300 dots per inch. Because a laser printer uses the same reproduction technology as the best photocopying machines, its output is always clear, sharp, and black.

Unlike other kinds of printers, laser printers are, in effect, small computers. In order to produce high-resolution graphics, laser printers must be able to process complex information quickly. Even the least expensive laser printers have large amounts of memory and sophisticated microprocessors that allow them to "understand" graphic-oriented computer languages.

The manufacturers of the most widely used laser printers are Hewlett-Packard, creator of the LaserJet family, and Apple, creator of the LaserWriter family. The major difference between these two families lies in the languages they use: commands to a LaserJet must be expressed in the Hewlett-Packard Printer Control Language (HP PCL), while commands to a LaserWriter must be expressed in the PostScript Page Description Language (PostScript PDL). Most competing manufacturers designate their laser printers as "HP-compatible" or "PostScript-compatible," depending on which of the two languages they build into their products.

Which type of printer to use depends chiefly on the capabilities of your computer and software. (Programs written for the Apple Macintosh generally use the PostScript language exclusively. Programs written for the IBM PC often "speak" both languages, although low-end software may not have PostScript capability.) Another important factor, however, is cost: a PostScript-compatible printer generally costs at least $1,000 more than an equivalent HP-compatible printer. This significant price difference is due, in part, to the very different ways these printers handle text.

The typical HP-compatible printer comes with two monospaced fonts installed—10-pitch Courier and a relatively useless line printer font. In order to take advantage of the printer's full capabilities, you have to add supplementary fonts yourself. One way to do this is to install hard fonts (font cartridges), which contain bitmaps of one or more typefaces in several point sizes. (A bitmap, to review, is a dot-by-dot representation of a graphic image.) Another way is to use soft fonts, which are bitmaps that are stored in the printer's memory rather than in plug-in cartridges. (Manufacturers of soft fonts provide software that allows you to load these fonts into the printer's memory. Unlike cartridge fonts, soft fonts disappear when the printer's power is shut off and have to be loaded into memory again the next time they are used.)

Once these extra fonts have been added, using them is quite simple. Graphics software is not necessary; an ordinary word-processing program can tell the laser printer which font to use by sending a series

Figure 3.10 Text printed in graphics mode from dot-matrix printer

of codes. After sending these codes, your word-processing program sends a series of letters to the printer—for example, *C, A, T*—and the printer automatically prints those letters in the designated font. In this way, using an HP-compatible laser printer is similar to using a dot-matrix printer in character mode. Unlike a dot-matrix printer, however, a laser printer can handle large and complex characters. If you have selected a 36-point Bookman Italic font, simply sending the letter *A* to the printer will cause a 36-point *A* to be printed in Bookman Italic with no further instructions necessary.

Unfortunately, there are limitations to this system. An HP-compatible printer can handle only a limited number of fonts at one time. If you decide to use 37-point type instead of 36-point type, you may have to delete the first font from the printer's memory and replace it with the second. (If you are using font cartridges, you may be out of luck entirely—since 37 points is not a standard size and may not be available on a cartridge at all.) You may also have to go through the trouble of "telling" your word-processing software about every font you have installed or deleted. (Without this information, the computer cannot send the proper font-selection codes to the printer.)

PostScript-compatible printers get around these limitations by using font outlines instead of bitmapped fonts. A *font outline* is a generalized, electronically coded description of a typeface that can be converted automatically into bitmapped characters of any size. For example, if you load a Bookman Italic font outline into a PostScript-compatible printer, you can print Bookman Italic characters in 2-point, 20-point, or 200-point sizes with no fuss. Your word-processing software simply specifies the point size, and the printer does the rest. Using the same font outline, a PostScript-compatible printer can rotate characters, create special effects such as shading and drop shadows, and print white on black.

All PostScript-compatible printers come equipped with a number of font outlines. (An Apple LaserWriter Plus, for example, comes with 35-font outlines built in.) PostScript-compatible printers also allow "soft" font outlines to be loaded into memory.

Of course, every laser printer can be used in graphics mode. In that case, the differences between HP-compatible and PostScript-compatible printers become less important. As you read earlier, many graphics programs contain their own font outlines and can generate bitmaps of text characters *within the computer.* These dot-by-dot instructions can be sent to a laser printer just as easily as to a dot-matrix printer (and most graphics programs do, in fact, work equally well with both kinds of printer). When bitmapped text characters from a graphics program are printed on a laser printer, they come out crisp and black—without the raggedness, streakiness, and grayness that plague dot-matrix output.

The versatility and high print quality of laser printers place them far above any other kind of printer. They do, however, have one great drawback—their price. Not only are the printers themselves quite costly (the least expensive HP compatibles cost about $1,000), but there are many associated expenses as well. Sophisticated word-processing and graphics programs that can take advantage of a laser printer's capabilities may cost as much as $500 each. A family of soft font outlines (that is, roman, italic, bold, and bold italic versions of a single typeface) usually costs well over $100. Maintenance costs for a laser printer can also be quite high. For these reasons, many libraries still rely entirely on dot-matrix printers, daisy-wheel printers, and typewriters.

This picture will change, no doubt, as prices for laser printers come down in the future. In the meantime, if your library doesn't have a laser printer, you may be able to rent time on one at a local service bureau. (See *Service Bureaus* in this chapter.)

Another drawback of laser printers is the difficulty of learning to use them effectively. The principles of soft fonts, font outlines, and printer control languages can be hard to grasp, and the learning process often takes weeks. This problem, too, may eventually become less significant as the technology "settles in" and manufacturers find ways to make these products easier to use.

Drawbacks   There are two restrictions that apply to computer-generated lettering in general, regardless of what kind of printer is used. The first is size: for the most part, the size of any lettering you print will be limited to what fits on an 8 1/2-by-11-inch sheet of paper. (Even if you have a wide-carriage printer that handles 11-by-17-inch sheets, you are unlikely to find a graphics program that will accommodate so large a drawing area.) You can, however, enlarge computer-generated lettering after it is printed (see *Photocopying* and *PMTs* in this chapter).

The second restriction is color: on most printers, you will be able to print only in black. Colored ribbons (for daisy-wheel and dot-matrix printers) and colored toner cartridges (for laser printers) may be found in some mail-order catalogs, but their quality is questionable, and most printer manufacturers do not recommend that you use them.

There are, of course, a number of full-color printers on the market, but it is unlikely that your library would have one (or would want to buy one). Dot-matrix color printers (sometimes available for as little as $200) use 9-pin print heads and multibanded colored ribbons to produce streaky, muddy output. Ink-jet color printers (generally $1,000 or more), which spray tiny bursts of colored ink onto paper, are notorious for their unreliability. The best color printers are thermal-transfer printers, which use tiny heating elements to melt bits of colored wax onto paper. These printers do produce high-quality output, but they are expensive—$8,000 or more, on the average.

Color printing technology promises to improve in the future; quality will undoubtedly improve and prices will come down. In the meantime, though color printers might be a good investment for a graphics-oriented business (such as an advertising agency), they remain impractical for most libraries.

Cutout Lettering

Outlining letters on paper or cloth and cutting them out individually is an excellent way to produce attractive, colorful lettering of any size. This technique is better suited to temporary displays than to permanent ones: letters cut from colored paper are easy to handle but tend to fade after prolonged exposure to sunlight; letters cut from cloth keep their color better, but their edges tend to curl up after they have been glued to a backing. For special effects, you might consider cutting letters from felt or foil.

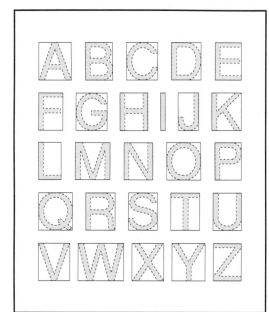

Figure 3.11 Simple block alphabet with cut lines

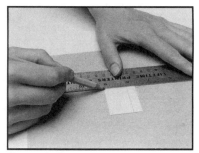

Figure 3.12 Copying the letter *L* onto rectangle

Figure 3.13 Copying a corner of the letter *O* onto rectangle

It is possible to make cutout letters in any style, but simple, block letters (especially uppercase letters) are easiest. By cutting your paper or cloth into strips, and then cutting off a rectangle for each letter, you can make sure your letters will be a uniform height. The dotted lines in figure 3.11 show the pieces of the rectangle you will need to cut away to make each letter.

The following is a suggested series of steps for producing the word LOOK in 2-inch-high cutout letters.

1. Using a pencil and a ruler, make a small mark 2 inches down one end of a sheet of colored paper. Make another mark 2 inches down the other end, and then connect the marks with a light pencil line.

2. With the ruler and a knife, cut along the line to make a 2-inch-wide strip of paper.

3. Following the directions from step 1, make a vertical line about 1 1/2 inches from the leftmost end of the paper strip. Use your ruler and a knife to cut off the rectangle marked by your vertical line.

4. Copy the letter *L* from figure 3.11 onto the rectangle (figure 3.12). Since you have to draw only two lines, you should be able to do this freehand, using your ruler to keep the lines straight.

5. Cut along the two lines you just drew and set the resulting letter *L* aside.

6. Repeat step 3 to cut another rectangle from the strip.

7. Copy one corner of the letter *O* from figure 3.11 onto the rectangle (figure 3.13). No tools will help you here; use your eye to guide you.

8. Cut off the corner you just outlined. Do not discard the piece you cut away.

9. Use the piece you cut away in step 8 as a template for the other three corners of the rectangle (figure 3.14). Line up the straight edges of the template with the edges of the rectangle; then trace the curved

portion lightly with your pencil. (This step is optional. You can, if you wish, simply copy the other three corners as you did the first, but this technique assures that your *O* will be as symmetrical as possible.)

10. Cut away the other three corners of the rectangle and discard them, leaving a neat oval. Then, using figure 3.11 as a guide, copy the center hole of the *O* onto your oval.

11. Carefully cut out the center of the *O* (figure 3.15). Then repeat step 3 to cut another rectangle from the strip.

12. Trace your finished *O* onto the newly cut rectangle. Keep your pencil lines as close as possible to the original shape. Then cut out the second *O*, keeping your knife blade just inside the pencil lines.

13. Follow steps 3 through 5 to make the letter *K*. Then carefully erase the pencil outlines on all four letters.

14. Draw a baseline on your backing material (for example, paper, cloth, or cardboard) and arrange the letters so their bottom edges are just touching the line (figure 3.16). When you are satisfied with the arrangement and spacing of the letters, glue them down. (For hints on letterspacing, see ***Spacing*** in this chapter. For suggestions on gluing, see ***Fastening/Mounting*** in chapter 5.)

If you wish, you can follow the same series of steps using a strip of graph paper. The grid on the graph paper will help keep your vertical lines vertical, your horizonal lines horizontal, and your curved lines steady. After you have cut your letters out of the graph paper, you can trace them onto a strip of colored paper or cloth and cut them out again.

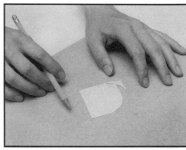

Figure 3.14 Template for tracing other corners of the letter *O* onto rectangle

Figure 3.15 Cutting out the center of letter *O*

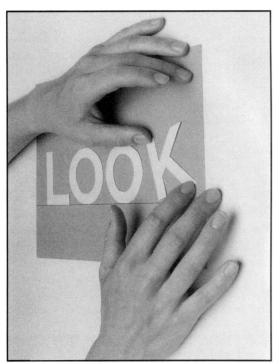

Figure 3.16 Arranging cut letters on baseline

Cutout letters are ideal for large signs and banners because they can be produced in virtually any size and color. They have the added advantage of flexibility: they can be moved and rearranged endlessly before being glued down. Their major drawback is that cutting out large numbers of letters can be very tedious work—especially if you decide to use a more complicated type style than the one illustrated here. Another drawback—at least for some people—is that outlining and cutting out presentable letters demands a steady hand and some degree of practice.

One way to get around these drawbacks is to use a letter-cutting machine from Ellison Educational Equipment, Inc. in Newport, California. The Ellison Letter Machine is an ingenious cookie-cutter device that can cut out letters in nine different styles and five different sizes. (See Appendix A for more information.) Unfortunately, using the Ellison machine is a far more expensive option than cutting out letters by hand: a starter set, including the machine and one set of dies, may cost anywhere from $795 to over $1,000 (depending on the type style you choose).

Enlargement/Reduction

For photomechanical methods, see *Photocopying* and *PMTs* in this chapter. For manual methods, see *Enlargement/Reduction* in chapter 4.

Felt-Tip Markers

The proper name for these is actually porous-tip markers, since the points of many markers (especially in smaller sizes) are made of plastic rather than felt. Nevertheless, felt-tip markers remains the usual term; it will be used here to refer to any writing instrument in which liquid ink flows through a porous tip.

The ink in felt-tip markers comes in two varieties, permanent and water soluble. Permanent ink is more opaque, more vivid, and more likely to "spread" or "bleed" when applied to paper. Water-soluble ink is easier to remove from skin or clothing, more likely to fade or change color, and (true to its name) more likely to run when it gets wet. Most markers are labeled either permanent or watercolor, but, if a marker is not so labeled, the best way to tell what kind of ink it contains is to sniff the tip. Permanent ink has a strong smell reminiscent of alcohol or gasoline; water-soluble ink tends to be odorless.

For letters and shapes drawn in one solid color, permanent markers are the better choice. If, however, you plan to use two colors that touch each other (for example, outlining a letter with one color and filling it in with another), your best bet is to use one marker of each type. The reason is chemical rather than aesthetic: if a permanent marker comes in contact with permanent ink of another color—even if the ink has dried completely—the new ink will dissolve the old and create a muddy smear. A watercolor marker has the same effect if it comes in contact with water-soluble ink. But if you outline a letter with one kind of ink and fill it in with the other, neither color will be disturbed.

Nearly every stationery store stocks several brands of felt-tip markers in eight or ten standard colors. If that selection is too limited for

```
ABCDE
FGHIJK
LMNOP
QRSTU
VWXYZ
```

Figure 3.17 Serif alphabet

your purposes, you will find that most larger art supply stores stock professional markers in dozens of additional colors.

The tips of felt-tip markers come in a dizzying range of sizes, from hairline (measurable in thousandths of an inch) to jumbo (about half an inch wide). The larger sizes usually have square or flat tips, similar to the nib of a calligrapher's pen. When such a marker is held with the broad edge parallel (or nearly parallel) to the bottom of the page, it makes narrow horizontal strokes and broad vertical strokes. For this reason, wide felt-tip markers are especially appropriate for serif typefaces.

Figure 3.17 illustrates a simple serif alphabet suitable for drawing with a felt-tip marker. Note that in the curved parts of letters (such as the right side of the uppercase *P*), the line grows gradually thicker as it moves from horizontal to vertical. There is no trickery necessary; simply holding the marker steady and keeping the flat edge in its proper orientation will achieve the desired effect. In those rare cases when a letter requires narrow vertical strokes (as in the upper serifs of the uppercase *T*), you can add them quickly by using the corner of the marker. To avoid unwanted spreading or bleeding of ink, never hold a marker in contact with a piece of paper any longer than necessary.

It is never a good idea to draw letters with a felt-tip marker unless you have sketched them first in pencil. (See ***Hand Lettering*** in this chapter.)

Felt-tip markers are easily obtained and convenient to use. They do, however, have drawbacks. Unlike paint, they are not opaque—when used on colored paper, they inevitably allow the background color to show through. Letters drawn with markers are rarely as vivid and striking as letters that have been painted or cut from colored paper. Because they do not come in widths greater than 1/2 inch, they are also less suitable than paint or paper for very large letters.

Glue Lettering

After you have outlined letters in pencil on a piece of cardboard (see ***Hand Lettering*** in this chapter), you can trace the outlines with

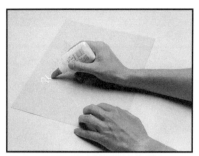

Figure 3.18 Glue bottle tracing pencil line

liquid glue, sprinkle on sparkles or sequins, and shake off the excess. The result is a glittery word or phrase that easily calls attention to itself.

This technique is especially appropriate for script letters, whose consistently narrow lines are easy to trace with the tip of a glue bottle. (See figure 3.18.) It is also possible to apply this technique to block letters such as those in figure 3.11, using rubber cement and a brush to fill in the outlines (figure 3.19). For more details on different kinds of glue, see *Fastening/Mounting* in chapter 5.

Sparkles, sometimes known as *glitter,* are available in many stationery stores and hobby shops. They most often come in a multicolored mixture, but it is possible to find them in individual colors (red, blue, green, and gold) as well. The single-colored sparkles are less garish and tend to work better in most designs.

Before you apply glue and sparkles to a piece of cardboard, spread out a large sheet of newspaper underneath. Apply glue to one letter—or even one part of a letter—at a time, so the glue will not have a chance to dry before you cover it with sparkles. Pour the sparkles on liberally, making sure they cover the entire glued area. Then carefully pick up your piece of cardboard, shake the excess sparkles onto the newspaper, and tap the edge of the cardboard gently against the newspaper a few times to jar loose any stragglers. After you have repeated this process for each letter, you can pour the excess sparkles back into their container. When recycled in this way, one small container of sparkles can be made to last for years.

Letters finished with glue and sparkles are a fine special effect, but they should be used sparingly. They are often more difficult to read than other kinds of lettering, and they may be too showy for all but the most festive displays.

Figure 3.19 Brushing in outlines with rubber cement

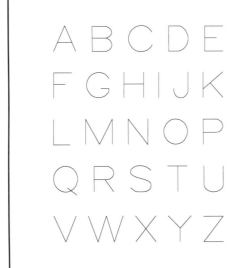

Figure 3.20 Stick-figure alphabet

Hand Lettering

The process of drawing letters by hand has three steps: planning, outlining, and finishing. The planning step includes making a preliminary sketch, determining the appropriate size, style, and color for your lettering, and laying out your space. These procedures were discussed at length in chapter 2. The outlining step, which involves drawing pencil guidelines and sketching each letter in its proper position, will be discussed here. The finishing step—giving each letter its final shape and color—is dealt with elsewhere in this chapter under the headings *Felt-Tip Markers, Glue Lettering,* and *Paint.*

In order to make your letters as consistent as possible, you will need to draw three guidelines for each line of text: a lower line, an upper line, and a middle line about one-third of the way down from the upper line. (The distance between the lower and upper lines should equal the intended height of your capital letters.) You may also want to draw left and right margins—the lines beyond which your lettering will not be allowed to go—and a center line midway between the margins. (See figure 6.1 for a sample set of guidelines.)

Then, using very light pencil strokes, outline each letter in its proper place. There is no need to draw the letter as it will look when it is finished; leave out details such as line thickness, serifs, and ornaments. All that is necessary is to sketch a simple "skeleton"—a stick figure—showing the letter's basic shape and size. Later, when you get to the finishing stage, you can add appropriate embellishments with paint or ink. (Figure 3.20 offers a sample stick-figure alphabet that will serve most of your outlining needs. Figure 3.21 shows how a stick-figure letter can be finished in several different ways.)

One important purpose of drawing these outlines is to make sure that all of your text will fit where it is supposed to. Therefore, as you sketch, keep a mental image of how the final letters will look. If you

Figure 3.21 Stick-figure letter finished in different ways

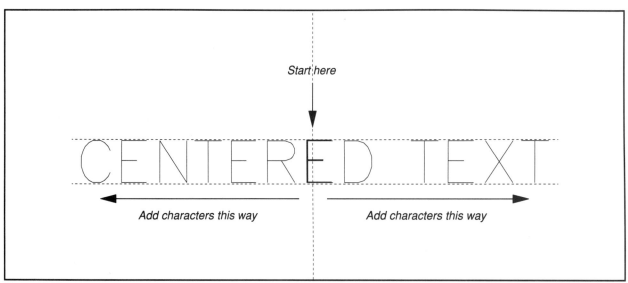

Figure 3.22 Centering from center line

intend to paint your letters with broad brushstrokes, for example, you will want to space your skeleton letters farther apart.

Lines of text are typically either left-aligned, right-aligned, or centered. If you want your text to be left-aligned, sketch the first letter at the left margin and add the remaining letters as you normally would. If you want your text to be right-aligned, you will need to go backwards: sketch the last letter at the right margin and then work your way left, adding one letter at a time.

Centering text is more difficult. One way to handle the task is to count the number of characters (letters and spaces) in the line that you intend to center and determine which character falls in the middle. Sketch that character on the center line (the vertical guideline midway between the left and right margins). Then add the remaining characters: those that precede the middle character must be added backwards, toward the left margin; those that follow the middle character are added normally, toward the right margin. (See figure 3.22 for an example.) This method is not foolproof, however: because not all characters are the same width, the character that is in the middle numerically may not really fall in the center of the line. Therefore, you may have to erase and redraw your outlines several times in order to get your text centered precisely.

Another way to center a line of text is to sketch it first on a separate piece of paper. (You will need to draw a set of guidelines on the paper first.) Then you can measure the actual length of the text line and determine exactly what margins you will need to center it on your display. For example, suppose you sketch out the word REFERENCE and discover that it is 7 inches long. If the empty line on your display is 11 inches long, you will need to place the first letter 2 inches from the left margin and the final letter 2 inches from the right margin in order to center the word. If you use this technique, be sure you sketch your letters on the display *exactly* the way you sketched them on the separate sheet of paper. (You may even want to trace them from the paper to the display: see *Tracing* in chapter 4.)

No matter which type of alignment you use, you may sometimes discover that the text you had intended to put on a line simply will not fit. In that case, you will need to erase the letters you have outlined and start again, making your letters slightly narrower. (Reducing the width of a character without reducing its height is called *condensing* the character. Figure 3.23 is a condensed version of the stick-figure alphabet shown in figure 3.20, for use when space is limited.)

Even though the letters you are sketching are merely skeletons and will never be seen by the public, it is important that they be drawn as carefully as possible. If you look closely at the stick-figure alphabets in figures 3.20 and 3.23, you will see that all the letters are the same height and the crossbars (for example, on the *E* and the *H*) are all halfway between the top and the bottom. (An exception is the *A*, whose crossbar is traditionally lower than those of the other uppercase letters.) There is no need for you to copy these alphabets exactly, but your outlines should be equally neat and consistent. If not, you will run into trouble in the finishing stage—any defects in your letters will become much more apparent when your pencil outlines are enhanced with paint or ink.

Hand-drawn lettering is the most flexible and versatile form of lettering. It can be produced in any size, color, or style. There are no limits to the ways it can be expanded, condensed, rotated, contorted, or modified. It is also the least expensive way to add lettering to a display, even when the costs of finishing materials (such as paint or markers) are included. The only drawback of hand lettering is that it takes some degree of skill and practice to do well. By following the directions given here, virtually anyone can turn out neat, legible, presentable lettering, and this is sufficient for many purposes—but if you want to produce a display that is slick, snazzy, or elegant, you may have to turn to some of the commercial sources or mechanical devices discussed elsewhere in this chapter.

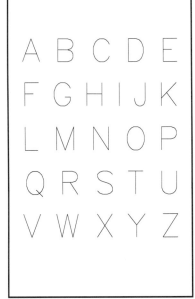

Figure 3.23 Condensed stick-figure alphabet

Light Box

A light box consists of a thick, white, translucent panel (usually coated glass or sturdy plastic) mounted on a box with fluorescent bulbs inside it. When the bulbs are turned on, the translucent panel diffuses the light, and thus any item placed on the light box is illuminated from behind with a soft, white glow. You have probably seen light boxes in doctors' offices, where they are used for viewing X-rays.

When used for graphic arts work, the light box itself becomes a sort of X-ray machine—it allows you to "look through" one layer of work at the layer beneath. Its primary use is for *pasteup*, the process of attaching graphic elements to a piece of white cardboard in preparation for reproduction or printing. (See *Mechanicals* in this chapter.) Without a light box, it can be difficult to position two sheets of paper so that the lettering on one sheet aligns with a pencil guideline on the other. When both sheets are placed on a light box, however, they become translucent—and, as a result, the text can be positioned precisely (figure 3.24).

Light boxes come in many sizes and levels of quality, but they are more expensive than you might expect. Even a relatively small light box (12 by 17 inches) usually costs over $100, and larger light boxes may cost

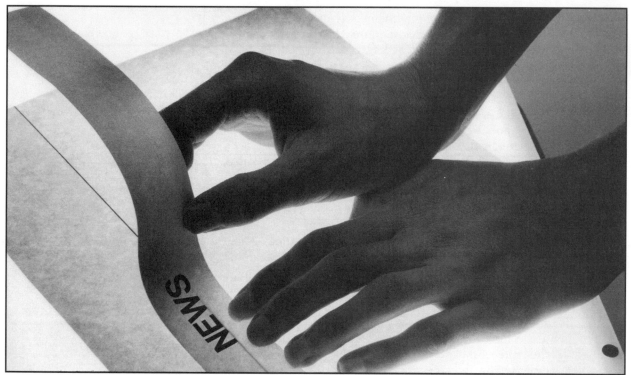

Figure 3.24 Using a light box

hundreds more. Fortunately, unless you intend to do a lot of pasteup work, a light box may be thought of as a luxury rather than a necessity. In a pinch, you can always use "nature's light box"—that is, you can tape your work to the inside of a window and let the sun illuminate it from behind.

Machine-Generated Lettering

You can choose from a number of automatic lettering machines (with brand names such as Kroy and Leteron) at art supply stores or in mail-order catalogs. These machines print professional-quality letters on strips of colored or transparent tape, which can then be applied to a variety of surfaces. If you want to avoid having strips of tape visible in your displays, you can generate black letters on transparent tape and then make a photocopy or PMT of the result. (See *Photocopying* and *PMTs* in this chapter.)

Lettering machines have many advantages. They are quick and easy to use, requiring only that you "dial" each letter and press a button to transfer the letter to the tape. They take care of proportional spacing automatically. They can be used for a variety of purposes, including name tags and equipment labels, as well as for displays.

There are some drawbacks, however. Each lettering machine comes with only one font, typically 24-point Helvetica. Additional fonts must be purchased separately, and the selection of typefaces and point sizes is rather slim. Color selection is slim as well: you may have to choose between red, blue, or black letters on transparent tape or black letters on red, blue, yellow, or green tape. The final drawback, especially for small libraries, is cost. The least expensive Kroy machine costs about $150, but it cannot print letters any larger than 24 points. Machines that can print larger letters, or that are built to withstand heavier use, may cost much more. (For example, a Leteron machine that can print 2-inch-high letters costs over $1,000.) If you cannot afford a lettering machine, you can achieve similar results with rub-on lettering (see *Rub-On Lettering* in this chapter).

Mechanicals

A *mechanical* is a black-and-white original that is intended for reproduction or printing. It typically consists of a number of graphic elements (text and/or illustrations) that have been pasted to a piece of white cardboard. Mechanicals are known informally as *boards*, and the process of making a mechanical is known as *pasteup*.

The easiest way to produce a mechanical is to use a commercially manufactured layout grid. This is a sheet of cardboard with non-reproducing blue guidelines printed on it (see *Nonrepro Blue* in this chapter). If you decide to use ordinary white cardboard instead, you'll have to draw the guidelines yourself. (Guidelines are absolutely necessary to assure that your lettering is straight and properly aligned. For tips on drawing them, see *Hand Lettering* in this chapter.)

You should never paint, glue, or rub individual letters directly onto a mechanical. Instead, cut a sheet of white paper into strips and draw a blue baseline on each strip. Then do your lettering one line at a time, putting each line of lettering on a separate strip. (For an example of this procedure, see *Clip-Art Alphabets* in this chapter.) If you are using graphics or illustrations, you will want those to be on separate sheets of paper as well.

After you have prepared each element individually, you can place the elements on your sheet of white cardboard and arrange them as you like. Match the blue baseline of each line of text with the proper guideline on the mechanical (figure 3.25). When you align text at the left or right margin, make sure that you align the letter itself—not the edge of the paper strip. Using a light box makes alignment easier—see *Light Box* in this chapter.

When you are satisfied with the arrangement of all your elements, you can paste them down. For suggestions on how to do so, see *Fastening/Mounting* in chapter 5.

Your finished mechanical will not look very presentable. It will be covered with strips and squares of paper whose cut edges are all too apparent and whose color may range from eggshell to pure white. Its grid of blue guidelines will still be at least partly visible.

All of these imperfections will disappear, however, when you make a good-quality reproduction of the mechanical. (See *Photocopying* and *PMTs* in this chapter.) For example, figure 3.26 shows an attractive sign; figure 3.27 shows the mechanical that this sign was reproduced from.

If you do not intend to reproduce your lettering by means of a photocopy or PMT, there is no reason to make a mechanical. Instead, use the layout techniques described in the section on hand lettering.

Figure 3.25 Aligning baseline on paper strip with guideline on mechanical

Figure 3.26 PMT of mechanical for sign

Figure 3.27 Original mechanical of sign

45

Nonrepro Blue

Nonrepro blue is the common name for a color that does not show up in black-and-white photographic reproductions. It is not, in fact, a single, specific color, but rather a range of light-blue tints that are invisible when photographed on high-contrast film.

Designers use nonrepro blue to draw guidelines on any item from which they intend to make a PMT. (A PMT is a high-quality, high-contrast reproduction—see *PMTs* in this chapter.) Guidelines drawn in ordinary pencil must be erased before a PMT is made, but guidelines drawn in nonrepro blue need not be. Figure 3.27, for example, shows a pasteup with nonrepro blue lines; figure 3.26 shows a PMT made from that pasteup.

Nonrepro blue does not work as reliably with photocopying machines (for example, Xerox copiers). Many older copying machines do pick up nonrepro blue lines, while most newer machines—designed with nonrepro blue in mind—do not. Some copying machines have a special button which, when pushed, forces the machine not to copy nonrepro blue. Even these machines, however, may pick up some blue lines that would be ignored by the PMT process. If you are planning to buy or lease a copying machine, you may want to test it with several nonrepro blue tints.

Art supply stores sell special pencils and pens that can be used to draw nonrepro blue lines. These pencils and pens are quite inexpensive and extremely useful. Some larger art stores also sell layout grids, sheets of white cardboard imprinted with vertical and horizontal nonrepro blue lines. These boards can come in very handy for pasteup work, because they save you from having to measure and draw your own guidelines.

If you have ordinary graph paper with light-blue squares, you may be able to use it as a substitute for a professional layout grid. Be aware, however, that the ink used for most graph paper is on the fringe of the nonrepro spectrum and thus may not "disappear" as you intend it to. The only way to know for sure is to test it.

Paint

Paint is an old, reliable, and very attractive way to finish hand lettering (see *Hand Lettering* in this chapter). It is easily obtained in stationery stores, art supply stores, and hobby shops. The kinds of paint you are most likely to encounter are acrylic, enamel, oil, tempera, and watercolor.

Acrylic   Acrylic paint is a plastic-based alternative to oil paint, used by fine artists as well as graphic artists. It comes in tubes with unusual color names such as cadmium red and cobalt blue. It blends easily, brushes on smoothly, and dries quickly to a smooth, matte finish. Because it is water soluble, it is easily removed from hands and brushes while it is still wet. Once it has dried, however, acrylic paint is permanent and waterproof. It resists fading, cracking, color changes, and other kinds of long-term deterioration.

To use acrylic paint, squeeze a small blob onto a palette (a clean piece of corrugated cardboard will work fine; no store-bought palette is necessary). Keep a cup of water nearby and dip your brush into it often as you work with the paint. You can mix colors by dipping your brush into two different blobs of paint and smearing them together on the palette. If you want a thinner consistency, add a few drops of water.

Acrylic paint is excellent both for lettering and for illustration. Because it is intended primarily for fine artists, however, it is more expensive than the general-purpose tempera paint that you are probably accustomed to using. You may want to reserve it for situations in which good quality and permanence are especially important.

Enamel   Enamel is a thick, durable, oil-based paint with a glossy finish. It is most often found in hobby shops (where it is sold in tiny bottles for painting plastic models) and in hardware stores. It is extremely difficult to remove from hands, brushes, or anything else. You will rarely need enamel for library displays unless you plan to paint on plastic or metal.

Oil   Oil paint is the medium of choice for fine artists, but it is never appropriate for library displays. Its primary drawback is that it requires days, or even weeks, to dry completely. If you need a high-quality appearance, use acrylic paint instead.

Tempera   Tempera paint, also known as *poster paint*, is the type of paint most often found in stationery stores and used in elementary school classrooms. It is available in tubes and in powdered form, but most people buy it as a liquid in jars. It is sold in a relatively limited number of colors, chiefly bright primary and secondary colors.

Because it is a liquid, tempera paint is very easy to use. You can dip your brush directly into the paint jar, or you can pour paint into a paper cup and dip your brush into that. You can mix colors by pouring paint from different jars into a cup. Tempera paint is water based, so you can clean up easily with water.

Because tempera paint is inexpensive, easy to get, and easy to use, it is well suited for most library display purposes. It does, however, have some drawbacks when compared to acrylic paint. Because of its high water content, it has a tendency to drip or to buckle the cardboard it is applied to. It dries to a dull, sometimes powdery finish and tends to fade or flake with time. It is not entirely opaque, so pencil lines and "slips of the brush" are sometimes difficult to obliterate. It is most appropriate for temporary posters or when a slick, professional look is not the highest priority.

Watercolor   Watercolor paints are available in liquid or powdered form, but they are most often sold as solid cakes. Multicolored assortments of these cakes are packaged in plastic or metal trays with hinged lids, often with a small brush included. To use watercolors, dip the brush into water and then rub it against a cake until it picks up a satisfactory amount of pigment. Then apply the paint gently to absorbent white or off-white paper.

The delicate, transparent colors of watercolor paint are usually not appropriate for library displays. In a pinch, watercolors might be used as a substitute for water-based markers to color a black-and-white line drawing. (See *Felt-Tip Markers* in this chapter and in chapter 4.) Watercolors should never be used for lettering.

ABCDEFGHI JKLMNOPQ RSTUVWXYZ

Figure 3.28 Casual brush alphabet

Brushes In order to use any kind of paint, you will need a brush. Brushes come in a variety of materials, shapes, and sizes, each of which is appropriate for different conditions.

The best kind of brush for serif lettering is broad, flat, and stiff. When the flat edge of such a brush is held parallel with the bottom of the page, it can be used to make narrow horizontal strokes and broad vertical strokes. (See *Felt-Tip Markers* and figure 3.17 in this chapter.)

For looser, casual lettering, you will want to use a soft, round brush. Figure 3.28 shows you an appropriate alphabet for this kind of brush, with rounded corners and easy curves.

When you find a brush shape and a lettering style that you are comfortable with, you will probably want to get the same brush in several different widths so you can draw letters in different sizes.

Applications As a way to finish hand-drawn letters, paint has several advantages over felt-tip markers. Unlike markers, which are available in only a limited number of colors, paint can be mixed to make any color imaginable. Those colors are also bolder, more vivid, and (in the case of acrylic paint, at least) more opaque than their felt-tip counterparts. Because it can be applied evenly and smoothly with wide brushes, paint is also more suitable for very large letters. (Cutting letters from paper is also appropriate for large sizes—see *Cutout Lettering* in this chapter— but painting is much less tedious.)

In many ways, however, felt-tip markers are preferable to paint. Because they do not require accessories such as palettes, brushes, and drop cloths, markers are simpler to use. Markers do not have to be washed as paint brushes do, and they do not drip on floors or furniture. Most important, people tend to feel more comfortable with a marker than with a brush: because of its solid, pencil-like feel, the marker is easier for a nonartist to manipulate and control.

It is certainly true that using paint well—especially for lettering—requires some degree of skill or experience. Do not, however, let your lack of experience steer you away from paint altogether. You may want to get a brush and a single color of paint to experiment with. (Remember to outline letters carefully in pencil before painting them, as described in the section on hand lettering.) You are likely to find that with a few hours' practice, you can turn out quite satisfactory lettering that will add color and energy to your displays.

Photocopying

Office photocopiers have come a long way in the thirty years since they first became widely available. At one time, a photocopy was simply a practical substitute for a carbon copy—it was convenient, but it did not look very good. Today, in contrast, a photocopy often looks better than the original. A good photocopier has become one of the most useful tools for producing library displays, even when multiple copies of the same display are not needed.

Here are some of the things you can do with today's photocopiers:

- *Cleanup.* A photocopier can make a "clean" copy of a mechanical, eliminating pasteup lines, guidelines, eraser smudges, and correction fluid spots. (See *Mechanicals* in this chapter.) If some elements on your mechanical are mottled or dark gray (for example, computer-generated lettering printed with a cloth ribbon), a good photocopier will convert them to a smooth, dark black. Similarly, if your mechanical includes several shades of white paper, a photocopier will usually ignore the variations and provide a uniform, white background.

  Most copiers made in recent years are designed to ignore nonrepro blue (see *Nonrepro Blue* in this chapter.) Many older copiers, however, will pick up nonrepro blue lines and print them in a faint gray. If your copier falls into the latter category, be sure to erase all outlines and guidelines from your mechanical before making copies.

- *Enlargement/reduction.* Many copying machines allow you to enlarge or reduce an image simply by pressing a button. Some copiers can enlarge or reduce only in fixed ratios (66 percent and 77 percent are typical); others allow you to choose any ratio you want in 1 percent increments. To determine the ratio you need, divide the size of the copy by the size of the original and multiply the result by 100. For example, if you have a line of type that is 3 inches high and you want a copy that is 4 1/2 inches high, divide 4.5 by 3 to get 1.5. Then multiply 1.5 by 100 to get 150 percent, the enlargement setting you need. Similarly, if you have a line of type that is 3 inches high and you want a copy that is 2 inches high, divide 2 by 3 to get 0.666. . . . Round that result to 0.67 and multiply it by 100 to get 67 percent, the reduction setting you need.

  There are, of course, some limits to how far you can go—many copiers, for example, will not accept reduction settings below 20 percent or enlargement settings above 150 percent. If necessary, it is possible to get around these restrictions by making a copy of a copy: for example, if you need a 175 percent enlargement, you can make a copy at 140 percent and then make a 125 percent enlargement of that copy. Keep in mind, however, that image quality deteriorates slightly with each new generation.

- *Printing onto different materials.* No law says that every photocopy must be made on plain, white paper. By replacing a copier's standard paper with colored paper, lined paper, or graph paper, you can achieve a number of interesting effects. Many photocopiers will even copy onto clear acetate, available at office supply stores.

  Some photocopiers have a slot that allows you to insert single sheets of alternative copy paper, automatically bypassing the copier's usual paper supply. If the machine you are using does not have this feature, you will have to remove the standard paper from the paper tray and replace it with your alternative paper.

  Keep in mind that some machines are pickier than others about accepting nonstandard copy paper. Check with the manufacturer, the key operator, or the service representative before experimenting with different kinds of paper; otherwise you may damage the machine.

- *Screening.* Photocopiers are designed to copy sharp blacks and whites rather than shades of gray. For this reason, photographs ordinarily do not copy well. Today, however, some photocopiers are equipped with a "photo" button that scans photographs and converts them into dot patterns. (To find out more about this process, called *screening,* see **Reproduction** in chapter 4.) Photocopies produced in this manner retain all the shadings of the original. They may be recopied, enlarged, or reduced with much better results than you might expect.

- *Stretching/squeezing.* The most sophisticated photocopiers on today's market can enlarge in one dimension while keeping the other dimension constant. Using such a machine, for example, you could "stretch" a line of Helvetica type (that is, extend the horizontal axis without changing the vertical axis) and end up with Helvetica Extended. Similarly, you could "squeeze" the same line of type (that is, reduce the horizontal axis without changing the vertical axis) to come out with Helvetica Narrow. Although copiers with this capability are still quite rare, they will probably become increasingly available in the next few years.

- *Color copying.* Full-color photocopiers have been around for quite a while, but they have never been very popular. The original color copiers tended to break down frequently. When they did work properly, they produced muddy-looking copies whose colors barely resembled those of the items they reproduced. Even so, the few commercial copy shops that offered color copying often charged as much as three or four dollars per copy.

  In the past few years, however, manufacturers have taken advantage of advances in laser-printing technology to design greatly improved color copiers. The machines themselves are more reliable, the copies are sharper and truer, and the per-copy cost has come down considerably. Photocopying has now become a viable way to reproduce color photographs and colored lettering.

All color copiers have screening capability built in, and many have enlargement and reduction capability as well. Color copiers cannot, however, be used to produce a "clean" copy of a mechanical. Pasteup lines will show up in shades of gray, and variations in whites and blacks may be accentuated rather than smoothed. Nonrepro blue will print as visibly as any other color. These restrictions make color copiers significantly less useful than ordinary black-and-white copiers.

A handy, low-cost alternative to a full-color copier is a monochrome copier that accepts colored toner cartridges. (The best known machines of this type are made by Canon.) Such a copier will not reproduce colored originals, but it will produce single-colored copies. For example, if you install a green cartridge and then copy a black-on-white mechanical, you will get a green-on-white photocopy. By feeding the same copy through the machine several times—using different mechanicals and different color cartridges—you can build a multicolored copy. (See Plate 3 for an example.)

If the photocopiers in your library were made during the past ten years, they are likely to have at least some of the foregoing capabilities. Enlargement and reduction, in particular, are now included on all but the most inexpensive machines. When you need to take advantage of a feature that your library's copiers do not have, you can go to a storefront copy center or a service bureau (see **Service Bureaus** in this chapter).

Self-service copy shops have become increasingly common in recent years; most communities have at least one, and some communities have dozens. Many copy shops have several kinds of photocopiers, with different capabilities and different per-copy prices. A typical shop might offer ordinary copies for seven cents each, high-quality copies for ten cents each, enlargements or reductions for twenty cents each, and "special effects" such as screening for fifty cents each. (Average prices may be higher in small communities or lower in large communities. In a major city or a college town, where competition is fierce, photocopies often cost as little as two and a half cents each.) Because the photocopiers in these shops are usually up to date and well maintained, they will probably produce better copies than you can get from the machines in your library. Therefore, you may want to use a commercial shop for all your display-related copying.

Despite its unmatched convenience, low cost, and growing versatility, photocopying does have some drawbacks. The most important is image quality: no matter how clean and clear a photocopy may be, it will never be quite as sharp as the original. Tiny, fine lines tend to get lost, and square corners tend to become rounded. These deficiencies become even more apparent when you make a copy of a copy.

Size limitations are another drawback. The copying machines in most libraries and offices are limited to 8 1/2-by-14-inch copies. Larger machines, which can handle 11-by-17-inch copies, may be found in many commercial copy shops. Some copy shops are now installing machines that can make poster-sized (20-by-30-inch) copies, but these machines are not yet widely available.

A final drawback of photocopying is that photocopies smear easily when they become wet or damp. If you try to color a photocopied image with paint or felt-tip markers, you are likely to smudge it. If you use liquid glue to fasten a photocopy to a cardboard backing, the glue may soak through the paper and ruin the image. If you use white correction fluid to cover an unwanted spot on a photocopy, you may end up with a muddy, gray blotch. (Liquid Paper correction fluid comes in a special formulation called Just For Copies, which largely solves this last problem.) For safety's sake, always make two or three photocopies even if you need only one. Then, if you accidentally smear one copy, you will be sure to have another available.

PMTs

PMT is an abbreviation for *photomechanical transfer,* a black-and-white reproduction that resembles a photocopy but is of much higher quality. To most graphic arts professionals, PMTs are known as *photostats* or, informally, as *stats.* The process of making a PMT is known even more informally as *statting.*

In order to make a stat, a technician uses a large-format camera to photograph the original onto high-contrast, light-sensitive paper. The copy, once developed, appears as a crisp black image on a glossy white background. Unlike an ordinary photocopy, a PMT is virtually as sharp and clear as the original. In many cases, only a trained eye can tell the difference between an original image and its PMT copy.

A PMT consists only of blacks and whites, with no grays. If an original includes any color or shade other than black and white, the PMT process either converts it to black or ignores it. Red and orange always become black on a PMT. Blue is generally invisible to the PMT process, and therefore light-blue lines on an original will not appear at all on a PMT. (See **Nonrepro Blue** in this chapter. For more information about statting images that include grays or colors, see **Reproduction** in chapter 4.)

A PMT can be used for some of the same purposes that photocopies are used for: making a "clean" copy of a mechanical, enlarging, reducing, and screening. (For fuller explanations of these terms, see **Mechanicals** and **Photocopying** in this chapter.) In fact, due to their far superior image quality, PMTs are clearly preferable to photocopies for all of these purposes. In addition, PMTs are extremely durable—they can be glued, painted, drawn on, or retouched without damage.

PMTs do have several drawbacks, chiefly involving convenience and cost. An ordinary photocopy is easy to get—you can make one yourself, either on your library's copier or at a commercial copy shop. A PMT, in contrast, must be made professionally at what may be a less accessible location. (To find a source for PMTs, look in the Yellow Pages for printing or typesetting shops that advertise camera work.)

PMTs, unlike photocopies, cannot be made instantly—setting up, photographing, developing, and drying a PMT usually takes about fifteen minutes. Because most printers are not willing to interrupt their work whenever somebody needs a PMT, you will usually be asked to leave your original at the shop and return the next day for your copy. Some businesses advertise "two-hour stats" or even "while-you-wait stats," but proprietors will often do their best to avoid being held to these promises.

Price is the area in which photocopies have the greatest edge over PMTs. At a neighborhood copy shop, a top-quality 8 1/2-by-11-inch photocopy might cost twenty cents at most. In contrast, an 8 1/2-by-11-inch PMT generally costs at least five dollars—a full 2,500 percent more! For this reason alone, you will probably want to use PMTs only when superior image quality is especially important.

In some cases, a choice between photocopies and PMTs is not necessary. Unlike photocopies, PMTs cannot be "stretched," "squeezed," made on different kinds of paper, or made in color. If you need to do any of these things, photocopying is your only option.

Rub-On Lettering

Rub-on letters are microscopically thin plastic characters that are fixed to the underside of a clear plastic sheet (the *carrier*). When the carrier is placed on a piece of paper and a selected letter is rubbed firmly, the letter is transferred to the paper.

Sheets of rub-on lettering are more properly called *dry transfer sheets*. This term, however, embraces a number of other items besides lettering (see, for example, *Rub-On Graphics* in chapter 4). Therefore, the more informal rub-on lettering will be used here to eliminate confusion.

Unlike clip-art lettering (see *Clip-Art Alphabets* in this chapter), rub-on lettering has no white paper background and no visible lines around each letter. Therefore, rub-on lettering can be transferred directly to colored paper or cardboard and used in a display. When transferred to a strip of white paper, it can, of course, be incorporated into a mechanical and reproduced. (See *Mechanicals* in this chapter.)

Before you can use rub-on lettering, you must draw a baseline on which the letters will rest. Different types of baselines are appropriate for different circumstances. If you plan to reproduce the lettering, it is best to draw the baseline with a nonrepro blue pen. (See *Nonrepro Blue* in this chapter.) This line will disappear when you make a photocopy or a PMT. However, if you plan to include the original lettering (rather than a reproduction) in your display, you will want your baseline to be thoroughly invisible. The trick for doing this is to draw the baseline on the *reverse side* of your sheet of paper. Then place the paper, blank side up, on a light box (see *Light Box* in this chapter.)

The baseline will show through from the other side, allowing you to transfer your letters neatly. When the light box is turned off, the baseline will disappear.

If you do not have a light box, or if you are using heavy paper or cardboard that light cannot penetrate, you have no choice but to draw a visible baseline. Draw it very lightly in pencil, so it can just barely be seen. Later, after you have finished transferring your lettering, you will have to erase the line very carefully. Be sure that your eraser does not touch any of the lettering—even the slightest contact with an eraser can damage or destroy a rub-on letter.

Rubbing the letters is best accomplished with a special burnishing tool, available for a few dollars at any art supply store. If you do not have a burnishing tool, use any firm, blunt instrument. The bowl of a

Figure 3.29 Rubbing letter with burnishing tool

spoon works well for large letters; the handle of a spoon works well for small ones.

The following is a suggested series of steps for producing the word LOOK with a sheet of rub-on lettering.

1. Draw a baseline using one of the three techniques described above.

2. Remove the protective backing from your sheet of lettering. Position the sheet so that the letter *L* rests on the baseline. Some brands of rub-on lettering print a positioning bar below each letter on the sheet. In that case, place the positioning bar—not the letter itself—on the baseline.

3. To make sure that the letter is perfectly horizontal, look at the adjoining letters on the sheet and make sure that they (or their positioning bars) are also resting on the baseline.

4. Rub the letter with a burnishing tool. Use smooth, firm strokes, starting from the upper left corner of the letter and working toward the lower right (figure 3.29). As you rub the letter, it will seem to turn gray.

5. Look closely at the letter to make sure it is entirely gray, without black spots indicating nontransferred areas. If you find any black spots, rub them until they turn gray.

6. Carefully lift away the lettering sheet and place the protective backing sheet (or any clean, thin sheet of paper) over the letter. Burnish it firmly to fix the letter permanently to your display (figure 3.30). Some burnishing tools have a hard, flat edge for this purpose.

7. Position the lettering sheet so that the letter *O* is next to the letter *L* you just transferred. In many styles of lettering, the letter *O* (as well as other round-bottomed letters such as *C, G, J, Q,* and *S*) is

Figure 3.30 Protective overlay on letter to be burnished

meant to dip below the baseline. To find out whether this is true for the style you are using, find an *O* that is next to a square-bottomed letter such as *N*. Position the *N* so that it rests on the baseline and note the position of the *O* (figure 3.31). If your brand of rub-on lettering uses positioning bars, place the bar over the baseline as usual. The *O* will automatically be positioned properly.

8. Repeat steps 3 through 7 for both *O*'s, and steps 3 through 6 for the final *K*. (For hints on letterspacing, see *Spacing* in this chapter.) The final result is shown in figure 3.32.

Figure 3.31 Position of letters *N* and *O* on baseline

If you make a mistake in positioning a rub-on letter, you can remove it by pressing a piece of transparent tape over the letter and carefully peeling off the tape. This procedure works best if done between steps 5 and 6—that is, before the letter receives its final burnishing. Once a letter is removed, it cannot be reused.

Rub-on lettering is the most convenient way to add professional-quality text to a display. It demands little skill or experience, requires no special equipment, and is easily obtained.

Most stationery stores and office supply stores carry rub-on lettering, but these mass-market sheets are available in only a few styles and are often of questionable quality. If possible, try to buy your lettering at an art supply store that carries high-quality brands such as Letraset or Chartpak. These manufacturers offer lettering in hundreds of different styles, and most styles are available in sizes from 24 points to 60 points. (Letraset offers its most popular style, Helvetica, in sizes from 6 points to 192 points.)

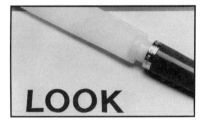

Figure 3.32 Completed word from rub-on letters

The primary drawback of rub-on lettering is its cost. A single sheet of Letraset lettering often costs about twelve dollars and fifty cents. That is fine for small sizes, but as the point size increases, the number of letters per sheet decreases. 120-point Helvetica requires two sheets for its uppercase letters and two sheets for its lowercase letters, or about fifty dollars for the entire font. In such cases, it may be less expensive to have your text professionally typeset. See *Typesetting (Commercial)* in this chapter.

Another drawback of rub-on lettering is its limited color selection. Selected lettering styles may be available in red, blue, green, white, or gold, but most are available only in black. One way around this restriction is to use an "outline" style, which can be colored in later with paint or felt-tip markers.

Service Bureaus

Large corporations can generally afford to buy all the computer equipment they need, but many smaller businesses and institutions cannot. In your library, for instance, the relatively infrequent occasions when you need high-quality graphics may not justify the cost of a laser printer.

In response to this problem, many entrepreneurs have begun to set up desktop publishing shops in which computer time is rented by the hour. Such a shop typically has a selection of Macintosh and IBM computers loaded with popular software, and a single PostScript-compatible laser printer accessible from every computer. (See *Computer-Generated Lettering* in this chapter.) If your library lacks a laser printer, you can store your word-processing or graphics files on a floppy disk, bring the disk to a desktop publishing shop, and print out your files at a typical cost of thirty cents per page. If your library has no computer equipment at all, you can do all your work on the shop's computers for six to ten dollars per hour.

Increasingly, desktop publishing shops are offering services beyond computer rental. Many are equipped with desktop scanners that can convert graphic images, such as photographs, into computer-readable format. (See *Computer Graphics* in chapter 4.) Some also have PostScript-compatible photocompositors, such as the Linotronic 300, that can generate professional-quality, typeset output from ordinary word-processing files. [For an explanation of photocomposition, see *Typesetting (Commercial)* in this chapter.] A few even have film recorders that can make color slides from computer graphics files. Shops with these kinds of advanced capabilities have taken to calling themselves *service bureaus* (an unfortunately inexplicit term, but one that has achieved widespread use).

Service bureaus are a relatively new phenomenon and are not yet available in every community. Finding one is sometimes difficult, especially because Service Bureaus is too vague to be used as a category in the Yellow Pages. Desktop Publishing *is* a valid Yellow Pages category, but not all service bureaus choose to list themselves that way. Your best bet is to look at ads for copy shops, typesetters, computer stores, and photo labs, and see which ones offer the services you need.

Silk Screen Lettering

Silk screening is primarily a graphics medium, but it is a good way to produce multiple copies of colored lettering. For a fuller explanation, see *Silk Screen* in chapter 4.

If you want to produce colored lettering but do not need multiple copies, silk screening is not appropriate. See *Cutout Lettering* and *Hand Lettering* in this chapter for alternative techniques. If you need multiple copies of black-and-white lettering, see *Mechanicals, Photocopying*, and *PMTs* in this chapter.

Spacing

Placing the proper amount of space between letters is an art, not a science. For best results, letterspacing must be done by eye rather than with a ruler.

The basic rule of letterspacing is that all of the letters in a word should *seem* to be equally spaced. Paradoxically, this rule requires most letters to be spaced unequally. For example, look closely at the word CLIMATE in figure 3.33. The *C* and the *L* have what might be considered an average amount of space between them. The *L* and the *I* are practically touching each other, yet they seem to be adequately separated due to the large amount of space "built into" the *L*. In contrast, the vertical strokes of the *I* and the *M* must be placed quite far apart in order for the space between them to seem reasonable.

Figure 3.33 Letterspacing

In some cases, it is necessary to overlap letters to give the impression of uniform spacing. If you look again at the word CLIMATE, for example, you will see that the *A* and the *T* in CLIMATE are slightly overlapped. This sort of overlap is generally not apparent to the untrained eye.

Computer graphics software and lettering machines tend to standardize the amount of space between letters. As a result, mechanically generated letters—especially in large sizes—may seem awkwardly spaced. Some computer programs allow you to make manual adjustments to the space between letters, a process called *kerning*. A few programs, such as WordPerfect, can kern automatically when they encounter certain combinations of letters.

Some manufacturers of rub-on lettering, such as Letraset, include positioning bars on their sheets of lettering. (See **Rub-On Lettering** in this chapter.) These bars are intended not only to show how each letter should be placed on the baseline, but also to indicate the recommended spacing between letters. In general, however, it is a good idea to ignore the bars and to handle letterspacing visually. Like other standardized spacing methods, positioning bars deal poorly with special cases such as the *A* and the *T* in CLIMATE.

When you draw your own lettering (see **Hand Lettering** in this chapter), you have only your own judgment to guide your spacing decisions. If you do not feel confident about your eye for letterspacing, you may prefer to start off with kinds of lettering that can be rearranged easily and then glued down. See, for example, **Clip-Art Alphabets, Cutout Lettering**, and **Stick-On Lettering** in this chapter.

Stencils and Templates

In theory, a *stencil* is an outline designed to be traced along its inside edge, while a *template* is an outline designed to be traced along its outside edge. When applied to lettering, however, these terms are often used interchangeably. In common usage, a lettering guide made of cardboard or metal is usually called a stencil, while a lettering guide made of transparent plastic is usually called a template. Do not look for any logic behind that distinction.

Stencils and templates are really shortcuts for producing uniform hand lettering. To use them, you must first draw baselines and margins as described under **Hand Lettering** in this chapter. Then you can use a stencil or template to outline your letters instead of drawing the outlines freehand.

Later, you can fill in the outlines with paint or markers. (See **Felt-Tip Markers** and **Paint** in this chapter.) When you do so, be sure to fill in the gaps that are characteristic of many stencil-drawn letters (figure 3.34).

Stencils are available at nearly every stationery store, hobby shop, and art supply store. They are made to produce letters in a wide range of sizes, generally from 1/2 inch high to 6 inches high. They are quite inexpensive—an entire alphabet can be had for a few dollars. Plastic templates cost somewhat more than cardboard stencils, but they are heavier-duty and easier to use.

Stencils and templates have serious drawbacks. They are made in very few styles, most of which are unattractive and instantly

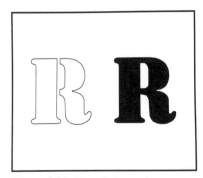

Figure 3.34 Stencil-drawn letter

recognizable as stencil lettering. Moreover, because tracing is an awkward process, letters made with even the best-designed stencils tend to have a cramped, graceless look to them. If you want professional-looking lettering, other commercial products may be preferable. (See, for example, *Machine-Generated Lettering, Rub-On Lettering*, and *Stick-On Lettering* in this chapter.) If you want a more homemade look, you might do better to draw your letters freehand as described in the section on hand lettering. Freehand lettering may be less uniform than stenciled lettering, but it is usually more graceful and easier to read.

Stick-On Lettering

Stick-on letters, also known as *sign letters*, are made of vinyl or plastic and have a self-adhesive coating. When peeled from their backing sheets and pressed into place, they adhere well to cardboard, glass, and metal.

Most stick-on letters have low-tack adhesive, meaning that they can be placed lightly on a surface so as to form a light bond. Only when they are pressed down firmly does the bond become permanent. Thus, using stick-on letters is similar to using cutout letters: you can move the letters around until you are satisfied with their arrangement before fastening them down. (See *Cutout Lettering* in this chapter.)

You can get inexpensive stick-on letters at many stationery stores. They are usually available in heights up to 6 inches, arranged in rows on conveniently sized backing sheets. A full set, including several copies of each letter, usually costs less than five dollars.

At larger art supply stores, you can get high-quality sign letters from manufacturers such as Letraset. They are often sold by the letter rather than in complete alphabets. These letters are better designed, are more carefully manufactured, and have stronger adhesive than their stationery store counterparts. They are also more expensive: a package containing five copies of a letter may cost as much as two dollars.

Stick-on letters are more durable and easier to use than virtually any other commercial lettering product. In many cases, they are less expensive as well. Their only real drawback is a severe lack of variety: stick-on letters are available in few styles or colors. The highest quality letters, in fact, tend to be available only in Helvetica and only in black or white.

One way to get around the color limitation is to use a can of spray enamel to paint your stick-on letters while they are still on their backing sheet. When they have dried thoroughly, they can be peeled off and used as usual.

Typesetting (Commercial)

Professional typesetters, also known as *compositors*, no longer set type in hot lead as their forebears did for hundreds of years. Instead, they set type electronically. They enter the text to be set, along with complex formatting commands, into a computer. The computer passes this information to a machine called a *photocompositor*, which translates the computer's instructions into a photographic image. When this image is printed onto high-contrast, light-sensitive paper, the result—called *repro*—is sharp, black text on a glossy white background.

If you want to have type professionally set, you must first prepare a manuscript for the typesetter. The standard way to do this is to type the text, double-spaced, on sheets of plain paper and to handwrite formatting instructions at the top and in the margins. These handwritten instructions are called *specifications*, or *specs* for short. (*Spec* is also used as a verb, as in "to spec type.")

Your specs must include, at the very least, the typeface, point size, and leading that you want the typesetter to use. In most cases, specs should also include a maximum line length, expressed in picas. (A *pica* is equal to 12 points, or about 1/6 inch.)

A number of traditions govern the way specs are usually written. For example, as you learned in the introduction to this chapter, line spacing is expressed as the sum of the type size and the leading size. Therefore, the spec "24/32 Korinna x 48 pi" would mean 24-point Korinna type with 8-point leading and a maximum line length of about 8 inches.

General formatting instructions (such as "center each line" or "do not hyphenate") may be expressed in plain English at the top of the page. Formatting instructions for individual words or lines, however, are better expressed using traditional editor's and proofreader's marks. (You can find these marks in *Words into Type* and other books listed in Appendix C.)

Once you have given your marked manuscript to the typesetter, you may have to wait anywhere from twenty-four hours to several days for the job to be done. At the end of that time, the typesetter will give you a copy to look at—either a photocopy of the repro (sometimes referred to by the old-fashioned term *galley proof*) or, more likely, the repro itself.

You will need to look very carefully at the copy you receive. If you find any spelling errors or formatting errors, you can correct them directly on the proof. Provided that they were not present on your original manuscript, these kinds of mistakes are called *printer's errors*, or *PE's*. If you label them as such, the typesetter will correct them without charge.

You may also decide, at this point, to make other revisions in the wording or formatting of the text. If you make such changes on the proof, label each with the abbreviation *AA* (for *author's alteration*). Typesetters normally charge a fee for making author's alterations.

When you return your marked copy to the typesetter, you will often receive finished, corrected repro within twenty-four hours. This repro can then be pasted to a mechanical (see **Mechanicals** in this chapter) or incorporated directly into a display.

The process of preparing specs, proofreading, and marking corrections can be much more involved than it may seem from this brief introduction. If you plan to deal often with commercial typesetters, you will probably want to read a book that deals more thoroughly with the subject. Several such books are listed in Appendix C.

In the context of displays, the greatest advantage of professionally set type is its high quality. The computer software used by typesetters is far superior to ordinary word processors in its ability to space letters properly and format text precisely. The sharpness, high contrast, and durability of a photocompositor's output are similar to those of a PMT. (See *PMTs* in this chapter.)

An additional advantage of most professional typesetters is that they offer a vast selection of typefaces to choose from. Usually, the only place you can find a greater variety of lettering styles is in the catalog of a rub-on lettering manufacturer such as Letraset or Chartpak. (See *Rub-On Lettering* in this chapter.)

The major disadvantages of commercial typesetting are its difficulty and its cost. Learning to spec a manuscript takes time and often involves several expensive mistakes. Professional typesetters typically charge at least forty dollars an hour for their work, and many charge much more. There is usually a half-hour minimum charge, even for the smallest corrections.

If you need lettering in a hurry, professional typesetting is probably not the best option. Most typesetters request at least twenty-four hours to complete a job and another twenty-four hours to make corrections, if they are required. Your own involvement can be time-consuming as well. For example, you will probably have to proofread your text at least three times: once before you give it to the typesetter, once when you get it back in typeset form, and once after corrections have been made.

You may be able to avoid most of these problems through use of the latest technology. An increasing number of typesetters have added PostScript-compatible "front ends" to their photocomposition systems. (For an explanation of PostScript PDL, see the section on laser printers under *Computer-Generated Lettering* in this chapter.) If you have access to a computer and software that can "speak" the PostScript language, you can include all necessary formatting codes along with the text in your computer file. You can then bring that file on a floppy disk to the typesetter, who will print it on a photocompositor—sometimes immediately, but usually within twenty-four hours—for a relatively small charge of five to eight dollars per page. (Many computer service bureaus now offer photocomposition as well—see *Service Bureaus* in this chapter.)

By "setting type" on your own computer, you avoid having to prepare formal specs for your lettering. You can preview the text on your computer screen and print out proofs on a PostScript-compatible laser printer. By the time you bring your file to the typesetter, you will know exactly what the final repro is going to look like.

Of course, there are disadvantages to this technique. Your selection of typefaces and your ability to format text precisely may be limited by the capabilities of your computer software. You also give up the right to label an error as a PE. Any mistakes in spelling or formatting become your responsibility, not the typesetter's.

Typewriter

Even in this age of computerization, most libraries and offices still have typewriters on hand. If you need to prepare explanatory notes, identification labels, or other small items for a display, a typewriter may be the best tool to use—especially if the only alternative is a dot-matrix printer. The print quality of an electric typewriter (especially a typewriter with a carbon film ribbon) is far superior to that of even the best dot-matrix printers. If your typewriter accepts interchangeable print elements, you may be able to print in a larger variety of typefaces than you can with a dot-matrix printer in character mode. (See the discussion of dot-matrix printers under the heading *Computer-Generated Lettering* in this chapter.)

Compared to any sort of computer printer—daisy-wheel, dot-matrix, or laser—a typewriter is usually able to handle small items such as file cards, labels, and scraps of colored paper much better. For many people, a typewriter is simply easier to use than a computer.

The drawbacks of a typewriter as a lettering tool are obvious. It can only type in small sizes, and its output has an instantly recognizable "typewriter look." Even on self-correcting typewriters, errors are difficult to fix gracefully once the paper has been removed from the typewriter. Nevertheless, a typewriter is often the best way to handle a small, quick lettering job.

CHAPTER 4

Illustration

Illustration is not a necessity for most displays, but it is always welcome. Drawings, cartoons, photographs, and cutouts attract attention to a display and help reinforce its message or theme.

Illustrations can serve a variety of purposes. Their most common role is to add visual interest or humor to an otherwise straightforward display. A chart explaining the Dewey decimal classification system, for example, can be enlivened by adding small, descriptive pictures next to each subject category. A sign about overdue fines can seem much less threatening if it shows a cartoon figure on a skateboard, racing to return a book to the library.

Illustrations are also effective for setting the tone of a display. Imagine, for example, an exhibit of books on environmental hazards. If accompanied by a stark, black-and-white photo of an oil-coated shorebird, the exhibit conveys a sense of gravity and immediacy. If accompanied instead by drawings of spirited young people picking up trash, the exhibit takes on a tone of energy and optimism.

Finally, illustrations can reinforce or add to the information in a display. In figure 2.2, for example, the diagram of the copying machine's control panel makes the directions for using the machine more easily understandable. In figure 6.11, the illustrated floor plan describes the library's layout much more effectively than any written material possibly could.

If you have a talent for drawing, you may want to create original illustrations for most of your displays. If not, you can rely on the virtually limitless assortment of illustrations available from commercial sources. You can use these commercial illustrations as is, or you can customize them by changing their size, style, color, and content.

TOOLS AND TECHNIQUES

The following tools and techniques for creating and modifying illustrations are arranged alphabetically for easy reference. Note, once again, that there is some overlap between techniques for illustration and those for lettering. Therefore, some techniques will be described only briefly, with a cross reference to a fuller explanation in chapter 3.

Clip Art

A number of publishers distribute collections of black-and-white line drawings for use by graphic designers. These drawings are intended to be clipped from the page (hence the term *clip art*) and used as illustrations in books, advertisements, and displays. They are designed to be easily enlarged, reduced, copied, modified, or colored.

Most clip-art publishers make it as simple as possible for you to use their illustrations. They provide several sizes of each drawing, and they print them on only one side of the paper. In practice, however, there is no reason to cut up a page of original clip art when you can make a good-quality copy and cut that up instead. (For reproduction techniques, see *Enlargement/ Reduction* and *Reproduction* in this chapter.)

Once you have reproduced a clip-art illustration, you can do anything you want with it. You can fasten it to a backing and incorporate it directly into a display (see *Fastening/Mounting* in chapter 5). You can add color to it, using any of a variety of finishing techniques [see *Felt-Tip Markers, Film (Self-Adhesive)*, and *Paint* in this chapter]. You can cut it apart, combine it with text or with other graphic elements, and paste it to a mechanical for further reproduction (see *Mechanicals* in chapter 3). You can scan it into a computer file, modify it with a graphics editor, and print it out on a laser printer (see *Computer Graphics* and *Scanning* in this chapter).

Clip art is typically sold in thirty-two-page books, which can be found for under ten dollars apiece at most art supply stores. Each book tends to have a specific theme, such as food, sports, business, or holidays. There are also clip-art books containing specialized graphic elements, such as lines, arrows, borders, and alphabets. (See *Clip-Art Alphabets* in chapter 3.)

Rather than pay for commercial clip art, you may be tempted to clip illustrations from newspapers and magazines instead. Before you do so, however, you should be aware that published drawings are protected by international copyright law and may not be reproduced without the copyright holder's permission. Cutting an illustration from a magazine and gluing it to a display is permissible, but reproducing the illustration in any way—by photocopying, electronic scanning, or even hand tracing—is a violation of the law. Clip art, in contrast, is always distributed with the publisher's explicit waiver of copyright protection.

Clip art is inexpensive, abundant, and easy to use. Its only real drawback is that its style is not always appropriate for library displays. Rather than pay artists to create—and give up their rights to—new illustrations, some clip-art publishers simply recycle nineteenth-century engravings. (Under U.S. copyright law, anything published before 1909 is considered to be in the public domain.) When publishers do create original clip art, it tends to be bland and commercial. As a result, you may have to look through dozens or hundreds of clip-art illustrations before you find one that suits your needs.

Computer Graphics

Computer graphics programs are tools for creating and editing images. They allow you to outline objects on the computer screen by manipulating lines, curves, and shapes. You can then fill in the outlines with colors or shades of gray. You can enlarge, reduce, stretch, squeeze, rotate, or copy an entire drawing or any part of a drawing. Some graphics programs allow you to draw freehand as well, using a mouse or a digitizing tablet. (See *Freehand Drawing* in this chapter.)

Figure 4.1 Computer-generated
drawing of open book

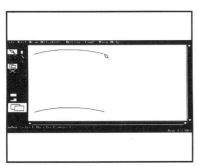

Figure 4.2 Curve on computer screen

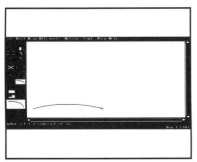

Figure 4.3 Duplicated curve on
computer screen

A computer graphics program automates much of the process of drawing. Therefore, for people with limited drawing ability, a graphics program is an ideal way to produce professional-looking illustrations. Look, for example, at the drawing of an open book in figure 4.1. This relatively simple picture would be difficult to draw by hand, since it requires so much accuracy and symmetry: the curve at the top of each page must match the curve at the bottom, and the right-hand page must be an exact mirror image of the left.

On a computer, however, a drawing like this one can be made in a few minutes. The following is a suggested series of steps for drawing this picture with a typical graphics program. Every graphics program is different. These steps may have to be modified to fit the capabilities and limitations of the program you are using.

1. Draw the curve that represents the bottom of the left-hand page. You can do this easily in most graphics programs by entering three points: the curve's starting point, its ending point, and one point in the middle. You can adjust the positions of all three points until they seem right to you; when you are satisfied, the computer will connect them with a smooth, solid line (figure 4.2).

2. Use your program's copying feature to make a copy of the curve and move it toward the top of the screen (figure 4.3). This new curve will represent the top edge of the page.

3. Use your program's sizing feature to reduce the new curve slightly in size.

4. Connect the top and bottom curves with straight lines. Drawing a line requires entering just two points: the beginning and the end of the line. In just a few seconds, you can draw the two lines that represent the left and right edges of the page (figure 4.4).

5. Add a stack of page edges at the bottom (figure 4.5). You can do this easily by making multiple copies of the original curve (as you did in step 2), and moving them to the bottom of the screen.

6. Draw a cover (figure 4.6), using the line-drawing technique you used in step 4.

7. Use your program's copying feature to make a copy of everything you have drawn so far. Move the copy to the right side of the screen.

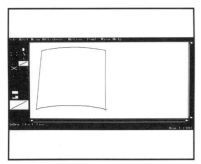

Figure 4.4 Lines on computer
screen connect curves to make page

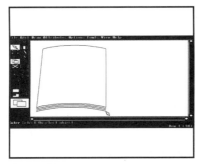

Figure 4.5 More curves on computer
screen represent edges of pages

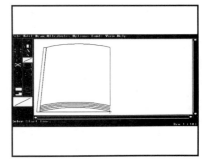

Figure 4.6 Lines on computer
screen represent book cover

Figure 4.7 Mirror-image copy of book on computer screen

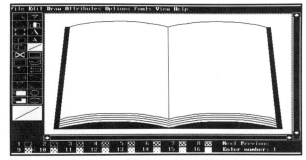

Figure 4.8 Book cover filled in with solid black on computer screen

8. Use your program's mirroring feature to flip the copy you just made, so it becomes a mirror-image of the original (figure 4.7). This mirror-image copy represents the right side of the book.

9. Move the left and right sides of the book together so they join seamlessly.

10. Use your program's "fill" feature to fill in the outline of the book cover, making it solid black (figure 4.8).

Once you have made a drawing in this manner, there are several things you can do with it. You can print it out and use the resulting paper copy as part of your display. You can use your graphics program to edit the drawing or to combine it with other elements (such as text). You can save it to a disk file, where it is kept in coded form for future use. You can "export" it in a file format that can be used by another program, such as your favorite word processor. In many cases, you will want to do all of these things.

Keep in mind that the example you have just seen is an unusually simple one. With a good graphics program, it is possible to create attractive and sophisticated illustrations that show no sign of having been produced on a computer. The more you experiment with your program's capabilities, the more you will be able to accomplish with it.

There are two basic types of graphics programs on the market. Both types allow the user to manipulate lines and shapes (as in the foregoing example), but the way they handle these lines and shapes is fundamentally different.

The first type is generally referred to as a *paint program.* A paint program treats an image as an array of tiny dots called *pixels*. When you draw a line or a shape with a paint program, you are manipulating hundreds or thousands of pixels at a time. (It would be possible, though not very practical, to produce the same line or shape by moving individual pixels around on the screen.) Images produced by paint programs are known as *bitmapped* or *raster* graphics.

The second type of graphics program is known as a *draw program.* A draw program treats an image as a series of instructions or formulas. When you draw a straight line, for example, a draw program records information about the line's starting point, direction, length, thickness, and so forth. Images produced by draw programs are called *vector* or *object-oriented* graphics. (A few high-end graphics programs combine drawing and painting capabilities in one package. See Appendix B for some examples.)

The best way to contrast paint programs with draw programs is to compare the way they store and retrieve files. Suppose you use a paint program to draw a simple shape—say, a circle—and save it to a file. The resulting file contains a very long string of codes, each code representing a single pixel. The file also contains a header that specifies how many pixels are in each row and how many rows are in the entire image. Later, when you retrieve the file into the paint program, the program reads the header and arranges the pixels according to its instructions, thereby reconstructing the image. It does not "know" that the image is a circle—from the program's point of view, the array of pixels could equally well represent a straight line or the *Mona Lisa*.

Suppose that you now create a similar circle with a draw program and save it to a file. The resulting file is very small, consisting only of the minimum information needed to define the circle—for example, the length of the circle's radius and the location of its center point. When you retrieve the file into the draw program, the program uses the stored information to reproduce the circle you drew earlier. Because different kinds of geometric shapes require different kinds of instructions, the draw program "knows" (in a way that a paint program does not) that it is drawing a circle.

Each type of program has its advantages and disadvantages. Paint programs are, on the average, less expensive than draw programs, and they are better at handling coloring and shading. Paint programs can also be used to edit scanned images (see *Scanning* in this chapter), while draw programs cannot. On the negative side, the bitmapped graphics produced by paint programs are inconvenient to handle and to store. Because it consists of a fixed number of pixels, a bitmapped graphic cannot be enlarged or reduced in size without a significant loss in image quality. (Enlarging the graphic usually requires enlarging the pixels themselves, giving the image a grainy appearance.) Also, saving a bit-mapped image to a file—a process that requires keeping a record of every pixel—can require a huge amount of disk space.

Draw programs tend to be more expensive and more complex than paint programs. Many draw programs—especially those that are sold as presentation graphics packages—have sophisticated charting and text-handling capabilities built in. The vector graphics created by draw programs are easy to store and to manipulate. A vector graphic can be enlarged, reduced, stretched, or squeezed with no loss in quality, since the draw program needs only to adjust a few numbers in a formula to change the characteristics of the image. The major disadvantage of draw programs is that each tends to use its own "language" to define and store graphics, and therefore files created by one draw program will not always work well in another draw program. This can be a problem if you expect to use lots of electronic clip art or to download free graphics from computer bulletin boards (see *Electronic Clip Art* in this chapter). In contrast, file formats for bitmapped graphics are well standardized, and therefore one paint program is likely to have little difficulty using files created by another.

No matter which type of program you decide to use, you will find that computer graphics software is an excellent tool for producing display graphics. The only real drawback is the large start-up cost. While low-end paint programs (or signmaking programs such as Print Shop) are generally available for under fifty dollars, the capabilities of these programs are limited. To produce top-quality graphics, you may have to spend as much as $500 for a good graphics program. You may also need to upgrade your computer with a lot of memory, a large hard disk, and a mouse. For best results, you will also want to use a laser printer, though this is not strictly necessary. (For a detailed discussion of the capabilities and limitations of different kinds of printers, see *Computer-Generated Lettering* in chapter 3.)

The same restrictions that apply to computer-generated lettering also apply to computer-generated graphics: ordinarily, the size of your graphics will be limited to what will fit on an 8 1/2-by-11-inch sheet of paper; and, unless your library can afford the expense and inconvenience of a color printer, your graphics will be restricted to black and white. You can, of course, enlarge computer graphics after they are printed (see *Enlargement/Reduction* in this chapter), and you can color them using traditional methods [see *Felt-Tip Markers, Film (Self-Adhesive),* and *Paint* in this chapter].

Cutouts

Simple designs or full illustrations may be traced, copied, or drawn onto paper or cloth, then cut out and fastened to a backing. Using cutouts is an easy way to add color and texture to a display.

The most elementary example of this technique is that old winter standby, the paper snowflake. To make a snowflake, draw or trace a circle onto a sheet of white paper and cut it out with scissors. Fold the circle in half; fold the semicircle in thirds along the lines shown in figure 4.9; and then fold the resulting wedge in half. Make a series of cuts in the folded paper—you can use the dashed lines in figure 4.10 as a guide, or you can experiment with your own designs. When you unfold your finished snowflake, it should look like the one in figure 4.11. You can use this fold-and-cut technique to make other symmetrical objects such as flowers, stars, and wagon wheels.

Cutouts can also be used to produce more complex illustrations. Suppose, for example, that you want to create a colorful bouquet of flowers. The usual way to do this would be to sketch the flowers on a piece of cardboard and color them with paint or markers. (See *Freehand Drawing* in this chapter.) In this case, however, you will use cutouts instead. Draw the leaves and stems on a sheet of green paper and cut them out. Draw assorted flower parts onto other sheets of colored paper and cut them out also. (See plate 4 for examples.) If you wish, use the cut-and-fold technique described earlier to create the flower parts.

When you are finished, place the cutout elements on a colored backing. You can arrange them in several different ways until you find a design you like. (For example, see plate 5.) When you are satisfied with the arrangement, glue the cutouts down. (For suggestions on gluing, see *Fastening/Mounting* in chapter 5.)

Using cutouts is one of the easiest and most flexible ways to produce eye-catching illustrations. By cutting and pasting pictures from different sources, you can create a colorful composite that would have

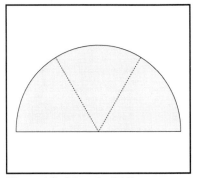

Figure 4.9 Lines for folding semicircle of paper in thirds

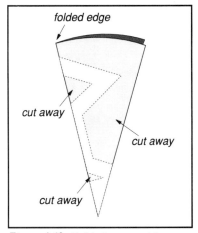

Figure 4.10 Folded paper with cut lines

Figure 4.11 Unfolded paper snowflake

been difficult to produce in any other way. (You might, for example, paste a hand-drawn scene onto the screen of a computer-generated television set, and then add a clip-art family to watch the show.) By experimenting with different arrangements before you glue the pieces down, you increase your chances of being pleased with the final result.

The only real drawback to cutouts is that they are often time-consuming. Cutting small or complicated shapes from colored paper can be a difficult task, especially for people whose hands are not naturally steady.

Electronic Clip Art

Electronic clip art is similar to ordinary clip art (see **Clip Art** in this chapter), but it is distributed as codes in a computer file rather than as ink on paper. A computer graphics program is needed to interpret the codes and reconstruct the drawing. (See **Computer Graphics** in this chapter.)

Unlike traditional clip art, electronic clip art is easily modified for any purpose. Within a graphics program, a clip-art drawing can be enlarged, reduced, rotated, copied, and colored. Most electronic clip art can also be edited—that is, elements of a drawing can be deleted or changed. For example, the left side of figure 4.12 shows a clip-art jack-o'-lantern. Next to it, you can see how the same jack-o'-lantern looks when its facial expression has been altered with a graphics program.

If you are not comfortable using the advanced functions of a computer graphics program, you can simply use the program to view and print an electronic clip-art drawing. Once the drawing has been printed on paper by a laser printer, it can be treated just like an ordinary piece of clip art—that is, it can be enlarged, reduced, hand colored, cut up, or pasted down.

Many computer graphics programs come with disks of assorted clip art. In recent years, a few software companies have begun to sell clip-art collections separately, in bitmapped and vector formats that are compatible with the most popular graphics programs. The quality and price of electronic clip art varies widely: at one end of the spectrum, a variety of drawings can be downloaded free from most computer bulletin

Figure 4.12 Computer-generated jack-o'-lantern

boards; at the other end, commercial clip-art libraries intended for business users often sell for hundreds of dollars. (See Appendix B for some suggested clip-art sources.)

If you have access to a computer, a printer, and graphics software, electronic clip art is a useful resource. It is more versatile and often more up to date than traditional clip art. It is not yet available in as great a variety as traditional clip art, but that situation is changing as use of computer graphics software becomes more widespread.

Enlargement/Reduction

Many illustrations can be enlarged or reduced instantly by means of photocopies or PMTs (see *Reproduction* in this chapter). These photomechanical techniques do have limitations, however. If a picture includes dot patterns (or has been printed on a dot-matrix printer), it may take on a jagged or grainy appearance when it is enlarged. If a picture includes thick lines, those lines may run together and produce a muddy effect when the picture is reduced; if the picture includes very thin lines or tiny dots, those features may disappear altogether. In such cases, it may be preferable to copy an illustration the old-fashioned way—by hand.

If you want to enlarge or reduce a drawing manually, you will need to choose among three different tools: the grid, the pantograph, and the projector.

Grid   The grid is the oldest known technique for enlargement and reduction; it goes back at least as far as the ancient Greeks. The principle is simple: the original drawing has a grid drawn over it, dividing it into squares of uniform size. A similar grid is drawn on another sheet of paper. (The duplicate grid may be larger or smaller than the original, but it must have the same number of squares.) To reproduce the drawing, the artist copies the contents of each square into the corresponding square of the duplicate grid.

This technique is not quite as simple in practice as it is in principle. There is, for one thing, the matter of drawing the grids. Drawing two grids by hand, and maintaining a good degree of accuracy when doing so, can be long and tedious work. Carefully erasing the grids afterward is not pleasant either.

Fortunately, a few shortcuts are available. Most art supply stores sell various-sized grids printed on sheets of clear plastic. By placing one of these grids over a drawing, you can subdivide the drawing without having to write on it. Of course, this shortcut works only for the original drawing. You cannot place a plastic grid over the copy, since you would then be unable to draw on the paper underneath.

Another shortcut is to place a sheet of graph paper into the paper tray of an office copier and photocopy the drawing onto the grid. (See the discussion of printing onto different materials under *Photocopying* in chapter 3.) Again, however, this technique works only for the original drawing. You cannot use graph paper for your enlargement or reduction, since there would be no way to delete the grid when you were finished.

A final shortcut is to use a light box. (See *Light Box* in chapter 3.) If you place a grid on a light box, and then place a sheet of paper over the grid, you can see the grid right through the paper. This technique will work equally well for the original or for the copy. (If you have only one small light box, use it for the copy, and use one of the preceding techniques to grid the original.)

If you do not have a light box, your only option is to draw a grid directly onto the paper that you are using for your copy. Draw the grid carefully, using a sharp pencil and a ruler. Keep your pencil lines as light as possible so you can erase them later.

Once you have found a satisfactory way to handle the grids, you can proceed with the rest of the process—copying the original, box by box. Make your copy in pencil, even if the grid lines are also drawn in pencil. Later, when the copy is finished, you can go over the pencil outline with paint or a felt-tip marker. When the paint or the ink has dried completely, you can erase the grid lines without erasing the drawing.

The advantages of using a grid to enlarge or reduce a drawing are that it requires no special equipment (the plastic sheet, photocopier, and light box are optional) and that it works with drawings of any size. You can use a grid to make a picture as large as the side of a barn or as small as a postage stamp.

The disadvantage of using a grid—apart from the possible tedium of having to draw and erase grid lines—is that it requires some degree of talent. Copying a drawing box by box is easier than copying a drawing freehand, but it is still a skill that is easier for some people than for others. It is worth your while to try the technique once and see whether the results are satisfactory.

Pantograph　　A pantograph is a simple mechanical device for copying, enlarging, or reducing a drawing. It consists of a stylus and a pen mounted on a jointed frame. When the stylus is traced over a drawing, the pen—with a sheet of paper beneath it—echoes the movements of the stylus. Depending on how the frame is adjusted, the scope of the pen's movements can be magnified or minimized to produce a drawing of the desired size.

The pantograph was popularized by Thomas Jefferson and was used frequently in the nineteenth century. Though pantographs are rarely used today, they remain available at larger art supply stores.

Projector　　A very practical way to enlarge a drawing is to project the original onto a large sheet of paper and trace the outlines of the projected image. The best kind of projector to use depends on the characteristics of the original drawing.

If the original drawing is black and white and is small enough to fit into a photocopying machine, your best bet is to copy it onto a sheet of clear acetate. (Once again, see the discussion of printing onto different materials under *Photocopying* in chapter 3.) You can then place the acetate on an overhead projector and project a clear, bright, sharp image.

If you cannot copy the original drawing onto acetate, your next best option is to place the original in an opaque projector. Opaque projectors (which are designed to project any flat, opaque item) tend to produce dim and somewhat fuzzy images. Still, these images are usually satisfactory for tracing purposes.

If the original drawing is too large to fit into an opaque projector— or if your library does not have an opaque projector—you have one option left: You can use a camera to photograph the original onto color slide film, have the film developed, and use a slide projector to project the drawing. Be aware, however, that most amateur cameras cannot focus on objects that are closer than 3 or 4 feet. Unless your camera has a suitable lens, you may not be able to get close enough to your original drawing to make a useful slide.

No matter what sort of projector you use, you are likely to encounter an annoying problem when you try to trace the projected image onto a sheet of paper: the shadow of your hand will get in the way. One way to deal with this problem is to grip the pencil as far up toward the eraser end as possible. Another, more drastic solution—if your projector is bright enough and your paper is translucent enough—is to mount the paper on a pane of glass and project onto it from the rear.

While a projector is a useful tool for enlarging, it can rarely be used for reducing. Very few projectors can focus on a screen that is less than a few feet away.

Limitation All of these manual enlargement and reduction techniques have one limitation in common: they are much more suitable to line drawings than to paintings or photographs. In order to be copied or traced easily, a drawing must have clear, sharp outlines. If you have a certain degree of artistic ability, you may be able to interpolate outlines where there are none; otherwise, you will be better off using photocopies or screened PMTs to reproduce illustrations that lack definite lines and shapes.

Felt-Tip Markers

Felt-tip markers are an excellent way to add color to clip art, computer-generated art, and other black-and-white drawings. Use straight, even strokes and be careful to stay within the black outlines.

If you use markers to finish a hand-drawn or hand-traced drawing, you will have only light pencil outlines to guide you. (See *Freehand Drawing* in this chapter.) Be especially careful when two areas of color meet at a pencil line: if one marker comes in contact with the ink from another, the result may be a messy smear. To avoid this possibility, use watercolor markers to fill in the areas bounded by the pencil lines, leaving narrow gaps around the lines themselves. Then use permanent markers to trace over the pencil outlines and fill in the gaps.

It is never a good idea to draw freehand with felt-tip markers; always outline a drawing in pencil first.

For a detailed discussion of felt-tip markers, along with their advantages and drawbacks, see *Felt-Tip Markers* in chapter 3.

Film (Self-Adhesive)

Self-adhesive colored films are often used by graphic arts professionals to add color to black-and-white drawings. In many situations, film provides smoother, more uniform, more vivid color than felt-tip markers or paint.

When you buy a sheet of self-adhesive film, it seems to be opaque—but this is because it comes attached to an opaque white backing sheet. When you peel a corner of the film away from the backing, you will see that it is, in fact, transparent. This "dual personality" is one of the best features of self-adhesive film. Its transparency makes it easy to work with, but its seeming opacity (when applied to a white surface) helps give drawings a bold, confident look.

Self-adhesive film is available in hundreds of colors. It is also available in dozens of black-and-white patterns: dot screens of various densities, textured effects, even imitation wood grain. The black-and-white versions are useful for simulating color and texture in drawings that will be reproduced photomechanically (see **Reproduction** in this chapter).

Self-adhesive film works best with drawings that have distinct, black outlines. If you are using it to color a hand-drawn illustration (see **Freehand Drawing** in this chapter), use a felt-tip marker to darken the pencil outlines *before* you apply the film.

The recommended way to use self-adhesive film is to cut a piece that is larger than the area you want to cover, apply this piece to the drawing, and cut away the excess. This process involves using a graphics knife on the surface of the drawing and therefore demands special caution. If your drawing is on thin paper, mount it on a piece of cardboard before you attempt to apply film to it. (See **Fastening/Mounting** in chapter 5.) Also, make sure your knife blade is clean and sharp to prevent grabbing and snagging.

The following is a suggested series of steps for applying film to the clip-art drawing of a pencil shown in figure 4.13.

1. With the tip of your knife blade, cut a rectangle on a sheet of yellow film. Use enough pressure to cut through the film but not through the backing. Be sure that the rectangle you cut is bigger than the area it is meant to cover.

2. Turn your knife sideways and gently slip the blade under one corner of the rectangle to separate it from the backing.

3. Using the knife and your index finger, pull the rectangle away from the backing sheet. For large pieces of film, you may prefer to grasp the corner gently between your thumb and your index finger. (See figure 4.14.)

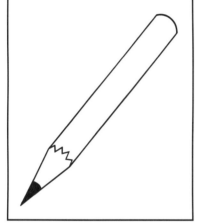

Figure 4.13 Clip-art drawing of pencil

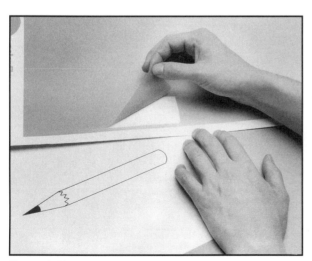

Figure 4.14 Pulling film rectangle from backing sheet

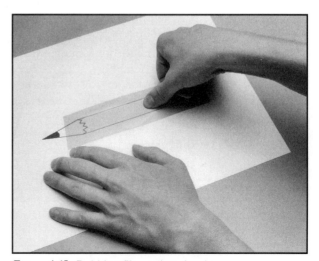

Figure 4.15 Rubbing film against drawing

4. Lay the rectangle gently on the surface of the clip-art drawing, positioning it correctly over the outline of the pencil.

5. *Very gently* rub the film with your fingers so that it lies flat against the surface of the drawing (figure 4.15). If you rub it too hard, it will adhere permanently.

6. With the tip of your knife, cut along the outlines of the yellow portion of the pencil (figure 4.16). Be careful to cut only through the film and not through the drawing.

7. Slip your knife blade under the edge of the rectangle and peel away the excess film. With your other hand, hold down the portion of the film that you want to keep on the drawing (figure 4.17).

8. Using a burnishing tool (see **Rub-On Lettering** in chapter 3), rub the film down. Begin at one edge and work your way steadily toward the other, using brisk, even strokes (figure 4.18).

9. If you encounter air pockets or bubbles along the way, gently lift the unburnished portion of the film with your knife blade. Peel it away from the drawing and smooth the irregular spot with your finger (figure 4.19). When the air has escaped, continue burnishing as before.

10. Repeat the process with light brown film for the pencil point. The completed illustration is shown in figure 4.20.

When you apply large pieces of film, you may sometimes find air bubbles under the surface after you have finished burnishing. Do not try to peel up the film at this point; you will damage the film, and you may damage the drawing as well. Instead, use a pin to prick the surface of the air bubble; then use your burnishing tool to rub the area flat. The repair will be virtually undetectable.

Self-adhesive film is not always as easy to use as it was in this example. Applying film to small areas, or to areas whose outlines are very irregular (for example, a map of Norway), demands painstaking work with the knife. Even a simple circle may be difficult to color with

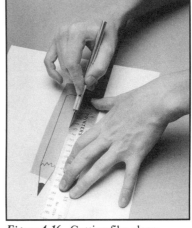

Figure 4.16 Cutting film along outlines of drawing

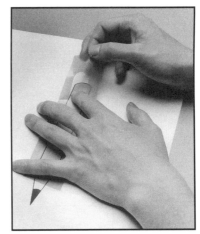

Figure 4.17 Lifting off excess film from drawing

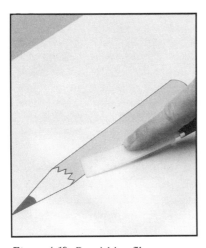

Figure 4.18 Burnishing film on drawing

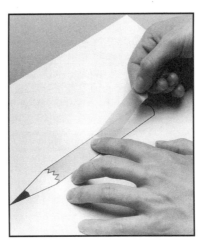

Figure 4.19 Flattening air bubble on film

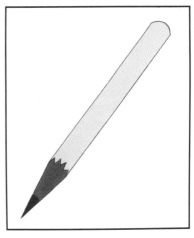

Figure 4.20 Finished illustration of pencil with film in place

self-adhesive film, because it is harder to cut neatly along a curve than to cut along a straight line.

The most serious drawback of self-adhesive film is its cost. It can generally be found only in the graphic art departments of larger art supply stores, where it usually sells for ten to twenty dollars per sheet. (For that price, you can buy a few tubes of acrylic paint or a whole collection of felt-tip markers.) Therefore, you may want to use self-adhesive film only when high quality is especially important.

Found Art

The easiest way to add illustrations to a display is to let professionals do the work—professionals such as Rembrandt or Rand McNally. Fine art reproductions, maps, commercial prints and posters, photographs, book jackets, magazine covers, and record album jackets can all be incorporated into displays. So long as these items are left intact and are not reproduced in any way, you will not violate copyright law by displaying them. (For a discussion of copyright, see *Clip Art* in this chapter.)

You can also solicit art from other sources. Students and community members are often happy to contribute illustrations for library displays. With the cooperation of an art teacher, you can often get entire classes to design and produce illustrations for you. Such an arrangement benefits everyone involved: you get artwork with a minimum of effort, the teacher gets a ready-made lesson plan, the contributors get the reward of seeing their work publicly displayed, and the library gets public-relations points.

Whenever you borrow artwork from other people—whether it is a lithograph lent by a local museum or a fingerpainting lent by a local third grader—you are responsible for protecting the item and returning it in its original condition. At the very least, this means mounting it in a way that avoids damage to the picture. (For mounting suggestions, see *Fastening/Mounting* in chapter 5.) It may also mean displaying the item in a well-supervised area or in a closed exhibit case where it is protected from vandalism.

Found art does not have to be presented as if it were in a museum. It can be integrated into a display as fully as any other kind of art, and it can serve the same purposes: attracting attention, setting a tone, conveying information. The only real drawback of found art is that much of it—particularly maps, book jackets, and reproductions of classic paintings—is cliché and familiar. For this reason, you may want to find ways to use it ironically, whimsically, or unpredictably.

Freehand Drawing

Even if you have little drawing experience, you may choose to enhance your displays with simple, handdrawn illustrations. Make a few practice sketches on a sheet of paper first; then, using very light pencil strokes, copy your sketch onto the sheet of paper or cardboard that you plan to use for the display. (If you have trouble making a satisfactory copy of your sketch, see *Enlargement/Reduction* in this chapter for some shortcuts that might help you.) Finally, add color to

Figure 4.21 Vertical rectangle becomes a book, a building, or a cereal box

your drawing using whatever finishing technique you prefer. [For finishing techniques, see *Felt-Tip Markers, Film (Self-Adhesive)*, and *Paint* in this chapter.]

If you have a high-end computer graphics program, you may prefer to do your drawing on the computer screen rather than on paper. Freehand drawing on a computer requires a mouse or other suitable input device. (A relatively new input device called a *digitizing tablet* allows you to draw with a stylus on a sensitized pad; the movements of the stylus are converted to cursor movements on the screen.) Once you have completed your on-screen "sketch," you can edit it, save it, or print it as you can any other graphic file. (See *Computer Graphics* in this chapter.)

If you lack confidence in your drawing ability, the best way to begin is with simple geometric shapes. A vertical rectangle, for example, can become a book, a building, or a cereal box (figure 4.21). A horizontal rectangle can become a truck, a dollar bill, or a radio (figure 4.22). A triangle can become a Christmas tree, a mountain, or a road vanishing into the distance (figure 4.23).

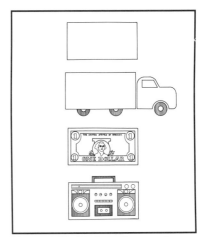

Figure 4.22 Horizontal rectangle becomes a truck, a dollar bill, or a radio

Figure 4.23 Triangle becomes a Christmas tree, a mountain, or a road vanishing into the distance

Figure 4.24 Cartoon faces

Figure 4.25 Smiling cartoon faces with varying eyebrows

One of the simplest things you can draw is also one of the most valuable: a face. Faces, even simple cartoon faces, can add an appealing human touch to almost any display. Even if you just use two dots for eyes and a curve for a mouth, it is possible to draw faces that do not look like "smile buttons." By varying the shapes and positions of different features, you can draw faces that represent a wide range of personalities (figure 4.24).

If you want your faces to reflect different moods, do not underestimate the value of eyebrows. When combined with a grin, upturned eyebrows indicate dazed bliss; horizontal eyebrows indicate confident satisfaction; and downturned eyebrows indicate amused, villainous scheming (figure 4.25). When combined with a sad mouth, upturned eyebrows indicate helplessness; horizontal eyebrows indicate resignation; and downturned eyebrows indicate hostility or anger (figure 4.26).

Figure 4.26 Sad cartoon faces with varying eyebrows

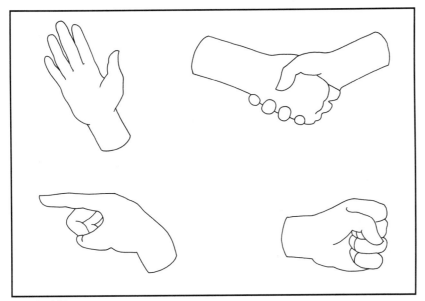

Figure 4.27 Hand poses

Hands are a bit more complicated to draw than faces, but they are equally useful. Figure 4.27 shows a number of hand poses that you might want to use in your displays: open, pointing, gripping, and clasped in a handshake.

Sometimes, of course, you will need to attach your hands and faces to bodies. Unfortunately, bodies—even cartoon bodies—are among the most difficult things to draw convincingly. Figure 4.28 shows a number of bodies in common poses: standing, sitting, walking, and running. If you try to copy these bodies line for line, your drawings will probably look awkward and stiff. Instead, use these bodies as guides, and experiment with a drawing style that feels right to you.

Figure 4.28 Body poses

Figure 4.29 Painted basketball

Even if your homemade drawings are not of professional quality, they will greatly enhance the attractiveness of your displays. Freehand drawings add a sense of liveliness, spontaneity, and humor that "canned" drawings cannot deliver. They also cost next to nothing to produce.

Paint

Like felt-tip markers and self-adhesive film, paint can be used to add color to black-and-white drawings. (See *Clip Art* and *Electronic Clip Art* in this chapter.) It can also be used to finish freehand drawings. (See *Freehand Drawing* in this chapter.)

The chief advantage of paint over markers and film is that its colors can be blended to produce more lifelike, three-dimensional effects. Look, for example, at the painted basketball in figure 4.29. You can see how the color of the ball gets gradually darker toward the bottom left and gets quite dark at the edge. This effect of light and shadow makes the ball seem solid and real.

To create an effect like this one you have to imagine the location of the light source that is illuminating the object. (In this case, for example, the light is coming from the upper right.) You can then simulate shadow by adding black to the basic paint color.

The most appropriate technique for applying the paint depends on the type and consistency of the paint you are using. One technique—suitable for liquid paints, such as tempera—is to mix your paint colors in a paper cup. Brush the upper right area of the ball with bright orange paint; then gradually add black to the mixture as you work your way to the lower left. Another technique—appropriate to more viscous paints, such as acrylic—is to blend your paint colors directly on the picture. After painting the entire basketball a uniform orange, quickly dip your brush in black paint and apply it to the lower left edge of the ball. The black paint will blend with the still-wet orange, creating a suitably shadowy color. By dipping your brush in water and brushing the shadow toward the upper right, you can blend it seamlessly with the rest of the basketball.

There are other color-blending techniques as well. Some artists, for example, prefer to put different colors on opposite sides of a broad brush; others prefer to apply shadow with a stiff, dry brush. To find the technique that works best for you, you will have to experiment with your own paints and brushes.

For a thorough discussion of the different kinds of paint, see *Paint* in chapter 3.

Reproduction

Illustrations may be copied either manually or photomechanically. For manual methods, see *Enlargement/Reduction, Silk Screen,* and *Tracing* in this chapter. This section will concentrate on photomechanical methods, specifically PMTs and photocopies.

PMTs   A PMT, or stat, is a high-quality, high-contrast, photographic reproduction. The PMT process copies blacks and whites cleanly and sharply, but it cannot reproduce colors or shades of gray. (See *PMTs* in chapter 3 for a fuller explanation.)

For the purpose of making PMTs, it is necessary to distinguish between two kinds of original drawings: line-art originals and continuous-tone originals.

Any black-and-white illustration with no shades of gray is considered line art. Despite its name, line art does not have to consist entirely of lines; it can include large, solid areas of black or white, or dot patterns that appear gray when viewed from a distance. Line art is often described as camera-ready because it can be statted as is.

Any illustration that includes colors or shades of gray is classified as a continuous-tone image. Nearly all photographs are continuous-tone images, as are paintings and charcoal drawings. Because the PMT process can reproduce only blacks and whites, continuous-tone originals are not considered camera-ready.

In order to make a PMT of a continuous-tone original, the original must first be screened. Screening is the process of converting colors or gray tones into patterns of black dots. It is accomplished by photographing the original image through a precisely etched grid. (If you look closely, you will see that all of the photographs in this book have been screened.)

A continuous-tone original has to be screened only once. The resulting PMT, because it consists of dot patterns rather than of colors or grays, is technically line art. If the screened PMT is pasted onto a mechanical for further reproduction, the mechanical will be considered camera-ready.

It is possible, under some circumstances, to stat a continuous-tone original without screening it—a process called "statting as line art." This technique can be used to create eye-catching, pop-art graphics from otherwise run-of-the-mill photographs. It works best with images that have large areas of white in them, such as a winter landscape or the face of a clown. Figure 4.30 shows an example of a continuous-tone photograph; figure 4.31 shows how the same picture looks when it has been statted as line art.

Photocopies

The distinction between line art and continuous-tone art is less important for photocopies than it is for PMTs. (See *Photocopying* in chapter 3.) Many photocopying machines have a limited ability to copy shades of gray; therefore, a photocopy of a continuous-tone original may be relatively presentable. For example, figure 4.32 shows a photocopy of the photograph from figure 4.30. It has many more gradations of tone than the line-art stat in figure 4.31.

Some state-of-the-art copying machines are able to screen continuous-tone originals with the press of a button. Your library is unlikely to have such a machine, but you can probably find one at a commercial photocopying shop. Screened photocopies are much faster and less expensive than screened PMTs, but, as you might expect, their image quality is much lower.

A color photocopier screens all originals automatically, whether they are line art or continuous-tone images. (For a discussion of color photocopying, see *Photocopying* in chapter 3.)

Applications

Reproducing illustrations (by means of PMTs or photocopies) serves the same purposes as reproducing lettering: you can enlarge, reduce, stretch, squeeze, or simply "clean up" a messy original.

Figure 4.30 Continuous-tone photograph

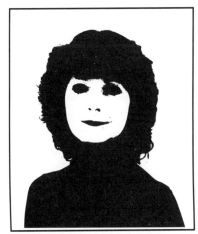

Figure 4.31 Photograph statted as line art

Figure 4.32 Photcopy of photograph

Color can be applied with a variety of finishing techniques. [See *Felt-Tip Markers*, *Film (Self-Adhesive)*, and *Paint* in this chapter.]

When a PMT or photocopy is made from a line-art illustration, the copy often looks better than the original. This is never true for continuous-tone illustrations—the screening process causes a great reduction in image quality. For this reason, you may want to avoid using screened PMTs or screened photocopies in your displays. Whenever possible, use the original drawing or photograph instead.

Rubber Stamps

Although rubber stamps are most often used for utilitarian purposes—marking a bill PAID or labeling an envelope FIRST CLASS MAIL—many manufacturers produce decorative and whimsical stamps as well. If you look long enough, you will find rubber stamps embossed with images of stars, flowers, food, abstract designs, household appliances, and practically every animal known to science.

Because the images they print are relatively small, rubber stamps are not especially useful for displays. Occasionally, however, you may find them handy for creating borders or spot illustrations. For an unusual and somewhat grotesque effect, you can enlarge a rubber-stamped image by means of a photocopy or PMT (see *Reproduction* in this chapter).

Rubber stamps generally cost between two and ten dollars apiece. They are available from toy stores, stationery stores, novelty stores, and mail-order distributors.

Rub-On Graphics

The major manufacturers of rub-on lettering also produce collections of rub-on graphics and symbols. Among their products are rub-on animals, houses, trees, cars, road signs, furniture, historical and holiday images, international flags (in full color), and decorative borders.

Rub-on graphics are very similar to clip art and can be used in much the same way. (See *Clip Art* in this chapter.) They have one great advantage over clip art, however: like rub-on lettering, they can be rubbed directly onto a display, without the need for cutting and pasting. You can apply them to practically any background with no visible seams. (For more information on rub-on products, see *Rub-On Lettering* in chapter 3.)

Rub-on graphics have three important drawbacks, however. The first is size: because their manufacturers try to squeeze as many illustrations as possible onto a single rub-on sheet, the size of each picture is quite small. You can enlarge rub-on graphics quite easily by means of photocopies or PMTs (see *Reproduction* in this chapter), but doing so takes away their only advantage over traditional clip art—their ability to be applied to any surface.

The second drawback is cost. A single sheet of rub-on graphics may cost as much as fifteen dollars. For that price, you can buy two or three thirty-two-page books of ordinary clip art.

The third drawback is availability. Most stores that sell rub-on lettering keep very few sheets of rub-on graphics in stock. You can look through the store's catalogs and special-order the sheets you want, but you may have to wait a week or more for them to arrive.

Scanning

A *scanner* is a device that allows a computer to "read" a graphic image from a piece of paper and convert it to a bitmap in the computer's memory. This bitmap can be saved to a file and retrieved into a paint program, where it can be edited and printed like any other computer graphic. (See **Computer Graphics** in this chapter.)

By using a scanner, you can convert ordinary clip art—or, for that matter, any kind of art at all, including photographs—into computer clip art. You can enlarge, reduce, copy, rotate, or modify the scanned image. You can combine it with text or with other computer graphics, and you can print it out on a dot-matrix or laser printer.

Scanned images have the same drawbacks as other bitmapped images: Their quality suffers if they are enlarged or reduced excessively, and they take up large amounts of disk space when saved to a file.

There are two kinds of scanners available: desktop scanners, which can usually scan images up to 8 1/2 by 11 inches; and handheld scanners, which can usually handle images that are 4 inches wide or less. Desktop scanners generally cost close to $1,000 (including software), but you can easily pick up a handheld scanner for less than $200.

Even a handheld scanner may not be worth the investment if you do not plan to scan images frequently. Many service bureaus and desktop publishing shops offer scanning services, sometimes for as little as five dollars a scan. (See **Service Bureaus** in chapter 3.) If you only need to scan an occasional image, this is obviously a much better deal.

Silk Screen

A silk screen is a device that allows you to make multiple copies of a sign or poster. In its simplest form, it consists of a large rectangle of silk stretched tightly over a wooden frame. When portions of the silk have been blocked with lacquer, ink can be squeezed through the unblocked portions to print an image.

Unlike other reproduction techniques discussed in this chapter, silk screening allows you to produce colored images on colored backgrounds. Using a silk screen, however, is a complicated matter. If you want to learn silk screening techniques, your best bet is to take an adult education course or to read one of the books listed in Appendix C.

Many hobby and art supply stores sell silk screen starter kits for under fifty dollars. They are not particularly useful, but they will allow you to try your hand at silk screening and to see whether it is practical for your circumstances. If you decide to pursue it on a larger scale, you may need to invest a few hundred dollars for equipment and supplies.

Stencils and Templates

Stencils and templates are useful tools for drawing basic shapes such as circles, curves, and arrows. They are available for a few dollars at most stationery stores, hobby shops, and art supply stores. For best results, use a pencil with your stencil or template; then go over the pencil line later with paint or felt-tip markers.

Tracing

Tracing is an easy, inexpensive way to copy simple line drawings. The only special equipment you need is tracing paper, which is available at art supply stores in pads of various sizes.

To use tracing paper, simply place the paper over the original drawing. Although the paper appears translucent, the drawing underneath will show through very clearly. Use a pencil to trace the outlines, being careful not to move the paper.

This, of course, is only half the process. A pencil drawing on tracing paper is not especially useful. If you want to use the drawing in a display, you have to transfer it to a heavier sheet of paper or cardboard (to be known hereafter as the *target sheet*). There are three ways to do this: you can use a ballpoint pen; you can use a pin; or you can create a template.

- *Ballpoint pen.* Under most circumstances, this is the most practical way to transfer a traced drawing. Place the sheet of tracing paper on top of the target sheet. (You may want to tape down both sheets so they will not move.) Use a ballpoint pen to trace over the pencil outlines on the tracing paper. Press down on the pen as firmly as you can without tearing the paper.

  When you are finished, remove the tracing paper. You will see that the ballpoint pen has made an impression on the target sheet. Use a pencil to trace over the impressed outlines, thereby recreating the original drawing.

- *Pin.* This method is useful only if you want to make several copies simultaneously. Stack a few sheets of paper on a piece of corrugated cardboard and place the sheet of tracing paper on top. Using an ordinary straight pin, make a series of closely spaced pin pricks along the outlines on the tracing paper. Push the pin down firmly enough so that it penetrates all the layers.

  When you are finished, remove the tracing paper. Then, as in the childhood game of connect the dots, use a pencil to connect the pinholes on each target sheet.

- *Template.* This method works only for very simple outline drawings with no internal detail. Use scissors to cut out the drawing from the tracing paper. Place this cutout on the target sheet and use it as a template, tracing along its edges with a pencil. If you wish, you can use this template to make several copies of the drawing on several target sheets.

  (The template method is also useful for transferring designs to cloth instead of paper. You can pin the tracing-paper template to the cloth and outline it with chalk—or you can cut around it with scissors, as you might do with a dress pattern.)

Each of these three methods leaves you with a pencil drawing on your target sheet. Compare this pencil copy to the original drawing and make any adjustments that seem necessary. When you are satisfied, you can finish the drawing in whatever way you like. [For finishing techniques, see *Felt-Tip Markers*, *Film (Self-Adhesive)*, and *Paint* in this chapter.]

Unlike photomechanical processes, tracing allows you to make copies of very large originals or to copy onto cardboard. It is, however, a slow and monotonous task. If your original drawing is 11 by 17 inches or smaller and if all you need is a copy on plain white paper, you are probably better off with a photocopy or a PMT (see *Reproduction* in this chapter).

CHAPTER 5

Construction

The illustration techniques discussed in chapter 4 were strictly two-dimensional: they involved drawing, painting, or printing onto a flat piece of paper or cardboard. Often, however, you will need to add a third dimension to your displays—you may want parts of a drawing to pop out, stand up, or hang down; you may want a display to occupy a three-dimensional space (such as an exhibit case or a tabletop); or you may want a display that can be used as well as looked at (for example, a sign that incorporates a functional suggestion box). These kinds of displays require elementary construction techniques.

In the visual arts, creating any three-dimensional object is considered construction. Most of the techniques in this chapter involve familiar materials such as cardboard, cloth, tape, and glue.

In library displays, constructed objects generally fall into two categories: structural and decorative. A structural object is intended to support other objects in a display. (Pedestals, shelves, book stands, and sign supports are examples.) The primary requirement for a structural object is that it be sturdy and strong.

A decorative object is, in effect, a three-dimensional illustration. Decorative objects serve the same purposes as two-dimensional illustrations: they add visual interest, create an atmosphere, and communicate information. Sculptures, papier-mâché animals, balloons, globes, and hobby shop models are all examples of decorative objects.

An object in a display may be both structural and decorative—for example, a book holder designed to look like a treasure chest (see plate 16). To add decorative elements to structural objects, you can use the lettering and illustration techniques presented in chapters 3 and 4.

While the construction techniques described in this chapter are most appropriate for exhibit cases, display windows, and tabletops, you may want to incorporate them into other kinds of displays as well. No law says that signs, posters, and bulletin boards must always be flat. Adding a third dimension to a wall-mounted poster is a sure way to grab the attention of library users. (See plates 10 and 11 for examples.)

TOOLS AND TECHNIQUES

The following construction tools and techniques are arranged alphabetically for easy reference.

Backdrops

Nearly every display has a *backdrop* or *backing*, a flat surface that forms a visual background for—and sometimes physically supports—the other elements of the display. There are several different kinds of backdrops, each of which is appropriate to a different kind of display.

Signs and Posters   As you may have gathered from chapters 3 and 4, the most suitable backing for most signs and posters is a sheet of cardboard. Lettering and illustrations may be drawn directly onto the cardboard, or they may be drawn on other materials and glued to the cardboard later.

For temporary, wall-mounted displays, the best backings to use are posterboard or stiff paper. (Posterboard, known in some areas of the country as *oaktag* or *tagboard,* is thin, flexible cardboard with a smooth finish on one side. It is generally sold by stationery stores in 22-by-28-inch sheets.) Because of their light weight, paper and posterboard are easily hung on a wall with tacks or tape. They are also easier to work with: they can be cut and folded with little effort and, in some cases, they can be placed on a light box to help you position text and illustrations. (See *Light Box* in chapter 3.) Neither paper nor posterboard is very durable, however, and paper is particularly likely to tear or curl. The main advantage of paper over posterboard is that it is available in a greater variety of colors and textures.

For more permanent signs, you will want to use a heavier grade of cardboard called *illustration board.* Most art supply stores stock illustration board in a range of sizes and in two varieties: hot press (with a smooth finish) and cold press (with a rougher, more textured finish). Because of its greater weight, illustration board cannot usually be hung using only tacks or tape. Fastening it securely to a wall requires nails, hooks, or self-adhesive squares, any of which can mar the wall permanently. (See *Fastening/Mounting* in this chapter.) Therefore, you may want to use illustration board only for displays that you expect to keep on the wall indefinitely.

If you plan to place your sign somewhere other than on a wall (for example, propped up on an easel or hanging from the ceiling), illustration board is the ideal backing. Paper and posterboard are simply too flimsy for these situations.

In many cases, the best backing is a combination of paper and illustration board. You can assemble your sign or poster on a paper backing, and then mount the entire display on a sheet of illustration board. (For mounting suggestions, once again see *Fastening/Mounting* in this chapter.) In this way, you can have the durability and stiffness of cardboard without giving up the attractiveness and versatility of paper.

Bulletin Boards   A bulletin board is, itself, a backdrop—it is designed for the sole purpose of showing off (and holding up) a variety of display elements. Unfortunately, the light-brown pressed board of which most bulletin boards are made has an unattractive, institutional look. If you want your bulletin boards to attract attention, you will need to cover them with materials that provide a more suitable background for your displays.

The easiest way to dress up a bulletin board is to cover it with colored paper. The usual drawback of this technique is that each sheet

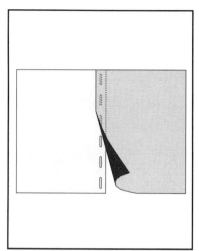

Figure 5.1 Overlapping paper to hide staples

of paper must be stapled on all four sides to connect it with other sheets, and the staples thus become the bulletin board's most prominent feature. There are two ways around this problem. The first is to use a single sheet of paper that is large enough to cover the entire bulletin board, and to staple it as close to the frame as possible. If you cannot get paper that large, the other solution is to overlap several sheets of paper so that each covers the stapled edge of the previous sheet (figure 5.1). In order to do this without exposing any staples, you will have to leave at least one edge of each sheet unstapled. When you are finished stapling, you can use liquid glue to fasten each unstapled edge to the sheet of paper it overlaps.

Whichever technique you use, you will still have lines of exposed staples along the outer edges of the bulletin board. You can mask them by gluing on a narrow border made from paper or ribbon (figure 5.2).

Paper is suitable only as a temporary covering for a bulletin board. It tends to fade quickly when exposed to sunlight, and it displays obvious holes when items that have been tacked to the bulletin board are removed.

If durability is important, you may want to cover your bulletin board with cloth rather than paper. You can achieve an elegant effect with tightly woven fabrics, or you can use coarse fabrics such as burlap for a warm, informal touch. Solid colors generally make better backgrounds than patterns.

The best way to apply a cloth covering is to cut a piece of cloth that is slightly larger than the bulletin board. If the frame of your bulletin board can be removed easily, remove it. Fasten the top center of the cloth to the top of the bulletin board with a few staples; then stretch the cloth tight and put a few staples in the bottom center. Stretch the cloth left and right and put a few staples on each side. Then add staples around the rest of the perimeter, stretching the cloth as you go.

If you were able to remove the frame from your bulletin board, prepare to put it back: cut away the excess cloth on all four sides, leaving

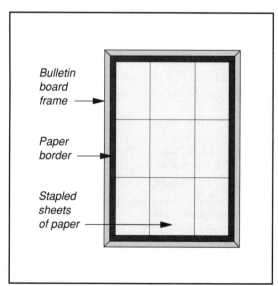

Bulletin board frame →

Paper border →

Stapled sheets of paper →

Figure 5.2 Hiding staples with paper border

half an inch or so to tuck under the frame. With the frame in place, the staples and the edges of the cloth should no longer be visible.

If you could not remove the frame, use a utility knife to cut off the excess cloth as close to the frame as possible. Then, as you would with paper, glue a border around the edges of the bulletin board to hide the exposed staples.

Cloth tends to fade much less quickly than paper, and it usually closes invisibly around the holes left by exposed tacks. It does, however, have a tendency to sag as time passes. If you plan to keep a cloth covering on your bulletin board for many months, you may want to restretch it and restaple it periodically to keep it looking fresh.

A final way to improve the appearance of a bulletin board is to paint it. You will get fine results with ordinary interior house paint (either the matte or the semigloss variety). The obvious drawback to this option is that paint is messy to apply: you will have to be very careful to protect the wall, the floor, and your clothing from dripping and splattering paint. Keep in mind also that paint tends to crack or chip on a frequently used bulletin board, so it is likely that you will have to repaint from time to time.

Exhibit Cases   The back wall of an exhibit case can be covered with paper or cloth just as a bulletin board can. If the wall is made of a material that does not accept staples, use tape or tacks instead. For a more elegant look, make the backdrop long enough to cover the floor of the case as well as the back wall.

Many exhibit cases have shelf standards built into the back wall. If so, you will need to trace their outlines onto the backdrop and cut openings for them.

If you do not plan to attach anything to the backdrop, you can achieve a "theater curtain" effect by tacking a piece of cloth at the top and letting it hang freely at the bottom. To enhance this effect, you may want to gather the cloth as you tack it.

Freestanding Backdrops   If you ever need to set up portable exhibits (at schools or community fairs, for example), a freestanding backdrop can come in very handy. You can also use freestanding back-drops in your own library, to set up displays on tabletops and in other areas that lack a back wall.

The easiest way to make a freestanding backdrop is to link several pieces of cardboard with hinges made from cloth tape. (For more on cloth tape, see *Fastening/Mounting* in this chapter.) Begin with two pieces of illustration board or other sturdy cardboard. Place them face down, side by side, making sure they are aligned perfectly. Fasten them together with a broad strip of cloth tape and cut off the excess tape with scissors. Fold the pieces of cardboard together like the covers of a book, with the strip of tape inside. Then add another strip of tape to the spine and cut off the excess neatly.

The result is a two-panel folding screen that can stand on its own. If you wish, you can add additional panels by following the same series of steps. If you want to make the cloth hinges less obvious, you can match the color of the tape to the color of the cardboard. You may, however, prefer to take the opposite approach: choose a tape color that comple-ments the color of the cardboard, and use the tape to make borders as well as hinges (figure 5.3).

Figure 5.3 Folding display screen with tape in contrasting color

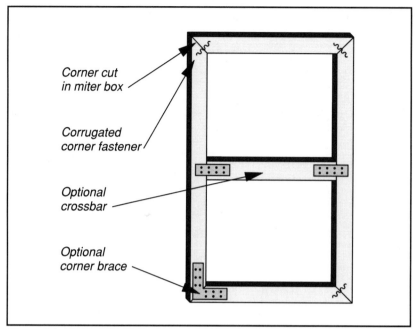

Figure 5.4 Wooden frame for display panel

The cardboard-and-tape backdrop is fine for tabletop displays, but it is not practical in very large sizes. It also is not especially durable: with the passage of time, the cardboard may warp and the tape may tear. If you need a larger or more durable backdrop, you are better off making your panels from wood instead of cardboard.

The diagram in figure 5.4 shows how to make a sturdy wooden frame from several pieces of 1-by-4-inch lumber. You can stretch a piece of cloth over this frame (following the directions in the section on bulletin boards, above) and fasten it with tacks or heavy-duty staples. If you build just one of these wood-and-cloth panels, you can make it stand by attaching feet from a building-supply store. If you build several panels, you can hinge them together into a folding screen, using metal hinges instead of tape.

Wood-and-cloth backdrops are attractive and lightweight, and they can be made in just about any size. Of course, building them requires a suitable workspace, a number of woodworking tools, and the ability to use those tools. If you lack these prerequisites, you can hire someone to do the work for you, or you can choose to buy professionally made freestanding panels that are available from library suppliers. (Ready-made panels generally cost $100 or more; see Appendix A for suggested sources.)

Freestanding backdrops for portable displays can also be made from boxes (see *Boxes* in this chapter). If you want to make freestanding signs, see *Sign Supports* in this chapter.

Book Supports

Books are among the most common objects included in library displays. They may be displayed open or closed, upright or lying down. It is possible to display books attractively using no special equipment—

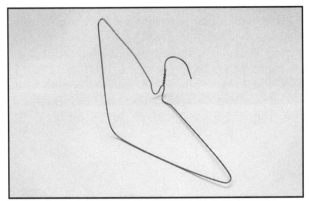

Figure 5.5 Bending wire hanger for bookend

Figure 5.6 Books in wire hanger bookend

for example, by opening a book slightly and standing it up. In some cases, however, you may want to take advantage of the extra flexibility and stability that book supports can offer.

To display a row of books spine-outward, you can use an ordinary set of bookends. Your library no doubt has hundreds of them but, if there are none to spare, you can make a bookend quite easily with an ordinary wire hanger. Using pliers, bend the hanger in half at a 90-degree angle and fold the hook up 90 degrees as well (figure 5.5). You can then slip one-half of the hanger under your row of books. The other half of the hanger supports the books, and the hook remains hidden behind them (figure 5.6).

To display a book face-outward, you can modify a metal bookend (either commercial or homemade) by bending its vertical side back slightly toward its horizontal base. You can then slip this angled piece between the book's back cover and its plastic jacket (figure 5.7).

Figure 5.7 Modified bookend displays, book face-outward

Displaying an open book requires a different kind of support—one that will not only hold the book upright, but will also hold it open to the desired page. Such supports (sometimes called *reading stands*) are available commercially, but you can make them yourself as well. Place a new wire hanger flat on a table and bend its ends toward each other (figure 5.8). Using pliers, fold each corner up slightly more than 90 degrees (figure 5.9). Fold the middle of the hanger up slightly less than 90 degrees (figure 5.10).

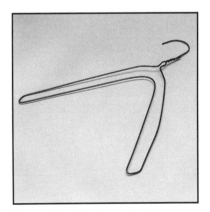

Figure 5.8 Wire hanger book support, step 1

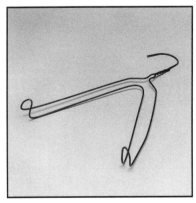

Figure 5.9 Wire hanger book support, step 2

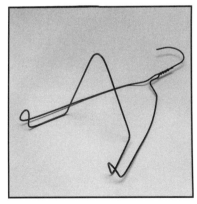

Figure 5.10 Wire hanger book support, step 3

Figure 5.11 Wire hanger book support, step 4

Figure 5.12 Decorated book support

Open the book that you want to display and place it on the stand as shown in figure 5.11.

To make your homemade book supports more attractive, you can decorate them with paper or cardboard cutouts. In figure 5.12, for example, a colored cardboard rectangle (with rounded corners and a painted border) has been taped to a wire-hanger bookend. Book supports can also be made from boxes. See *Boxes* in this chapter.

Boxes

Boxes are the most versatile items you can use in a library display. As decorative objects, they can be modified to represent houses, televisions, computers, fish tanks, fireplaces, or many other things. As structural objects, they can be used to support, protect, or frame other items. Boxes can also be used to hold pamphlets for distribution, or they can act as receptacles for suggestions, coupons, contest entries, and so forth.

Ready-made boxes are available from a variety of sources. Virtually everything you buy in a store comes in a box. Books and supplies are delivered to your library in boxes. Stationery stores sell archive boxes, and shipping companies sell shipping boxes. Supermarkets, liquor stores, and other retailers often have plenty of used boxes to give away.

Ready-made boxes are not always suitable for library displays, however. Most of them have printed words or pictures that are difficult to cover with paint or paper. Used boxes often have bent sides or crushed corners that detract from their visual appeal. Also, because boxes are inconvenient to store, it is unlikely that you will have a box of a particular size and shape on hand when you need it.

In cases where ready-made boxes will not do, you can easily make your own boxes out of paper or cardboard. Figure 5.13 shows a standard box template. The following is a suggested series of steps for using this template to make a paper box. (NOTE: Whenever the directions call for making a fold, fold the paper so that the dashed line is inside the fold.)

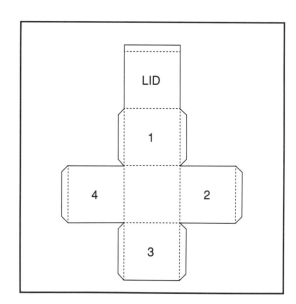

Figure 5.13 Template for standard box

1. Make an enlarged photocopy of the template, or use the technique of your choice to copy the template onto a sheet of paper or tagboard. (For reproduction techniques, see **Enlargement/Reduction** and **Tracing** in chapter 4.) Your copy should be significantly larger than the original.

2. Cut out your copy of the template along the solid black lines.

3. Fold the tabs attached to sides 1 and 3. Then fold sides 1, 2, 3, and 4 so that they are perpendicular to the base (figure 5.14).

4. Glue the tabs on sides 1 and 3 to the inside of sides 2 and 4.

5. Fold the tabs on sides 2 and 4 so they are parallel to the base of the box. Then fold the lid so it is parallel to the base of the box (figure 5.15).

6. Fold the tab attached to the lid and tuck it into the box.

Figure 5.14 Folding sides of box

You can follow these steps to make a box of virtually any size or shape. To alter the dimensions of the box, you need only to revise the template. (Figure 5.16, for example, shows what the template for a short, square box might look like. Figure 5.17 illustrates a template for a tall, rectangular box.) To make a box without a lid, you can eliminate the lid from the template. To make a removable lid (for example, the kind of lid you would find on a gift box), simply make a second box whose base is slightly larger than that of the first.

Once you get used to the way boxes are put together, you can design custom templates with very little effort. Once you have sketched out your desired box on paper, you can use a pencil and ruler to transfer the necessary cutting and folding lines to a piece of sturdy cardboard. (**Enlargement/Reduction** and **Tracing** in chapter 4 offer some suggestions that may help you make the transfer accurately.)

Whether you use ready-made boxes or make your own, you can use boxes to make a variety of useful display items. The following is merely an introductory sampling.

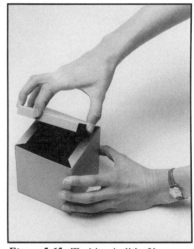

Figure 5.15 Tucking in lid of box

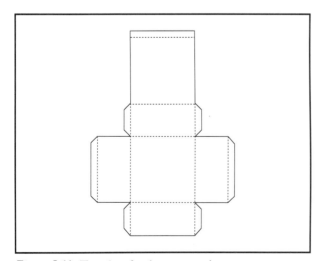

Figure 5.16 Template for short, square box

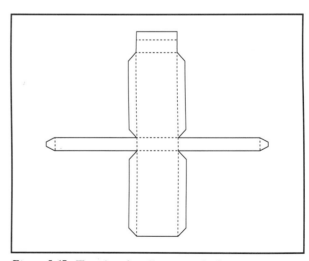

Figure 5.17 Template for tall, rectangular box

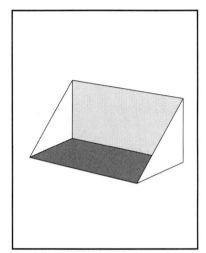

Figure 5.18 Shelf made from box

Figure 5.19 Dummy book with jacket

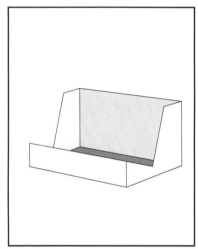

Figure 5.20 Reading stand made from box

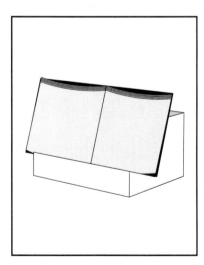

Figure 5.21 Reading stand holding book

- *Pedestal.* A sturdy box can be used as a base for displaying books, sculptures, or other objects. The easiest way to turn a box into an attractive pedestal is to drape a cloth over it. Alternatively, you can paint the box with spray enamel or cover it with paper (as if you were wrapping a gift). A box without a lid can still make an excellent pedestal; simply turn the box so the open side is down.

- *Shelf.* A rectangular box with its top and front cut away makes a fine display shelf for books or other objects. You can make the shelf more attractive by cutting away the sides on a diagonal line (figure 5.18). If the shelf is made of sturdy cardboard—or if the items it is supporting are not very heavy—you can mount it on a wall; otherwise, you can place it on a table or on top of another box.

- *Substitute book.* Many librarians prefer not to use real books in library displays, because they want every book to be available for circulation. Therefore, you may want to make a collection of book-shaped boxes to use as stand-ins. Paint three sides of the box white, and draw page lines with a black felt-tip pen. You can paint a realistic-looking cover on your dummy book, or else wrap a real book cover around it (figure 5.19).

- *Book support.* By cutting away the sides of a box as shown in figure 5.20, you can make a stable, attractive book support. Be sure that the box is at least slightly narrower than the cover of the book it is intended to support (figure 5.21).

- *Pamphlet holder.* A tall, shallow box (made with a template similar to that in figure 5.17) can be used to dispense pamphlets, newsletters, bulletins, schedules, or other printed items. (To make the pamphlet holder both more attractive and more functional, you can cut away portions of the front and sides.) Depending on the weight and size of the box, you may choose to stand it on a table, mount it on a wall, or attach it to a poster.

- *Freestanding exhibit case.* With its front cut away, a large box can be used as a portable exhibit case. You can use it to hold an entire three-dimensional display, either mounted on a wall or resting on a tabletop. You

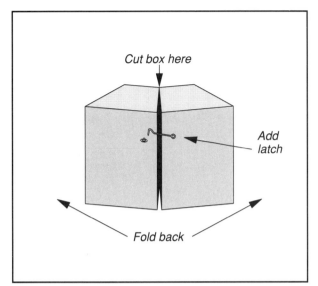

Figure 5.22 Portable two-sided display case

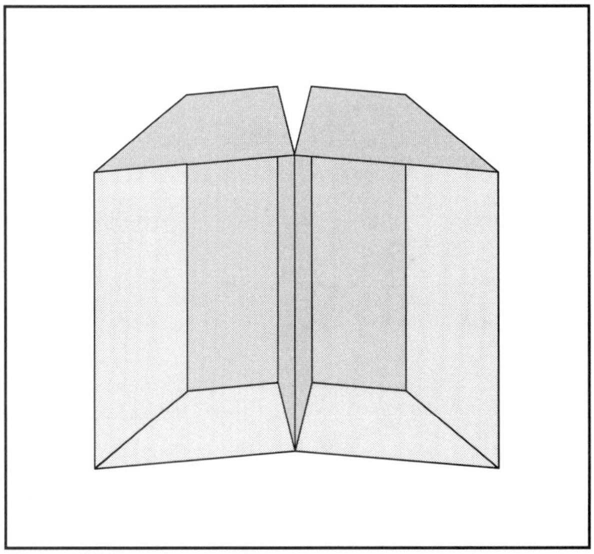

Figure 5.23 Box cut open for two-sided display case

can decorate it just as you would decorate a real exhibit case: you can hang a cloth on the back wall (see **Backdrops** in this chapter) or install shelves inside (see **Shelves** in this chapter).

One variation on the exhibit case idea is the "traveling show box" shown in figure 5.22. This two-part case is made by cutting a box nearly in half and then folding it along one side, as shown in figure 5.23. You can attach small hook-and-eye latches (available at any hardware store) by screwing them through the wall of the box into a small piece of wood. One latch goes in the rear to hold the box open; the other goes in the front to hold the box closed when you are traveling.

Fastening/Mounting

Nearly every time you produce a display, you will have to attach or fasten one item to another. Among your most frequent tasks will be mounting a paper sign on a cardboard backing, attaching illustrations or three-dimensional objects to posters or bulletin boards, or mounting a finished display on a wall.

Stationery stores and art supply stores provide dozens of fastening and mounting supplies, each of which is ideal for certain tasks and relatively useless for others. It is up to you to decide which you are most comfortable using and want to keep on hand. In general, fastening supplies fall into four categories: glue, wax, tape, and metal fasteners.

Glue   One of the most practical, versatile supplies you can buy is a white liquid glue such as Elmer's. When handled correctly, it can be used on everything from small pieces of paper to large pieces of wood.

The most common mistake people make with liquid glue is applying too much. (The variable-flow cap on the Elmer's bottle exacerbates the problem, since it is hard to know how fast the glue is going to come out.) Applying excess glue can cause paper to buckle or wrinkle, create stains and smears, and inhibit drying. Therefore, unless

Figure 5.24 Applying glue to pamphlet holder

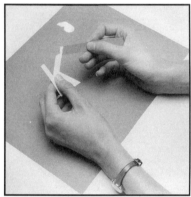

Figure 5.25 Paper dauber to apply glue

you are applying glue to a very porous surface, you will want to use just a thin ribbon of glue. Keep the glue away from the edges of the object you are fastening. Figure 5.24, for example, shows how you might apply glue to the back of a pamphlet holder that you want to mount on a poster.

It is necessary to apply glue only to one of the two surfaces. Press the glue-covered item firmly and slowly onto the dry surface, watching for any beads of glue that might squeeze out from between them. If any such beads appear, wipe them away immediately with a tissue.

When you are using liquid glue on paper—for example, in attaching cutout letters to a backing—even a thin ribbon of glue may be too much. To be safe, do not apply the glue directly from the bottle. Instead, squeeze a small pool of glue onto a sheet of scrap cardboard. Cut a thin strip of paper and dip the end of the strip gently into the pool of glue. Use this strip to apply the glue to the cutout letter (figure 5.25). You can use this same technique to do touch-ups on items that do not seem adequately glued.

Another kind of glue that you may want to keep on hand is rubber cement. Rubber cement is not as versatile as white liquid glue—it is not effective on wood, for example, and it is difficult to apply to very small items. It is, however, quite useful for attaching one sheet of paper to another, or to a sheet of cardboard. You can use it for making mechanicals (see ***Mechanicals*** in chapter 3), for mounting illustrations and photographs, or for fastening a paper sign to a cardboard backing. One advantage of rubber cement is that it does not create an especially strong bond. An item that has been glued down with rubber cement can usually be peeled up again. It will not be clean—that is, it will probably have a permanent glue residue—but that will not matter if you intend to fasten it to another surface later.

The best way to apply rubber cement is with a brush—in fact, most containers of rubber cement are sold with brushes built into their caps. As with liquid glue, rubber cement should be applied sparingly. Always wipe your brush several times against the mouth of the container before touching it to the paper. If rubber cement is brushed on too heavily, it may soak or bleed through the surface it is applied to.

The longer rubber cement is kept on your shelf, the thicker it is likely to get. If your rubber cement begins to congeal, you can buy a can of thinner from a stationery store. Adding a small amount of this liquid will bring your rubber cement back to its proper consistency.

If you find liquid glues too messy to use, you may want to try a nonliquid glue product. For example, many art supply stores and hobby shops sell spray-on adhesive in aerosol cans. You hold the can a few inches from the item that you want to glue, spray on a thin, even coat of adhesive, and burnish the item down in its proper position. (See ***Rub-On Lettering*** in chapter 3 for information on burnishing.) Like rubber cement, spray adhesive is convenient for mounting large items such as photographs and illustrations. It does, however, require a sizable, well-ventilated workspace. Spray adhesive, like spray paint, cannot be aimed with great precision, and thus everything within a few feet of your target is likely to acquire a thin, sticky coating. Also, breathing spray adhesive in a poorly ventilated room can cause discomfort or illness.

Another useful nonliquid product is the glue stick. The glue sticks sold in stationery stores are little more than toys, but many art supply stores sell professional-quality glue sticks that can produce reasonably good bonds. Glue sticks are most effective when used on paper—either for gluing one piece of paper to another, or for gluing small pieces of paper (such as cutout letters) to a cardboard backing. They may also come in handy for making mechanicals.

Most glue sticks come in lipstick-style containers that allow you to expose just as much of the stick as you want to use. Some manufacturers add color to their glue sticks so you can easily keep track of where the glue has been applied. The color disappears when the glue dries.

To use a glue stick, place the item you want to glue—for example, a square piece of clip art—face down on a sheet of scrap paper. Hold down the square with one hand and apply the glue with the other. Use firm, uniform strokes that begin on the square and end on the scrap paper. Then turn the square around, hold down the portion you have glued, and apply glue in the same way to the unglued portion. When the entire square is covered with a thin coat of glue, place it face up in its proper position and burnish it down.

Like white liquid glue, glue sticks can be used for touch-up work. Cut a thin strip of paper and press it against the tip of the glue stick to give it a coating of glue. Then insert the strip under the edge of the item you want to glue down. By pressing down on the item with your finger as you pull the strip out, you can transfer the glue from the strip to the item. When you are finished, burnish the item firmly.

Wax   Many graphic artists use hot wax to fasten one piece of paper or cardboard to another. Wax is most often used to make mechanicals, but it can also be used to mount photographs and illustrations.

In order to use this technique, you need a machine called a *waxer.* You can get a small, hand-held waxer in many art supply stores for under seventy dollars. The waxer contains a low-power heating element that melts pellets of specially formulated wax. By rolling the waxer across a surface, you can apply a thin, coating of liquid wax (figure 5.26).

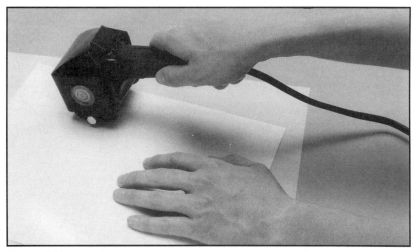

Figure 5.26 Using a waxer

Using a waxer is similar to using a glue stick. Place the item you want to wax—for example, a stat that will be placed on a mechanical—face down on a sheet of scrap paper. Hold it down with one hand and apply the wax with the other. Roll the waxer quickly but firmly, using long strokes that begin on the scrap paper, cross the stat, and end on the scrap paper. Each stroke should overlap slightly with the preceding stroke.

The wax will harden immediately after it is applied—unlike glue, it does not have to be wet to produce a bond. Once your stat has been waxed, you can set it aside indefinitely before you decide to fasten it down. The wax coating will be equally effective after days or even months have passed.

When you are ready to attach the stat, place it wax side down on your mechanical. Because the wax is dry, you can move the stat around and try it in different places. If you press down on the stat with your fingers, the wax will adhere loosely to the mechanical. Even after doing so, you can peel the stat up again and move it around some more. (Pressing the stat down and peeling it up again may leave a slight wax residue on the mechanical. You can remove the residue easily with a cotton swab dipped in alcohol.)

When the stat is positioned exactly the way you want it, cover it with a sheet of paper and burnish it with the flat end of a burnishing tool (see **Rub-On Lettering** in chapter 3). Once it has had firm pressure applied to it, the wax forms a strong, nearly permanent bond. It is possible to peel the stat up at this point, but doing so requires some effort. A waxed item that has been burnished down will almost never come off by itself.

Clearly, wax offers a good deal more flexibility than glue. It does, however, have several drawbacks: it can be applied only to paper or thin cardboard and it can be used only for low-stress bonds. (For example, wax is *not* appropriate for putting together a homemade box.) It also cannot be applied spontaneously: unless you keep your waxer plugged in all the time (as many graphic artists do), you will have to wait up to an hour for the wax to melt before it is ready to use.

Tape Transparent tape (such as Scotch tape), though extremely useful in offices, is usually not appropriate for display work. Despite manufacturers' claims, transparent tape is not invisible—it is, in fact, rather obvious, and it can greatly detract from the appearance of a display. If you must use tape in a place where it can be seen (for example, see the section, "Freestanding Backdrops" under **Backdrops** in this chapter), you are better off using a tape that announces its presence in a visually appealing way.

Most hardware stores sell bright cloth and plastic tape in a variety of widths and colors. These kinds of tape are both attractive and strong. If you need to make a box in a hurry, and you do not have time to wait for glue to dry, you can put the box together with cloth tape instead. Strips of contrasting tape along the seams of the box will not only hold the box together, but they will also give it a distinctive look. You may want to complete the effect by putting strips of tape along the top of the box, where they serve no purpose other than decoration (figure 5.27).

In cases where you need an invisible bond, glue is usually preferable to tape. Glue is stronger, less expensive, and less bulky. Nevertheless, there are situations in which glue is inappropriate—for example, when it comes time to hang a sign or poster. Unless you intend

Figure 5.27 Box with tape in contrasting color

a sign to become a permanent fixture, it is unlikely that you would want to glue it to the wall of your library.

If your sign or poster is not especially heavy, the most convenient way to hang it is with ordinary cloth or plastic tape. Make loops of tape, sticky side out, and stick them to the reverse side of the poster. (Usually one in each corner is sufficient.) Then place the poster on the wall and push on the corners to flatten the tape loops. If the poster is flexible (for example, if it is made of paper or thin cardboard), you must take special care to keep it from buckling. Fasten the top corners against the wall first; then gently flatten the poster against the wall from the top down.

Some signs and posters—for example, signs made of illustration board or posters with three-dimensional objects attached to them—are too heavy to be held up with tape loops. For cases like these, you may want to get some heavy-duty double-sided tape from your hardware store. Double-sided tape—which, as its name implies, has adhesive on both sides—comes on a roll like ordinary tape, but one side is covered with a backing. To use this tape, you cut a piece from the roll, press its exposed side onto the poster, and then peel away the backing to expose its other side.

Double-sided tape is stronger than it looks; it is certainly much stickier than any transparent or cloth tape. With a strip of double-sided tape in each corner, even a relatively heavy sign can be mounted securely on a wall. This strength, however, is also a drawback: some double-sided tape is so sticky that it will actually harm your wall when you try to remove it. Before you use double-sided tape to hang a sign, test a small piece in an out-of-sight area to see how it behaves.

Hardware stores also sell self-adhesive mounting strips and mounting squares, which are close relatives of double-sided tape. They consist of an even stickier adhesive bonded to a thick pad with a foam core. Mounting strips can be used to hang very heavy objects, such as framed paintings. Use them with caution, however; they are even more likely than double-sided tape to harm your wall when you remove them.

Metal Fasteners   Metal fasteners used for displays include nails and picture hooks for walls; and staples, thumbtacks, and pushpins, for bulletin boards.

It is unlikely that you will ever want to nail a sign or poster directly to a wall. If you need to hang a sign permanently, placing self-adhesive mounting squares on the back (see above) is much preferable to driving nails through the corners: mounting squares are easier to use, less likely to harm the sign, and certainly less conspicuous. If you do use nails, however, be sure that they have large heads: nail holes in cardboard can expand, and thus a small-headed nail may be able to slip through your sign.

If you want to mount a heavy sign or poster temporarily, you might consider using a picture hook. Hardware stores typically carry two kinds of picture hooks: the old-fashioned kind that you nail into the wall, and the stick-on kind that are attached to a swatch of adhesive-coated cloth. You will probably find the latter to be more trouble than they are worth: to use them, you must clean the wall thoroughly, moisten the adhesive with water, apply a hook to the wall, and let it dry overnight. Even then, these hooks tend not to adhere as reliably as the claims on their packages lead you to believe. The only real advantage of stick-on hooks is that they can often be removed without leaving a permanent mark on the wall.

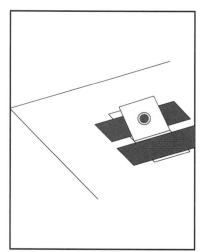

Figure 5.28 Eyelet reinforced with tape

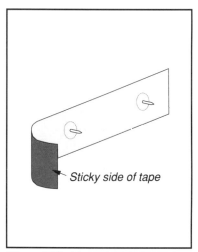

Figure 5.29 Tape with hidden tacks

Even if you do not buy stick-on picture hooks, you probably will want to buy the stick-on eyelets that are made to complement them. Because you cannot screw metal eyelets into a cardboard sign the way you can into a wooden picture frame, these cloth-mounted eyelets are ideal. Their adhesive is, of course, no more reliable than that of stick-on hooks, but that does not matter—once you have stuck an eyelet to the back of your sign or poster, you can reinforce it firmly with tape (figure 5.28).

To mount especially wide or heavy signs—or to make sure that your sign will not sway back and forth—you can use two picture hooks and two eyelets on a single sign. If you do so, however, you must measure carefully to make sure your hooks and your eyelets are mounted exactly the same distance apart.

Mounting items on bulletin boards requires different kinds of metal fasteners: staples, thumbtacks, and pushpins. The same rule that applies to tape applies to these fasteners: They should be hidden if possible, but, if they are visible, they should be made to look appealing.

You can use a simple technique to hang a pict're (or any other item) on a bulletin board, without exposing the mea's of support. Cut off a length of cloth tape and, with the sticky side facing you, push two thumbtacks through it (figure 5.29). Press the tape onto the reverse side of the picture you want to hang. Then place the picture in its proper position on the bulletin board and push the tacks in. If you want to hold the picture more securely, you can use two sets of tacks—one set at the top, another at the bottom. A variation on this technique is to tack or staple strips of tape, sticky side out, directly to the bulletin board. You can then press the picture onto the tape.

These techniques have two advantages: first, they allow you to display a picture without the distraction of tacks or staples; and second, they allow you to do so without making holes in the picture or otherwise damaging it. (Cloth tape can be peeled away from most items without harming them. If the item you want to display is especially delicate, you may want to use masking tape instead.)

Figure 5.30 Clamp with pushpin

Another way to display an item without harming it is to grip it at the top with a small metal clamp. You can then use a thumbtack or pushpin to fasten the clamp to the bulletin board (figure 5.30). This technique is not as elegant as the tape-and-tacks method, but it takes much less time. It is especially suitable for hanging items that change frequently (such as a weekly NEW ARRIVALS list).

If taking the time to hide your fasteners is impractical, then be sure to display them as attractively as possible. Staples should be straight and should be used sparingly. If several thumbtacks are used to hold a single item, they should be uniform in size and color. Small-headed thumbtacks are better than large-headed ones; pushpins are even better than thumbtacks. If you want your bulletin board to appear serious or businesslike, use transparent or white pushpins; otherwise, use colors chosen to match the rest of the display.

Found Objects

The concept of found objects is similar to that of found art (see *Found Art* in chapter 4). Virtually anything can be used as part of a display: dolls, stuffed animals, sea shells, flowers, sports equipment, household gadgets, or any other interesting-looking items you can find.

Found objects can be displayed in a variety of ways, depending on their size and weight. Large or heavy objects can be placed on a tabletop, on a pedestal (see *Boxes* in this chapter), or on the built-in shelf of an exhibit case. Lighter objects can be placed on a homemade display shelf (see *Shelves* in this chapter), attached to the back wall of an exhibit case, or even hung from the ceiling by cords or wires.

Three-dimensional objects can also be incorporated into signs and posters. If an object is relatively small or lightweight, you can fasten it to a poster with glue or double-sided tape (see *Fastening/Mounting* in this chapter). If the object is somewhat heavier—and if the backing of your poster is sturdy enough—you can attach it by means of cord or wire. To do so, simply cut two small holes in the poster, loop a piece of cord around the object and through the holes, and tie the cord in the back. (To mount the object more securely, you might want to make holes in the object and pass the cord through them as well.) Items can be mounted on the back wall of an exhibit case in the same way they can be mounted on a poster.

If you plan to exhibit a valuable or fragile object, be sure to place it in a locked display case in a well-supervised area.

Mobiles

Mobiles suspended from the ceiling are an excellent way to attract the attention of library users, especially if you are short on conventional display space. A mobile can include lettering on strips of cardboard, illustrations mounted on cardboard backings, and lightweight three-dimensional objects. All are kept in constant, mesmerizing motion by the natural movement of the air.

A basic mobile has a pyramidal structure, starting with a single piece of string and ending with a collection of suspended objects. The most interesting mobiles, however, avoid the strict symmetry of a pyra-

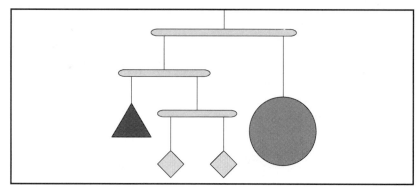

Figure 5.31 Asymmetrical mobile

mid in favor of a more asymmetrical arrangement. (See figure 5.31 for an example.)

The horizontal bars of a mobile may be made of cardboard, lightweight strips of wood, or thin dowel rods. Depending on the weight of the horizontal bars (and on the weight of the objects hanging from them), you may want to use thread, kite string, fishing line, or heavy cord to suspend the mobile and its elements.

The most important characteristic of a mobile is balance: in order for each bar to remain horizontal, the weight of the objects hanging from its ends must be exactly equal. Achieving this perfect balance requires planning, ingenuity, and a good amount of trial and error. When you first assemble a mobile, put it together loosely: hold it together with tape and with loosely tied knots, so that you can easily remove and rearrange elements. Suspend the mobile at a height where you can reach it. Then make whatever adjustments are necessary to distribute the mobile's weight evenly.

If a particular bar is not hanging straight, the easiest solution is to move the string that is supporting it. Bit by bit, nudge the string toward the heavier end of the bar until you achieve the proper balance.

You can also level a crooked bar by changing the weight of the objects that are hanging from it. Heavy objects can be made lighter through judicious cutting or trimming. Light objects can be made heavier by taping paper clips or coins to them. (This added ballast should, of course, be hidden under paper or cardboard.)

Once the mobile has been balanced to your satisfaction, you can fasten its elements more securely. Use a pencil to mark each spot where a string meets a horizontal bar. Then punch a small hole at each pencil mark, loop the string through the hole, and knot it. (If you cannot easily make a hole—for example, if your bars are made of wood—carve a groove instead and knot the string tightly into the groove.) Keep in mind that these final changes may alter the balance of the mobile slightly, and that you may have to do a bit more fine-tuning before the mobile is ready to hang.

Origami

Origami, the Japanese art of paper folding, is an inexpensive way to add elegant, unusual objects to your displays. Because origami figures weigh nearly nothing, they can be displayed in any number of ways: You can hang them from threads, glue them to posters, mount them on vertical rods, or arrange them on lightweight display shelves (see *Shelves* in this chapter).

Folding origami figures requires no special skills other than the ability to follow directions. It also requires no special materials. You can use virtually any sheet of paper, so long as you first cut it into a perfect square.

Many people prefer to use commercial origami paper, which is precut to the proper shape, is thin enough to fold easily, and comes in a variety of attractive colors. Assortments of origami paper, often packaged with directions for folding a few basic figures, are available at most craft stores, stationery stores, and art supply stores.

Because the steps for folding even a simple figure tend to be long and detailed, it is not possible to offer a sample set of directions here. If you are interested, however, you can consult an origami or paper-folding book. Such books typically offer directions for making dozens of figures, from elementary to complex. A number of origami books are listed in Appendix C.

Papier-Mâché

Papier-mâché (literally, chewed paper) is a technique for making durable, lightweight sculptures out of very simple materials. You can use papier-mâché to produce decorative containers, masks, animals, and even human figures.

To produce a papier-mâché object, you must begin with either an armature or a mold. An *armature* is a rough skeleton—usually made of paper, wire, or both—that will remain permanently at the core of the finished sculpture. A *mold* is a solid object that is used initially to shape the papier-mâché, but is later removed.

The only other materials needed to make papier-mâché are newspaper and wheat paste. You can find wheat paste in most hardware stores, where it is sold as an adhesive for hanging wallpaper. Wheat paste comes as a powder; before you use it, you must mix it with water according to the directions on the package.

Papier-mâché may not be practical for most of your displays: it is messy, tedious, and time-consuming. Also, although the technical aspects of papier-mâché are easy to learn, applying those techniques effectively demands some degree of artistic skill or experience. If you are comfortable with freehand drawing, you will probably be equally comfortable expanding those drawings into three dimensions. If your artistic ability is limited, however, you may prefer to use other people's sculptures instead of creating your own. (See *Found Objects* in this chapter.)

The last sample project in chapter 9 involves making undersea boulders from papier-mâché. For other papier-mâché techniques and projects, see the books listed in Appendix C.

Pop-Outs

An ordinary two-dimensional display can be much more eye-catching if several of its elements are made to extend toward the viewer.

Figure 5.32 Letters mounted on cardboard

Virtually any item on a poster or bulletin board—a line of text, a drawing, or a photograph—can be turned into a pop-out with a minimum of effort.

The following is a suggested series of steps for turning the word LOOK into a pop-out. (The word was originally produced by gluing cutout letters to a sheet of paper; see *Cutout Lettering* in chapter 3.)

1. Mount the word LOOK on a piece of cardboard and trim it to the desired size (figure 5.32). For suggestions on mounting, see *Fastening/Mounting* in this chapter.

2. Cut a strip from a second piece of cardboard, following the diagram in figure 5.33. The two segments labeled *A* should be about 1 inch long; the segments labeled *B* should be about half an inch long (or more, depending on how far you want your pop-out to extend). The length of segment *C* will vary according to the size of the item you mounted in step 1.

3. Fold the strip along the dashed lines; then glue the tabs labeled *A* to the back of the word LOOK (figure 5.34).

4. Wait for the glue to dry. Then glue segment *C* to your poster, or else use tacks or staples to fasten it to a bulletin board.

Another form of pop-out is the angled pop-out. To make this kind of pop-out, fold a strip of cardboard into a triangular wedge and tape the ends together. Glue one long side of the wedge to a display element—an

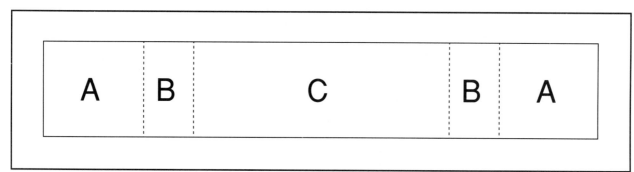

Figure 5.33 Diagram for pop-out

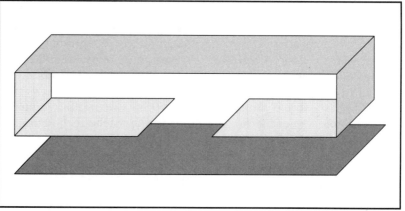

Figure 5.34 Folded pop-out strip

Figure 5.35 Angled pop-out

arrow, for example—and attach the other long side to your poster or bulletin board (figure 5.35).

Shelves

One of the best ways to display books, book jackets, and other small objects is to place them on shelves. Many exhibit cases have shelves already built in; for some displays, however, you may have to provide your own shelves.

The best way to acquire shelves may be to buy them rather than make them. In thrift stores and discount stores, you will find dozens of different kinds of shelves, including freestanding shelves, wall-mounted shelves, and adjustable shelves. If you look long enough, you are likely to find what you need at an affordable price.

If you are in a hurry, however, you can make serviceable shelves yourself. The simplest possible homemade shelf consists of a sheet of heavy cardboard folded in half and braced with cloth tape (figure 5.36). The tape is not especially attractive, but it is the most effective way to add support. If you want to sacrifice a degree of strength in favor of aesthetics, punch holes at the top and bottom and substitute knotted cord for the tape (figure 5.37).

You can make another very simple shelf by folding a sheet of heavy cardboard into a wedge (figure 5.38). Glue the shelf together by means

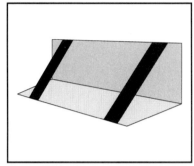

Figure 5.36 Cardboard shelf braced with cloth tape

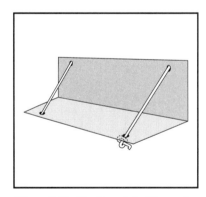

Figure 5.37 Cardboard shelf braced with knotted cord

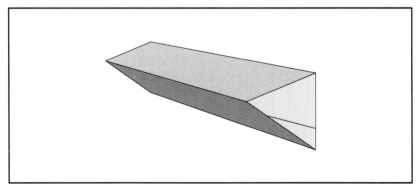

Figure 5.38 Wedge-shaped shelf

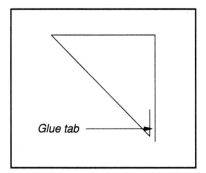

Figure 5.39 Wedge-shaped shelf with glued tab

of a tab at the bottom (figure 5.39). To make this shelf as sturdy as possible, you should make the vertical segment equal in length to the horizontal segment. (If you remember how to use the Pythagorean theorem—$a^2 + b^2 = c^2$—you can easily determine how long to make the diagonal segment. If not, you can figure it out by trial and error.)

A third type of shelf can be made from a cardboard box. See **Boxes** in this chapter for details.

All of the preceding suggestions work only for wall-mounted shelves. (For mounting suggestions, see **Fastening/Mounting** in this chapter.) If you need freestanding shelves, you will have to make them from wood—cardboard just is not strong enough. You can find plans for wooden bookshelves in any elementary carpentry book, but you are probably better off buying the shelves you need.

Whether your shelves are store-bought or homemade, you may want to dress them up for use in displays. You can give new life to a plain-looking shelf by covering it with colored paper or cloth. If the shelf is made of cardboard or unfinished wood, you may choose to give it a coat of paint instead.

If you want to include books in your exhibit, but you are afraid that your homemade shelves will not support them, use dummy books with real book covers. For more details, see the discussion of substitute books under **Boxes** in this chapter.

Sign Supports

There are many occasions when you will want your signs to stand by themselves instead of being hung on a wall. You may want to add explanatory cards to objects on a display shelf; you may want to post information that can be seen easily by people working at tables; or you may simply be short of wall space. In any of these cases, you can turn an ordinary sign into a freestanding sign in just a matter of minutes.

A sign must first be mounted on heavy cardboard to stand up properly. (For information on types of cardboard, see **Backdrops** in this chapter. See **Fastening/Mounting**, also in this chapter, for mounting suggestions.)

For lightweight signs, a picture frame stand works best. To make one, simply cut an isosceles triangle from a sheet of cardboard and fold it down the middle. (For best results, the triangle should be at least two-thirds as tall as the sign.) Glue one-half of the triangle to the back of your sign, and extend the other half at a 90-degree angle (figure 5.40).

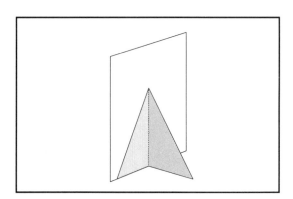

Figure 5.40 Triangular cardboard sign support

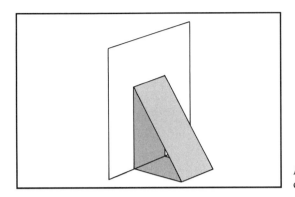

Figure 5.41 Wedge-shaped cardboard sign support

To support heavier signs, fold a strip of cardboard into a wedge and glue it to the back of the sign (figure 5.41). Seen from the side, the wedge should take the form of a right triangle. Its longest side should be at least two-thirds the height of the sign. For unusually wide signs, simply use a wider wedge.

If you expect people to approach your sign from more than one direction, you may want to make a sandwich board out of two identical signs. Place the signs face down, head-to-head, and hinge them together with a strip of cloth tape. Then, from another piece of cardboard, make a base similar to the one in figure 5.42. The length of the base (measured along the folds) should be equal to the width of each sign.

Apply liquid glue to the upturned sides of the base, and attach the base to the bottom edges of both signs. (You may want to hold the signs and the base together with masking tape until the glue dries.) The result should look similar to figure 5.43.

In a pinch, book supports can also be used as sign supports. For information on the different types, see ***Book Supports*** in this chapter.

The techniques described here work best with relatively small signs (no larger than 11 by 17 inches). The oversized supports required for larger signs are unwieldy, and the signs themselves may begin to sag under their own weight. If you need to make a larger sign stand on its own, your best bet is to use an easel.

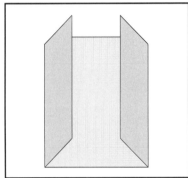

Figure 5.42 Base for sandwich board

Figure 5.43 Sandwich board sign

COLOR PLATES

Plate 1

See page 13.

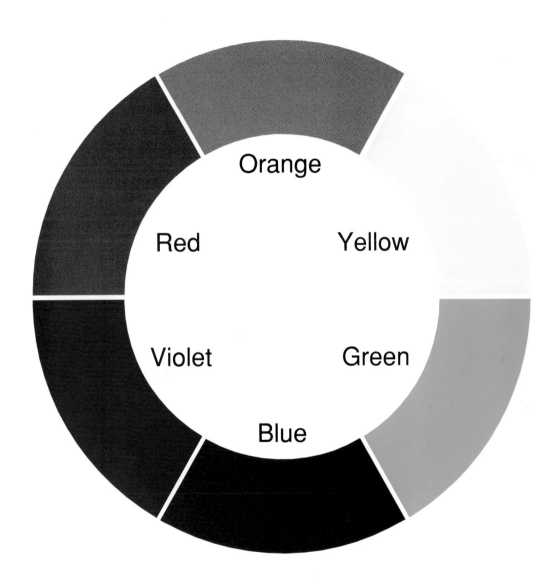

Plate 2

See page 13.

Yellow-Green

Yellow-Orange

Blue-Green

Yellow

Green

Orange

Blue

Red

Violet

Red-Orange

Blue-Violet

Red-Violet

Plate 3

See page 51.

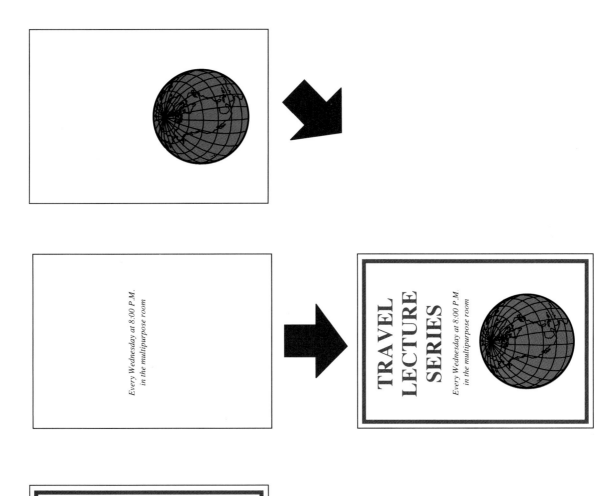

Plate 4

See page 67.

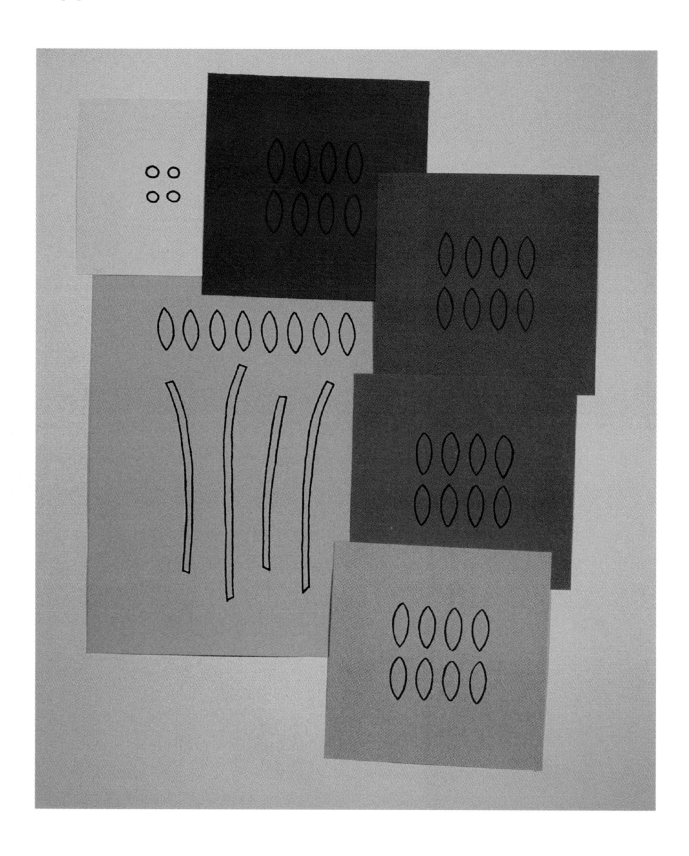

Plate 5

See page 67.

Plate 6

See page 109.

Plate 7

See page 111.

Plate 8

See page 114.

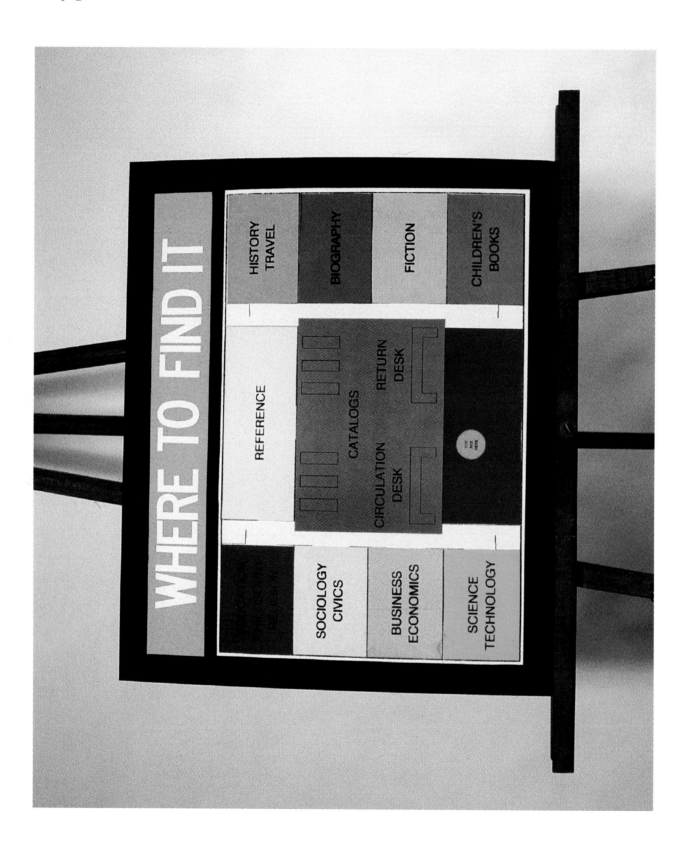

Plate 9

See page 118.

MAY 25 IS AMNESTY DAY

RETURN YOUR OVERDUE BOOKS
NO FINES — NO QUESTIONS ASKED

Plate 10

See page 119.

Plate 11

See page 125.

Plate 12

See page 133.

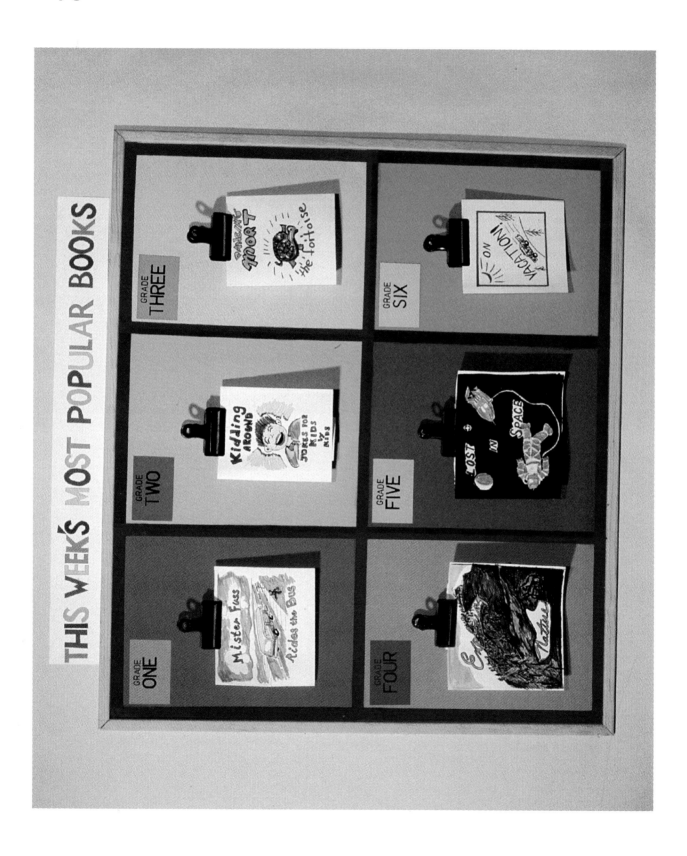

Plate 13

See page 137.

Plate 14

See page 144.

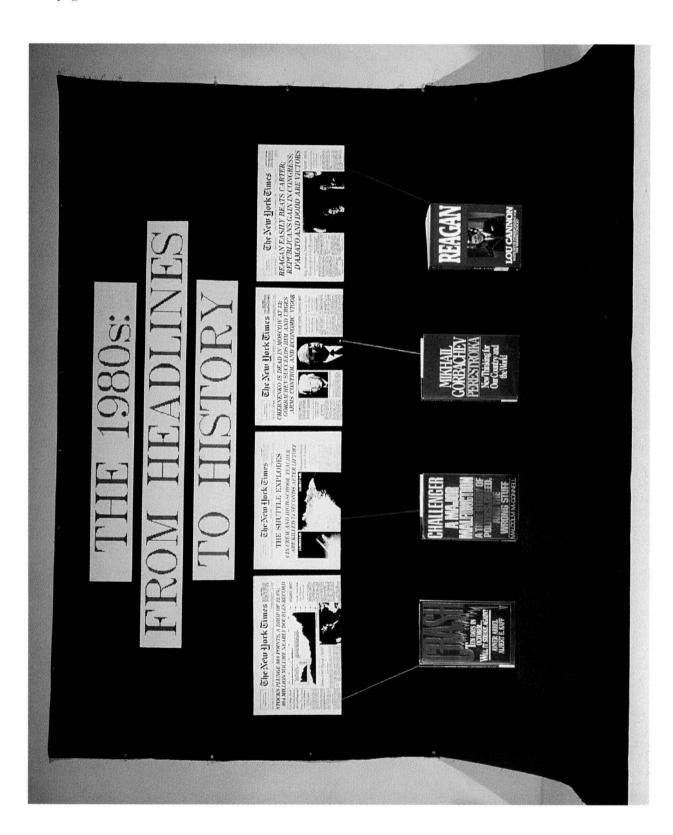

Plate 15

See page 147.

Plate 16

See page 151.

Part Two: *IDEAS*

CHAPTER 6

Signs

Signs serve a number of functions within the library. They identify places and things (for example, REFERENCE DESK), they give instructions, they state policies, and they help orient library users. Some signs, such as BIOGRAPHIES HAVE BEEN MOVED TO SECOND FLOOR, are merely temporary; most, however, are intended for long-term or permanent use.

Clear, well-placed signs make the library easier to use. They make library users feel more comfortable and they cut down on the time you and other members of the staff must spend answering routine questions. Signs are only effective, however, when used in moderation. Library users who are faced with dozens of different signs, each demanding attention to a new set of facts, may end up feeling intimidated and confused.

Whenever you design a sign, you must walk a thin line between function and attractiveness. Because their primary purpose is to provide clear, direct information, signs should be free of extraneous text or ornamentation. At the same time, they should always be pleasant to look at. The best signs are those that fit comfortably into the library environment, but that stand out enough to get their message across.

This chapter will illustrate a few ways in which you can satisfy these requirements. The sample signs presented here are not meant to constitute a comprehensive guide to signmaking; they simply show how some of the techniques from preceding chapters can be put to creative use. Each sample sign is accompanied by step-by-step instructions, but you may feel free to change the design or the production steps to suit your own needs and fancies.

SAMPLE PROJECTS

The samples in this and the following chapters make use of nearly all the production techniques described in chapters 3, 4, and 5. In some cases, you may not be able to use the technique that is illustrated—it may require tools or supplies to which you do not have access, it may be impractical within your time and budget limitations, or it may require skills that you feel you do not possess. For these reasons, each set of instructions includes a number of suggested alternatives for each step. You can find out more about these alternative techniques by consulting the alphabetical reference sections of the earlier chapters.

The samples are presented in approximate order of difficulty, from simple to complex. Each sample project begins with a list of the tools and supplies you will need. (Certain very basic items, such as a pencil, a ruler, and a pair of scissors, are not included on the supply lists. The supplies needed for the suggested alternative steps are also not included.)

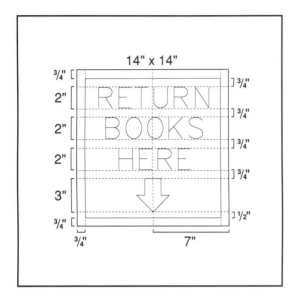

Figure 6.1 Penciled guidelines in dashes

Remember that these sample projects are not "recipes" to be followed exactly. They are meant only to spark your imagination, and to encourage you to use your own ideas and skills to their best advantage.

SAMPLE PROJECT 1
SIGN: RETURN BOOKS HERE

(See plate 6.)
Supplies needed:
> White illustration board, 14 by 14 inches or larger
> Vinyl sign lettering (uppercase, black, 2 inches high)
> Sheet of red paper
> Masking tape
> Dark-brown tempera paint
> Stick-on eyelets
> Picture-hanging wire

1. Cut a piece of illustration board to a 14-by-14-inch square.

2. Draw a set of light pencil guidelines as shown in figure 6.1. (There is no need to sketch in the letters. The text is shown in figure 6.1 so you will know where to position it later.)

3. Apply strips of masking tape 3/4 inch in from the edges of the board, following the guidelines you drew in step 2.

4. Paint a border around the sign with brown tempera paint (figure 6.2). Wait for the paint to dry, and peel the masking tape away. *Alternatives: Create the border with brown cloth tape, cut a border from a large sheet of paper and glue it to the sign, or use a felt-tip marker.*

5. Pick out the letters for RETURN BOOKS HERE from a set of vinyl sign letters. *Alternatives: Use rub-on lettering, cutout lettering, or hand-drawn lettering.*

Figure 6.2 Painting border

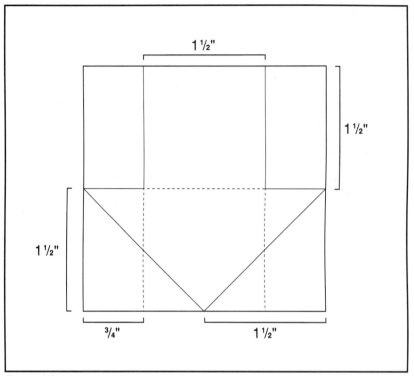

Figure 6.3 Diagram for arrow

6. Without removing the backings from the vinyl sign letters, arrange them on three lines as indicated in figure 6.1. (If all your letters are attached to a single backing sheet, peel them off and place them lightly on the illustration board so they can be moved around.) Use a ruler to make sure each line of text is centered.

7. One at a time, peel the backing from each letter (if necessary) and press the letter in place.

8. On the reverse side of a sheet of red paper, draw a set of pencil guidelines as shown in figure 6.3. Then, with a ruler and pencil, draw the outline of an arrow (indicated by the solid lines in figure 6.3). *Alternative: Draw the arrow directly on the illustration board and finish it with red paint, or use a premade vinyl arrow (available from some manufacturers of vinyl sign lettering).*

9. Cut out the arrow with scissors or a knife. Apply rubber cement to the reverse side of the arrow (the side on which you drew the guidelines), position the arrow as shown in figure 6.1, and smooth it down. *Alternatives: Use white glue, spray-on adhesive, or wax instead of rubber cement.*

10. Attach two stick-on eyelets to the reverse side of the sign, one in each top corner. Cut off two lengths of picture-hanging wire (2 feet or longer, depending on the height of your library's ceiling) and twist the end of each piece of wire through one of the eyelets (figure 6.4). *Alternatives: Use lengths of string or cord rather than wire and tape them*

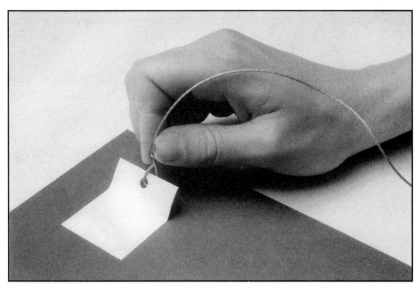

Figure 6.4 Attaching wire to eyelet

directly to the back of the board. To prevent slippage, tape them twice as shown in figure 6.5.

11. Suspend the sign from the ceiling over the book return desk.

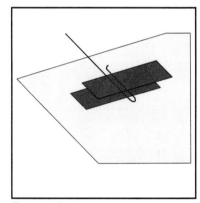

Figure 6.5 Twice-taped string

SAMPLE PROJECT 2
SIGN: THIS TABLE RESERVED FOR INDEX USERS

(See plate 7.)
Supplies needed:
    Computer with graphics software
    Sheet of light-blue paper, 8 1/2 by 11 inches
    Narrow felt-tip markers
    Piece of white tagboard, at least 8 1/2 by 16 inches
    Spray-on adhesive
    White liquid glue

1. Choose a graphics program that can handle a variety of fonts and start it on your computer. *Alternatives: Produce the text by means of rub-on lettering or machine lettering instead of a computer.*

2. Set the program for a standard 8 1/2-by-11-inch page in portrait orientation. Set 1/2-inch margins on all four sides.

3. Using your program's Line Draw feature, draw a horizontal line halfway down the page (that is, 5 inches down from the 1/2-inch top margin). The line should extend from the left margin to the right.

4. From the font selection menu, choose a serif typeface (for example, Times Roman) with a size of about 48 points. (The actual height of a 48-point uppercase letter is about half an inch.)

5. Position your cursor so that the top of the first line of text will be half an inch below the horizontal line you drew earlier.

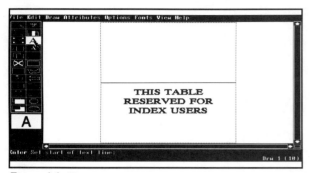

Figure 6.6 Sign text on computer screen

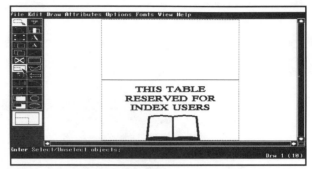

Figure 6.7 Book added to computer screen

6. Type THIS TABLE RESERVED FOR INDEX USERS, formatted as shown in figure 6.6. Allow 12 points of leading between each line. (With 12-point leading, the distance from the bottom of the first line of text to the top of the second line of text will be about 5/16 inch.)

7. If your graphics program has automatic centering capability, use it to center each line of text. If not, center each line manually with the program's Move feature.

8. Draw a book at the bottom of the screen, following the directions under **Computer Graphics** in chapter 4. *Alternatives: Use electronic clip art, or scan conventional clip art and retrieve it into your graphics program. (If you are not using a computer for this project, glue the text and the clip art to a mechanical.)*

9. Use your program's Size feature to enlarge or reduce the book to approximately 3 by 2 inches. The bottom edge of the book should be flush against the bottom margin, half an inch from the bottom of the page (figure 6.7).

10. Use your program's Copy feature to make a duplicate of the text and illustration. Position the copy above the horizontal line. Then use your program's Rotate feature to turn the copy upside down (figure 6.8). *Alternative: If your program does not have a Rotate feature, leave the copy right side up. Later, when you print out the page, you can cut it in half and turn the top half around.*

11. Use your program's Delete, Erase, or Clear feature to delete the horizontal line. Then use your program's File Save feature to store a copy of your work.

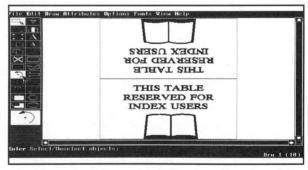

Figure 6.8 Sign copied and rotated on computer screen

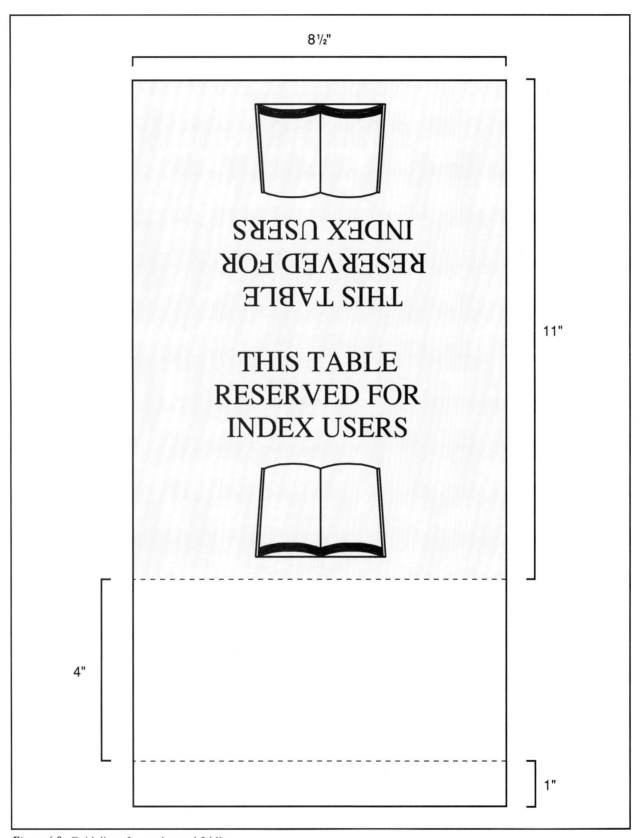

8½"

11"

THIS TABLE
RESERVED FOR
INDEX USERS

4"

1"

Figure 6.9 Guidelines for cutting and folding

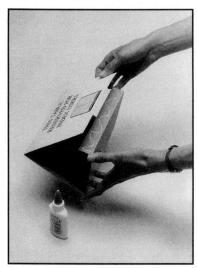

Figure 6.10 Gluing tab to sign

12. Print the finished page onto light-blue paper. *Alternatives: Print the page on white paper. Then photocopy it onto blue paper, or apply transparent self-adhesive film to turn the white paper blue.*

13. Use felt-tip markers to add color to the two line drawings. *Alternatives: Use paint or self-adhesive film.*

14. Use spray-on adhesive to mount the sign on a sheet of tagboard. *Alternatives: Use rubber cement or wax.*

15. With a pencil and a straightedge, draw the guidelines shown in figure 6.9. Cut along the solid lines with scissors or a knife, and fold along the dashed lines.

16. Use white liquid glue to fasten the tab to the back of the sign, as shown in figure 6.10. *Alternative: Use double-sided tape instead of glue.*

 ## SAMPLE PROJECT 3
SIGN: WHERE TO FIND IT

(See plate 8.)
Supplies needed:

    White graph paper with blue grid
    Black felt-tip marker with fine tip
    Black illustration board, 15 by 20 inches
    Waxer with hot wax
    Burnishing tool
    Self-adhesive film, various colors
    Sheet of green paper, at least 11 inches long
    Sheet of white paper, any size
    White glue
    Typewriter with 10-pitch print element
    Stencil or template with 1-inch-diameter circle

1. With a ruler and a pencil, draw a simple floor plan of your library on a sheet of graph paper. If possible, measure the actual floor area of each section of the library in order to make an accurate, reduced-scale diagram. *Alternative: Obtain an existing floor plan from the library's architects or from archival records.*

2. Use a fine, black felt-tip marker to darken the pencil lines on your floor plan. Add identifying labels with rub-on lettering (figure 6.11). *Alternatives: Use machine lettering or hand lettering.*

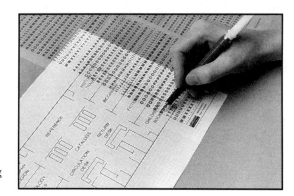

Figure 6.11 Adding rub-on lettering

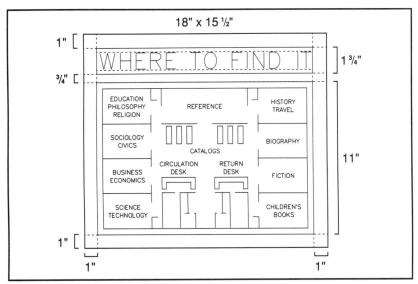

18" x 15 ½"

1" [

WHERE TO FIND IT

1 ¾"

¾" [

EDUCATION PHILOSOPHY RELIGION	REFERENCE		HISTORY TRAVEL
SOCIOLOGY CIVICS	CATALOGS		BIOGRAPHY
BUSINESS ECONOMICS	CIRCULATION DESK	RETURN DESK	FICTION
SCIENCE TECHNOLOGY			CHILDREN'S BOOKS

11"

1" [

1"   1"

Figure 6.12 Diagram for sign

3. Have a commercial copy service make an 11-by-17-inch enlargement of your floor plan. A PMT enlargement is best (it is clear and sharp, and it is unlikely to reproduce the blue lines of your graph paper), but you can make the enlargement on a photocopying machine if cost is an issue. *Alternatives: Make your enlargement manually by means of a projector, a pantograph, or a grid.*

4. Trim the enlargement so that your floor plan is surrounded by a uniform area of white space. In figure 6.12, for example, the 11-by-17-inch enlargement has been trimmed to 11 by 16 inches.

5. Cut a piece of black illustration board so that it is 2 inches wider and 4 1/2 inches longer than the trimmed enlargement. (In this case, therefore, the board is cut to 15 1/2 by 18 inches.) *Alternative: If black illustration board is not available, cover a piece of white illustration board with black paper. Do not paint the board black; glue and wax do not adhere well to paint.*

6. Using a pencil and a straightedge, draw a light guideline 1 inch from each edge of the illustration board.

7. Coat the back of the enlarged floor plan with hot wax and position it so that its bottom edge is framed by the pencil guidelines at the bottom of the illustration board (figure 6.12). Burnish it down. *Alternatives: Use rubber cement or spray-on adhesive.*

8. Choose portions of the floor plan that represent distinct areas (for example, the reference room, the audiovisual department, the children's section) and highlight them with several different colors of self-adhesive film. To highlight the reference room in yellow, for example, peel a piece of yellow film from its backing and place it carefully over the reference room on your floor plan. Smooth it down gently with your fingers. Then cut away the excess with a sharp knife (figure 6.13) and burnish the remaining film firmly. *Alternatives: Add color with paint or felt-tip markers (but be careful if your floor plan is a photocopy—it may smear).*

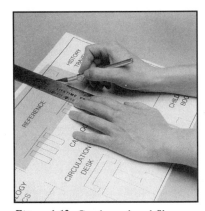

Figure 6.13 Cutting colored film

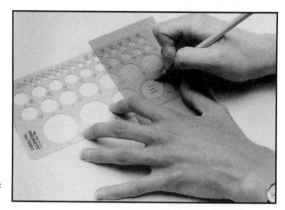

Figure 6.14 Tracing circle using stencil

9. Cut a strip of green paper 1 3/4 inches wide. The strip should be as long as your floor plan is wide—in this case, 16 inches. Draw light pencil guidelines 1/4 inch in from the two long edges of the strip.

10. Cut a strip of white paper 1 1/4 inches wide. From this strip, cut a series of 1 1/4-inch-high block letters. *Alternatives: Use white stick-on or rub-on letters.*

11. Arrange the white letters on the green strip so they spell out WHERE TO FIND IT. The bottom of each letter should rest on the lower pencil guideline; the top of each letter should touch the upper guideline. Use your ruler to make sure that the words are centered between the left and right edges of the strip.

12. Pick up one letter at a time, carefully apply white glue to its reverse side, and press it in place on the green strip. (To apply glue, squeeze a small amount onto a sheet of scrap paper. Dip a narrow paper strip into this pool and use it to put a very thin layer of glue on the backs of the cutout letters.) *Alternatives: Use rubber cement or a glue stick rather than white glue.*

13. Coat the back of the green strip with wax and place it on the illustration board so that its top edge is framed by the top pencil guidelines (figure 6.12). Cover it with a protective sheet of paper and burnish it down. *Alternatives: Use rubber cement or spray-on adhesive.*

14. Use a typewriter with a 10-pitch print element to type the words YOU ARE HERE on a leftover piece of green paper. Place each word on its own line and center it. (If your typewriter has a half-space key, use it to center the word HERE more precisely.) *Alternatives: Use a letter-quality computer printer, rub-on lettering, or hand lettering. Letters should be equivalent in size to 10- pitch (12-point) typewriter type.*

15. Using a stencil or template, trace a circle 1 inch in diameter around the words YOU ARE HERE (figure 6.14). Cut out the circle with scissors. *Alternatives: Use a compass instead of a template, or trace a circular object (such as a spool of thread) whose diameter is about 1 inch.*

16. Use white glue or rubber cement to attach the circle to the appropriate place on the floor plan. *Alternative: If you want the circle to be movable (that is, if you plan to change the location of the sign), use a loop of transparent tape to attach the circle to the sign.*

17. Display the sign on an easel, or use self-adhesive mounting squares to attach it to a wall.

CHAPTER 7

Posters and Wall Displays

It is tempting to say that a poster is merely a more elaborate kind of sign, but in fact posters and signs differ fundamentally in appearance and in function. Unlike a sign, whose purpose is to communicate information simply and clearly, a poster typically presents ideas or facts in an attractive, interesting, exciting, or thought-provoking manner. While most signs consist of plain text, posters usually feature colorful illustrations and decorative typefaces. Some posters draw further attention to themselves by means of elaborate pop-outs or constructions. (Posters with three-dimensional elements are often referred to as *wall displays*. In this chapter, *posters* will be used to refer to both the two-dimensional and three-dimensional varieties.)

In the library, posters may be used to inform (for example, HALLO-WEEN MASQUERADE—EVERYONE INVITED), to educate (AMERICA'S FIRST LIBRARY), to amuse (AUTHORS WITH THE ODDEST NAMES), or to inspire (READ WITH A FRIEND). Posters make the library seem friendlier by portraying it as a place that cares about its users and by adding color and interest to the physical environment.

Unlike signs, which are usually intended to be permanent (or at least long term), most posters are temporary. Posters that publicize one-time events, or that are tied thematically to seasons or holidays, must be taken down once the appropriate time has passed. Even posters with "timeless" subjects, however (such as those that encourage general reading), can rarely be displayed for more than a few weeks or a few months. The more offbeat or eye-catching a poster is, the sooner it is likely to lose its impact or wear out its welcome.

Because they are not meant for long-term display, posters can be made with relatively lightweight or perishable materials. For example, felt-tip markers and construction paper, which are unsuitable for signs because they tend to fade after long exposure to light, are ideal for posters. Tagboard, which is inexpensive and easily hung on a wall with double-sided tape, is much more appropriate than illustration board as a backing for posters.

If you have put a good deal of time into designing and producing a poster, you may be reluctant to retire it after only a few weeks. Fortunately, most posters can be reused, in whole or in part, in future years. See chapter 10 for information about disassembling and storing displays.

SAMPLE PROJECTS

As in the preceding chapter, the remainder of this chapter consists of three sample projects presented in approximate order of difficulty. The instructions for each sample project include suggested alternatives for most of the steps in case you lack the materials or expertise to produce the poster exactly as it is described. Feel free to use your imagination and to depart from the instructions whenever you wish.

SAMPLE PROJECT 1
POSTER: AMNESTY DAY

(See plate 9.)
Supplies needed:
    Yellow tagboard, 22 by 28 inches
    Red felt-tip marker (permanent) with 3/8-inch tip
    Red felt-tip marker (permanent) with 1/8-inch tip
    Watercolor markers, various colors
    Black felt-tip marker (permanent) with 1/8-inch tip

1. Turn a sheet of 22-by-28-inch yellow tagboard so it is horizontal (that is, in landscape orientation). *Alternative: Use a large sheet of paper.*

2. Draw a set of light pencil guidelines as shown in figure 7.1. Notice the empty space where you will place the illustration later.

3. Sketch in the text as shown in figure 7.1. In order to center the text accurately, sketch the middle letter of each line first, and then work outward to the left and right. (For further information, see the discussion of center alignment under **Hand Lettering** in chapter 3.)

4. Use a red felt-tip marker with a 3/8-inch-wide tip (often called a *jumbo* marker) to finish the first two lines of text. Refer to the sample alphabet in figure 3.20 for help in forming the letters. *Alternatives: Finish the letters with red paint, cut letters from red paper, or use red vinyl sign lettering.*

5. Use a narrower red marker (with a standard 1/8-inch-wide tip) to finish the next two lines of text. *Alternatives: Same as in Step 4.*

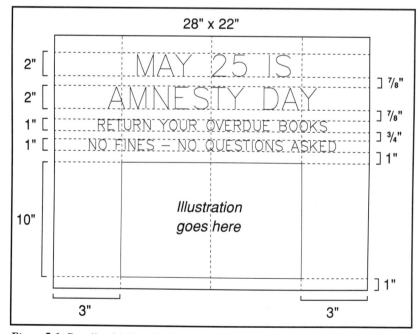

Figure 7.1 Pencil guidelines in dashes

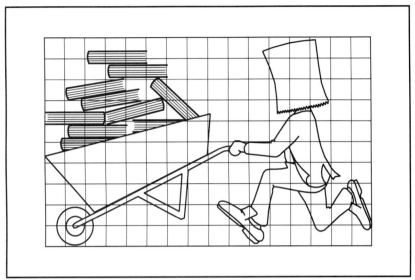

Figure 7.2 Illustration for poster

6. (Optional) Draw a light pencil grid in the part of the poster reserved for the illustration. The grid lines should be spaced 1 inch apart, and the grid should measure 16 squares horizontal by 10 squares vertical. This grid will help you copy a simple cartoon onto the poster. If you have a good eye for drawing or copying, the grid may not be necessary.

7. Copy the illustration from figure 7.2 onto the poster. (If you decided to skip step 6, ignore the grid lines in the figure.) For best results, use tools to guide your pencil lines—for example, use a straightedge when you outline the wheelbarrow and use a compass or a round template when you outline the wheel. *Alternatives: Use an opaque projector to project figure 7.2 onto the poster, and trace the outlines with a pencil; or use an appropriate piece of clip art or found art instead of the cartoon from figure 7.2.*

8. Color in the drawing with watercolor markers. Use the colors shown in plate 9, or choose colors of your own. *Alternatives: Use acrylic paint, poster paint, or self-adhesive film.*

9. Darken the outlines of the drawing with a permanent black felt-tip marker. *Alternative: Use black paint.*

10. Carefully erase all visible pencil guidelines.

SAMPLE PROJECT 2
POSTER: ENJOY THE GIFT OF READING

Make a poster for the holiday season. (See plate 10.)
Supplies needed:

      1 piece of white illustration board, at least 12 inches by 15 inches
      2 strips of white tagboard, at least 8 by 28 inches
      Stencil with 1 1/2-inch block letters
      Felt-tip markers (permanent), assorted colors

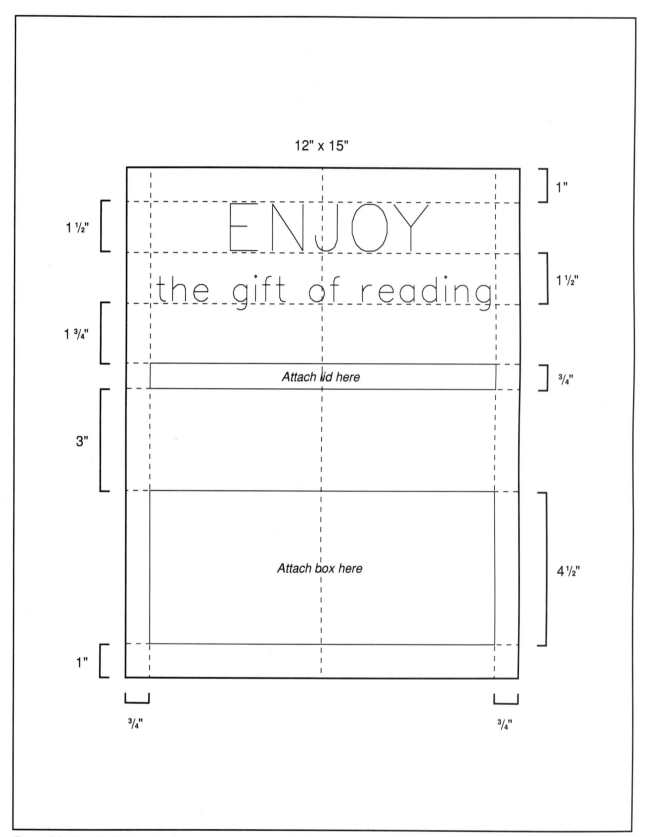

Figure 7.3 Pencil guidelines in dashes

Rubber cement
Red glitter
Rub-on lettering, 96-point Times Roman Bold Italic lowercase
White glue
Festive holiday wrapping paper
Stick-on bow
Scraps of colored paper or cardboard, assorted colors
Tape (any kind)

1. Measure and cut a 12-by-15-inch rectangle from a sheet of white illustration board.

2. Draw a set of light pencil guidelines as shown in figure 7.3. Sketch in the lines of text as shown.

3. With a pencil and a stencil, outline the word ENJOY in 1 1/2-inch-high block letters. Begin with the *j* on the center guideline, and then work outward to the left and right. *Alternative: Draw the letters freehand, using the alphabet in figure 3.11.*

4. Use a permanent black felt-tip marker to darken the outlines of the letters. For best results, use a straightedge to guide your marker when you need to make straight lines (that is, for the *e*, *n*, and *y*). Be sure to close up the "stencil gap" in the *o* (as in figure 3.34).

5. Carefully brush rubber cement or white glue onto the interior of the *E* and sprinkle red glitter over it. Shake the excess glitter onto a sheet of newspaper. Repeat with the *n*, *j*, *o*, and *y*. When you are finished, pour the "recycled" glitter back into the container for future use. *Alternative: Fill in the letters with red marker or paint, or cut letters from red decorative foil and glue them in place.*

6. Use rub-on lettering (96-point Times Roman Bold Italic) to produce the line THE GIFT OF READING. Once again, begin at the center (between the *o* and the *f*) and work your way outward. *Alternative: Hand letter the text in pencil and finish with a black felt-tip marker.*

7. Use a ruler and pencil to copy the box template from figure 7.4 onto white tagboard. Use the dimensions indicated in the figure.

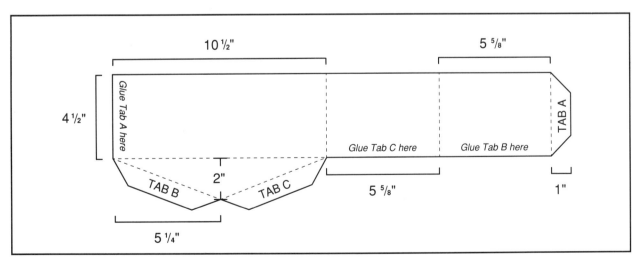

Figure 7.4 Box template

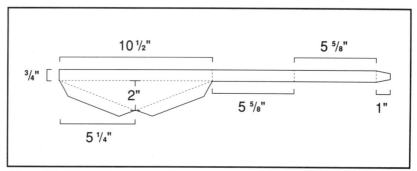

Figure 7.6 Lid template

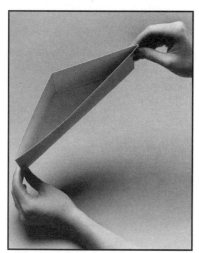

Figure 7.5 Triangular box

8. Cut and fold the triangular box as shown in figure 7.5. Glue it together with white glue. (For general instructions on folding boxes, see **Boxes** in chapter 5.) *Alternative: Use tape (any kind) instead of glue.*

9. To make a lid for the box, repeat steps 7 and 8 using the template shown in figure 7.6.

10. On the reverse (unprinted) side of a sheet of wrapping paper, draw 2 rectangles: one 7 1/2 by 11 1/4 inches, the other 3 3/4 by 11 1/4 inches. (The larger piece will be used to cover the box; the smaller piece will be for the lid.) Cut out the rectangles. *Alternative: Instead of using wrapping paper, paint the box to simulate wrapping paper.*

11. Fold each rectangle in half, making the fold parallel to the short dimension. The printed surface of the wrapping paper should be on the outside. Make a sharp crease along the fold, and then unfold the paper.

12. Place the triangular box with its long (10 1/2 by 4 1/2 inch) side resting on the table and its open end facing away from you. Apply rubber cement to the two 5 5/8-inch sides.

13. Place the larger piece of wrapping paper on the box, with its crease resting on the ridge between the two 5 5/8-inch sides. Allow 1/2 inch of paper to extend past the top of the box and 2 1/2 inches to extend toward you (figure 7.7). Smooth the paper down over the glued portion of the box.

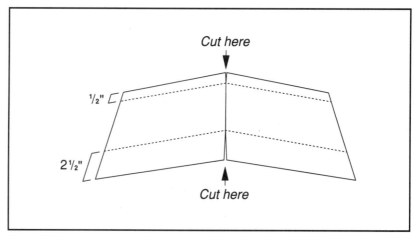

Figure 7.7 Cutting and gluing wrapping paper

14. Make 2 cuts along the crease in the unglued portions of the wrapping paper. The first cut goes from the edge nearest you to the bottom of the box; the second goes from the edge farthest from you to the top of the box.

15. Fold the two 1/2-inch flaps over and glue or tape them flat against the inside of the box.

16. Apply rubber cement to the reverse side of one of the 2 1/2-inch flaps. Fold the flap down onto the bottom of the box and press it in place.

17. Apply rubber cement to the reverse side of the remaining flap. Fold the flap down onto the bottom of the box where it will partially overlap the first flap. Press it in place.

18. Cut away the excess wrapping paper (that is, the ends that are hanging off the box).

19. Repeat steps 13 through 18, using the smaller piece of wrapping paper to cover the lid. Center a lightweight stick-on bow on the lid and press it in place. *Alternative: Make your own bow from ribbon or strips of colored paper.*

20. (Optional) Add ribbons, a tag, or other ornaments to the box and lid.

21. Lay the poster flat on your work table. Apply a rectangle of white glue to the back (unwrapped) side of the box and press the box onto the poster. Do the same for the lid. (Refer to figure 7.3 for proper placement.)

22. To keep the lid from drooping, you will want to make sure that the glue that holds the lid to the poster reaches the very upper edge. To do so, squeeze a pool of glue onto a sheet of scrap paper. Dip the end of a narrow strip of paper into the glue and insert it under the upper left-hand corner of the lid. Press the lid firmly against the poster and pull the strip out. Quickly wipe away any excess glue with a tissue. Repeat this process along the entire upper edge of the lid until you reach the right-hand corner. (For more information, see "Glue" under *Fastening/Mounting* in chapter 5.)

23. Cut seven rectangles, each measuring 2 3/4 by 4 inches, from different-colored scraps of paper and cardboard. Hand letter a book title of your choice on the upper half of each rectangle. Use different sizes, colors, and styles of lettering to suit the variety of titles. *Alternative: Use rub-on lettering instead of hand lettering.*

24. With the poster still flat on the table, arrange the 7 rectangles in the area between the box and the lid. Place them in 2 rows: a back row of 4 and a front row of 3. The rectangles in each row should tilt at various angles and should overlap their neighbors slightly. (Refer to plate 10 for a suggested arrangement.)

25. Lightly mark the position of each rectangle with a pencil. Trace the corners of each rectangle onto the rectangles it overlaps so you can re-create the arrangement precisely.

26. Pick up 2 contiguous rectangles from the front row and, referring to the pencil lines you made in step 25, overlap them in their proper positions. Fasten the rectangles together by applying one or more strips of tape to the reverse side.

27. Add the third rectangle to the row and tape it in place (figure 7.8).

Figure 7.8 Taping rectangles

123

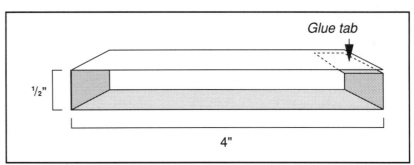

Figure 7.9 Glue tab for rectangle pop-out

28. Repeat steps 26 and 27 to fasten together the four rectangles of the back row.

29. To make the rows of rectangles pop out from the poster, cut 2 strips of cardboard 1 inch wide and 9 1/2 inches long. Fold each strip into a 4-by-1/2-inch rectangular support, and glue its ends together with a 1/2-inch tab as shown in figure 7.9. (See *Pop-Outs* in chapter 5.)

30. Place the 3 connected rectangles of the front row face down on the table. Lay one of the folded cardboard supports across the middle of the row of rectangles and tape it in place.

31. Repeat step 30, using the back row of rectangles and the other cardboard support.

32. Use white glue to fasten the front row assembly to the back row assembly. The result should be a "sandwich" consisting of a row of 3 rectangles, a cardboard support, a row of 4 rectangles, and the other cardboard support.

33. Apply white glue to the back of the second cardboard support. Insert the entire "sandwich" into the gift box and press it in place against the poster (figure 7.10).

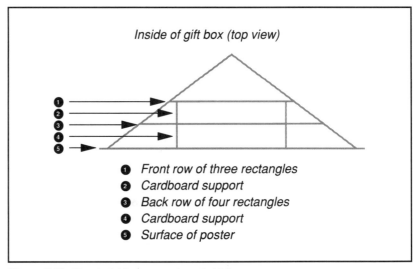

Figure 7.10 "Sandwich" construction of gift box

34. Erase all visible pencil lines, and allow the glued areas to dry thoroughly before you hang the poster.

SAMPLE PROJECT 3
POSTER: BOOK TALKS

(See plate 11.)
Supplies needed:
Light-blue tagboard, 22 by 28 inches
Piece of string, about 20 inches long
Sheet of dark-blue paper, any size
White glue
White tagboard, 22 by 28 inches
Rubber cement
Paint (tempera or acrylic), various colors
Pieces of yarn and patterned cloth (optional)
Scraps of illustration board or corrugated cardboard
Cloth tape, any color
Large paper clip
Book jacket
Dark-blue tagboard, 22 by 28 inches
Kroy (or similar) lettering machine with 36-point type
   sheet of white paper, any size

1. Draw a light, vertical pencil line down the middle of a sheet of light-blue tagboard. Assuming that the tagboard is standard size (22 by 28 inches) and is in portrait orientation, the line should be 11 inches from the left edge.

2. Use a ruler and pencil to place 4 small tick marks on the vertical line, at 1 1/4, 3 1/4, 3 3/4, and 4 1/2 inches from the top of the poster. Then make a small *x* on the vertical line, exactly 17 inches from the top of the poster.

3. Tie a piece of string around the point of a pencil. Place the pencil point on the first tick mark (1 1/4 inches from the top). Pull the string taut and hold it down tightly with your thumbnail at the spot where you made the *x*. Holding the pencil perpendicular to the surface of the tagboard, draw a smooth arc across the width of the poster (figure 7.11). *Alternative: Lay the poster on a sheet of corrugated cardboard, insert a pushpin at the* x, *and tie the string to the pushpin.*

4. Use the same technique to make arcs that pass through the other 3 tick marks. Be sure to use the same center point (the *x*) for all 4 arcs.

5. Cut a strip of dark-blue paper 2 inches wide. From this strip, cut the words BOOK TALKS in 2-inch-high block letters. *Alternatives: Use vinyl sign lettering (spray-painted blue while still on the backing sheet), or use hand-drawn lettering finished with markers or paint.*

6. From the same sheet of dark-blue paper, cut 2 or 3 strips 3/4 inches wide. From these strips, cut the words FIND OUT WHAT'S HAPPENING IN THE LIBRARY in 3/4-inch-high block letters. *Alternatives: Same as step 5.*

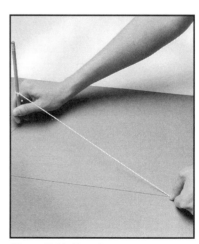

Figure 7.11 Drawing an arc

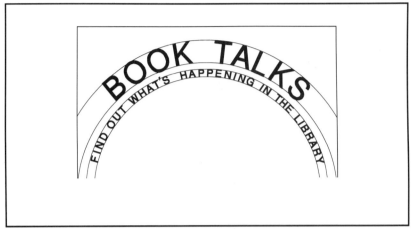

Figure 7.12 Cutout letters on pencil arcs

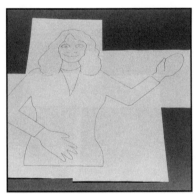

Figure 7.14 Drawing reassembled from 4 photocopies

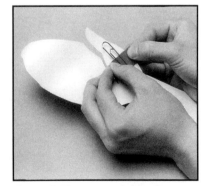

Figure 7.15 Taping paper clip

7. Arrange the cutout letters on the pencil arcs as shown in figure 7.12. Fasten them down with white glue. *Alternatives: Use rubber cement or a glue stick instead of white glue.*

8. The cartoon woman in figure 7.13 is divided into 4 quadrants by dashed lines. Use a photocopying machine to enlarge each quadrant so it fills an 11-by-17-inch sheet of paper. *Alternative: Ignore the dashed lines and enlarge the entire drawing to 22 by 34 inches by means of a grid or a projector.*

9. Place the four 11-by-17-inch photocopies onto a sheet of white tagboard, and reassemble them into a single 22-by-34-inch drawing (figure 7.14). Glue the photocopies to the tagboard with rubber cement, overlapping them if necessary. (Since a standard sheet of tagboard is only 28 inches long, you will have to cut away 3 inches of paper on each side. This space has deliberately been left blank in figure 7.13.) *Alternatives: Use hot wax or spray-on adhesive instead of rubber cement.*

10. Cut out the cartoon figure with scissors. The result is a stiff "paper doll."

11. Paint the cartoon figure with poster paint or acrylic paint. Use the colors shown in plate 11, or choose colors of your own. *Alternatives: Use felt-tip markers or self-adhesive film instead of paint.*

12. (Optional) Enhance the appearance of the cartoon figure by attaching a variety of textured materials with rubber cement. Add yarn or cotton for hair, patterned cloth for a dress, and bits of foil or glitter for jewelry.

13. To stiffen the cartoon figure's outstretched arm, lay the arm on a piece of illustration board or corrugated cardboard. Use a pencil to trace the outline of the arm and hand onto the cardboard and cut out the duplicate arm.

14. Use white glue to fasten the stiff cardboard arm to the back of the cartoon figure's arm.

15. Use cloth tape to attach a large paper clip to the back of the cartoon figure's thumb, as shown in figure 7.15. Be sure to thread the tape

Figure 7.13 Figure divided in four quadrants

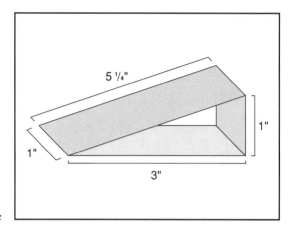

Figure 7.16 Wedge

through the paper clip as if it were a sheet of paper, so that only one layer of the paper clip is taped down.

16. Turn the cartoon figure right side up and position it on the poster. The bottom edge of the cartoon figure should be flush with the bottom edge of the poster, and the woman's head should be approximately centered on the vertical guideline you drew earlier. Use a pencil to trace a very light outline of the cartoon figure onto the tagboard.

17. Turn the cartoon figure over and apply a ribbon of white glue around its perimeter. (Do *not* apply glue to the cardboard-reinforced arm.) Press the cartoon figure onto the poster, using the outline you drew earlier as a positioning guide.

18. Cut a 1-inch-wide strip from a piece of illustration board or corrugated cardboard. Fold it into a wedge as shown in figure 7.16, and glue or tape the ends together.

19. Apply white glue to the two long sides of the cardboard wedge. Gently lift the cartoon figure's outstretched arm away from the surface of the poster and insert the wedge beneath it (figure 7.17). Do not perform this step until the glue from step 17 has dried.

Figure 7.17 Inserting wedge

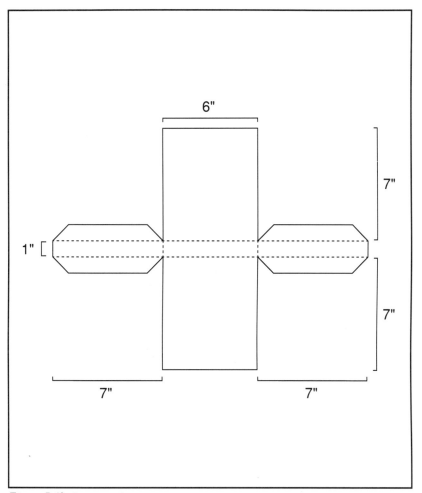

Figure 7.18 Box template

20. Choose a book that will be discussed in an upcoming book talk, and remove its jacket. Place the jacket in the cartoon figure's hand, holding it in place with the paper clip. (The book jacket should be replaced periodically as new titles are scheduled for book talks.) *Alternative: Simulate a book jacket by lettering the title of a book onto a rectangle of colored paper or cardboard.*

21. Use a ruler and pencil to copy the box template from figure 7.18 onto the reverse (dull) side of a sheet of dark blue tagboard. Use the dimensions indicated in the figure.

22. Cut out the box, fold it, and glue the tabs in place. (If you need help, see **Boxes** in chapter 5.) The result is a 6-inch-by-7-inch-by-1-inch pamphlet holder. *Alternative: Find an existing box of the appropriate size, cut away the top, and color the box with blue paint or blue paper.*

23. Use a Kroy lettering machine (or a similar device) to produce the words PLEASE TAKE A SCHEDULE in black, 36-point Helvetica type on a strip of transparent tape. Cut the strip between A and SCHEDULE. Center the resulting 2 strips, one above the other, on a sheet of white paper. Burnish them firmly. *Alternatives: Use rub-on lettering or computer-generated lettering.*

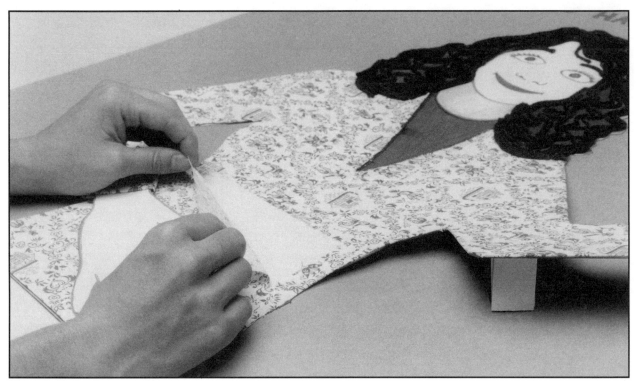

Figure 7.19 Peeling away cloth

24. Use a ruler and a pencil to draw a 5-by-1 1/2-inch rectangle around the 2 lines of lettering, making sure the lettering is precisely centered within the rectangle. Cut out the rectangle with scissors or a sharp knife.

25. Use your ruler to position the rectangle on the front of the pamphlet holder. The strip should be about 1/2 inch down from the opening and 1/2 inch in from the left and right sides. When you are satisfied with the position, mark the corners of the strip with light pencil lines.

26. Apply rubber cement to the back of the strip and fasten it in place using the corner marks as guides. *Alternatives: Use white glue or a glue stick.*

27. Position the pamphlet holder on the poster. Its bottom edge should be flush with the bottom edge of the poster, and it should be centered between the left and right sides. (If the poster is 22 inches wide and the pamphlet holder is 6 inches wide, it should be placed 8 inches from each side.) Mark the position of the pamphlet holder by tracing its top and sides onto the poster.

28. (Optional) If you used cloth to finish the cartoon figure's dress, the pamphlet holder will probably be positioned on top of the cloth. To strengthen the bond between the pamphlet holder and the poster, it is best to remove the portion of cloth that lies beneath the pamphlet holder. Use a sharp knife to cut along the 3 pencil lines you drew in step 27. Then peel away the rectangle of cloth that lies within the lines (figure 7.19). If you used rubber cement to attach

the cloth (as recommended in step 12), you should be able to remove the cloth easily without damaging the poster.

29. Apply a rectangle of white glue to the back of the pamphlet holder and press the pamphlet holder into place. Use the pencil lines you drew earlier (or the cut edges of the cloth) for help in positioning.

30. Carefully erase all visible pencil guidelines.

31. Photocopy book talk schedules onto 8 1/2-by-11-inch paper and fold them in half to fit the pamphlet holder.

32. Hang the poster, and fill the pamphlet holder with schedules. (Do not put schedules into the pamphlet holder until the glue applied in step 29 has dried thoroughly.)

CHAPTER 8

Bulletin Boards

Every library has bulletin board space that needs to be filled. Like chalkboards in classrooms, bulletin boards are often fixed permanently to library walls. They may be inconveniently sized or awkwardly placed, as if they had been installed to take up wall space rather than to serve a practical purpose. Their narrow wooden or metal frames usually surround an expanse of institutional, light brown, corklike material that librarians must do their best to cover up.

In theory, a bulletin board is a repository for temporary information: notices, schedules, and advertisements whose life span is a few days to a few weeks. In private offices, a bulletin board may also be used as a sort of vertical desktop—a place to put notes, clippings, and jottings that have no other place to go.

Neither of these functions, however, is especially suitable to library bulletin boards. Once you exclude internal memos and other items that are of interest only to library employees, you may find that you have enough public notices to fill, perhaps, one medium-sized bulletin board. In many libraries, that would leave a good deal of bulletin board space unaccounted for.

Even if you do have enough bulletins to fill your bulletin boards, there is the added problem of aesthetics. In most libraries, bulletin boards are an essential part of the decor—they are often the first thing people see when they come through the door. A board cluttered with haphazardly arranged cards and papers does not add to the appeal of the library environment, and it does not reflect the kind of image you would like your library to present.

The easiest way to deal with these problems is to stop treating your bulletin boards as bulletin boards—instead, treat them as framed signs and posters. The WHERE TO FIND IT sign in chapter 6, for example—as well as any of the posters in chapter 7—could easily be produced on a bulletin board rather than on a sheet of tagboard, using hidden staples or tacks instead of glue. (For hiding techniques, see "Metal Fasteners" under *Fastening/Mounting* in chapter 5.) Even if you produce a poster in the conventional manner, by gluing elements to a sheet of paper or cardboard, you can simply hang the finished poster on a bulletin board rather than on a wall.

If a bulletin board is too large to be used for a single poster, you can divide the space visually by means of different backgrounds and borders. (For a detailed discussion of backgrounds, see "Bulletin Boards" under *Backdrops* in chapter 5.) A long, horizontal bulletin board, for example, can be made to resemble a row of smaller, vertical bulletin boards (figure 8.1).

Compartmentalization is also the key to effective use of bulletin boards *as* bulletin boards. By subdividing the contents of a bulletin board

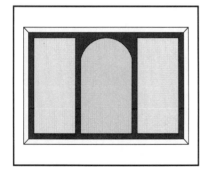

Figure 8.1 Divided bulletin board

into logical categories (for example, notices, advertisements, schedule changes, and so forth), you can make the entire bulletin board more attractive and more useful.

SAMPLE PROJECTS

The two sample projects in this chapter are examples of compartmentalized bulletin boards. The first is more suitable to a public library and the second is more suitable to an elementary school library, but the techniques demonstrated can be used just about anywhere.

Unlike the instructions in chapters 6 and 7, those in this chapter will generally not include precise measurements. The dimensions of bulletin boards are not standardized—they vary from board to board and from library to library—and, unlike paper or cardboard, a bulletin board generally cannot be cut to fit a particular project. Therefore, it will be up to you to adapt the instructions to suit the space you are working with.

Read the instructions thoroughly before you begin, and sketch each design on graph paper so that you can work out the best size and proportions for the bulletin board elements. (You may want to review the section called "Practical Steps for Creating Designs" in chapter 2.) Several of the illustrations in this chapter have grids superimposed on them so that you can easily calculate relative positions and proportions. As you refer to the illustrations, feel free to make any changes that suit the size and shape of your bulletin board. For example, the bulletin board in plate 12 is divided into six equal sections, but you may decide to divide yours into four or even eight sections.

SAMPLE PROJECT 1
BULLETIN BOARD: THIS WEEK'S MOST POPULAR BOOKS

A horizontal (landscape-oriented) bulletin board in an elementary school library. (See plate 12.)
Supplies needed:
　　6 large sheets of colored paper (6 different colors)
　　Stapler
　　Spool of broad, red ribbon (1/2 inch wide or more)
　　Rubber cement
　　Pushpins, transparent
　　Piece of white tagboard
　　White glue
　　Cloth tape, any color
　　Black felt-tip marker (permanent)
　　6 metal clamps
　　6 sheets of white paper, 8 1/2 by 11 inches or larger
　　Paints or markers, assorted colors

1. Collect 6 large pieces of paper, each a different color. (Use any 6 colors that go well together, excluding red.) Cut each sheet of paper into a rectangle whose width is about one-third the width of your bulletin board and whose height is about half the height of your

bulletin board. Round fractions up—not down—to the nearest half inch. (For example, if your bulletin board is 40 by 25 inches, each sheet of paper should be about 13 1/2 by 12 1/2 inches.) After you have cut the rectangles, save the remaining scraps of paper for use in steps 9 and 15. *Alternative: Make rectangles from cloth instead of paper.*

2. Staple the colored rectangles to the bulletin board in 2 rows of 3. Put the staples as close as possible to the edges of each sheet of paper. *Alternative: Arrange the sheets of paper face down on a wide table (or on the floor), glue or tape them together, and then staple them to the bulletin board as one large sheet.*

3. From a spool of broad red ribbon, cut 3 pieces whose length is equal to the width of your bulletin board. Cut another 3 pieces whose length is equal to the height of your bulletin board. (For example, if your bulletin board is 40 by 25 inches, you should cut 3 40-inch-long pieces of ribbon and 3 25-inch-long pieces of ribbon.) *Alternatives: Use strips of red paper, yarn, crepe paper streamers, or other decorative border material.*

4. Brush a narrow line of rubber cement along the top of your bulletin board, extending across its full width from the left side to the right. The rubber cement should cover the top row of staples holding up the sheets of colored paper. *Alternative: Use white glue instead of rubber cement. Apply it sparingly so it does not drip.*

5. Quickly, before the cement dries, cover it with one of the long strips of ribbon that you cut in step 3. Hold the ribbon in place with pushpins. When the rubber cement dries, remove the pushpins.

6. Repeat steps 4 and 5 to attach 5 more pieces of ribbon. (The strips of ribbon are represented by thick, black lines in figure 8.2.)

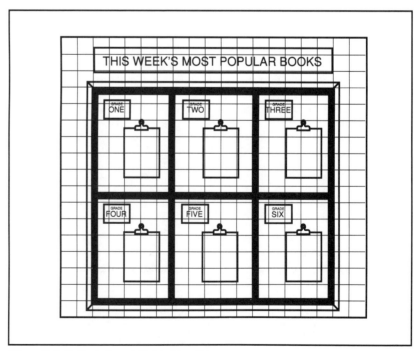

Figure 8.2 Bulletin board divided by ribbon

7. Cut a 28-inch-long strip from a sheet of white tagboard. The width of the strip should be about one-tenth the height of your bulletin board. (For example, if your bulletin board is 25 inches high, the strip should be about 2 1/2 inches wide.)

8. With the strip horizontal (that is, in landscape orientation), draw 2 pencil guidelines along its length. One guideline should be near the top edge of the strip, the other near the bottom edge. The distance between the guidelines should be about one-half the width of the strip. (On a 2 1/2-inch-wide strip, for example, each guideline would be 5/8 inch from the edge, and the distance between the guidelines would be 1 1/4 inch.)

9. Cut a strip from each scrap of colored paper that was left over at the end of step 1 or use fresh sheets of identical colored paper. The strips may be of any length, but the width of each strip should be equal to the distance between the 2 pencil guidelines you drew in step 8.

10. From the various strips of colored paper, cut letters to spell THIS WEEK'S MOST POPULAR BOOKS. (For the apostrophe, cut a small right triangle.) Cut the letters randomly from among the 6 different colored strips. The height of each letter should be equal to the width of the strip. *Alternatives: Use stick-on lettering painted with various colors of enamel, or use hand lettering finished with paint or markers.*

11. Arrange the letters between the guidelines on the tagboard strip you made in steps 7 and 8. When you are satisfied with the positions of the letters, fasten them down with white glue. *Alternative: Use rubber cement.*

12. Cut away the ends of the tagboard strip so that the text is centered on the piece that remains. Erase any visible pencil lines.

13. Tear off 2 pieces of cloth tape and fold them into loops, sticky side out. Press them onto the back of the tagboard strip. *Alternative: Tape thumbtacks to the back of the strip. (See figure 5.29 and the accompanying text on metal fasteners under* **Fastening/Mounting** *in chapter 5.)*

14. Rest the tagboard strip on top of the bulletin board frame. Use a ruler to center it between the left and right sides of the bulletin board. When you are satisfied with the strip's position, press it against the wall. *Alternative: Attach the strip to the front of the bulletin board frame rather than to the wall above it.*

15. To make labels for the 6 sections of the bulletin board, cut out 6 rectangles—one from each piece of colored paper left over from step 9. The dimensions of each rectangle should be about one-twelfth the dimensions of the bulletin board. (For example, if your bulletin board is 25 inches by 40 inches, each colored rectangle should be about 2 inches by 3 1/2 inches.)

16. Decide which label will go in which section of the bulletin board. Try to get the best combinations of foreground and background colors. (You can use the combinations in plate 12, or devise your own.) Make sure that no label will be the same color as its background.

17. Draw light pencil guidelines on each label as shown in figure 8.3. Pencil in the text as well, replacing the word ONE with TWO, THREE,

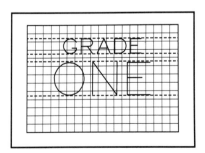

Figure 8.3 Label with pencil guidelines

135

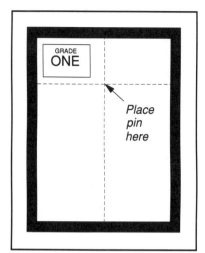

Figure 8.4 Position of pushpin on section of bulletin board

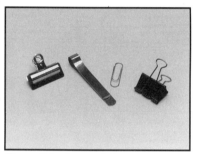

Figure 8.5 Assorted clamps

and so forth on each successive label. (Note that the grid in figure 8.3 is to help you calculate the proper positions for your own guidelines and text. There is no need to copy the grid onto your labels.)

18. Finish the text on each label with a permanent, black felt-tip marker. Erase the pencil guidelines. *Alternatives: Use rub-on lettering, machine lettering, or stick-on lettering.*

19. Use a ruler to position each label in the upper left-hand corner of its proper section of the bulletin board. (Refer to figure 8.2 for help with positioning.) Use a pencil to mark the position of each label's corners on the bulletin board.

20. Apply rubber cement to the back of each colored label and press it onto the bulletin board, following the pencil guidelines you made in step 19. *Alternative: Attach each label with hidden tacks or staples.*

21. Return to the first section of the bulletin board. Use a ruler and a pencil to mark a point halfway across and one-quarter of the way down from the top of the section (figure 8.4). Mark the point with an X. Repeat for the other 5 sections.

22. Gather 6 metal clamps of the kind used to hold large stacks of paper together. (Figure 8.5 shows a few different clamps that you may consider using.) Insert a transparent pushpin through the hole in the handle of each clamp and push it into one of the marks you made in step 21. *Alternative: If the clamp has no hole, fasten it to the paper backing with strong cloth tape, then staple the tape to the bulletin board. (The tape and staples will be hidden by the book cover you add in steps 23 and 24.)*

23. Cut 6 sheets of white paper down to the size of a typical book cover, about 6 by 9 inches. On each sheet of paper—one for each grade— sketch a mock-up of the cover of the week's most popular book. Finish the mock-up with markers or paint. (See figure 8.6 for a

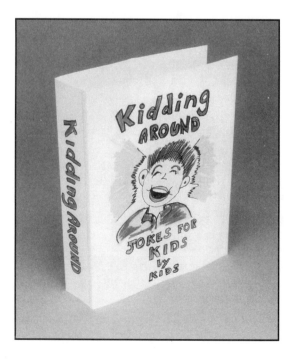

Figure 8.6 Mock-up of book jacket

sample.) *Alternatives: Use real book covers on the bulletin board, or photocopy real book covers and color the copies with markers or paint.*

24. Post each mocked-up book cover in its appropriate section by inserting it into the metal clamp. *Alternative: Omit the clamps and attach each book cover directly to the bulletin board with pushpins, thumbtacks, staples, or tape. (Note, however, that the clamps have several advantages over these other fasteners: they allow book covers to be replaced easily and positioned consistently; they also allow book covers to be reused indefinitely without damage.)*

25. Repeat steps 23 and 24 weekly to update the display of popular books. (You will rarely have to draw 6 new book covers in one week, since many books will remain popular for several weeks in a row.) *Alternative: Once a week, select a student from each grade to draw that grade's book cover.*

SAMPLE PROJECT 2
BULLETIN BOARD: MULTIPURPOSE BOARD

A vertical (portrait-oriented) bulletin board in a public library. (See plate 13.)
Supplies needed:

> Large piece of brown burlap (or other coarse cloth)
> Stapler
> Spool of craft yarn, off-white or tan
> Transparent tape (for example, Scotch tape)
> Pushpins, transparent and assorted colors
> Sheet of yellow tagboard
> Felt-tip markers (permanent), assorted colors
> Thumbtacks
> Cloth tape, any color
> Sheet of white tagboard
> Typewriter
> Index cards, assorted colors

1. Cut a piece of brown burlap (or any other rough, dark, coarsely woven cloth) to a rectangle slightly larger than your bulletin board. *Alternative: Use textured paper instead of cloth.*

2. Staple the top center of the cloth to the top center of the bulletin board; then stretch the cloth straight down and staple it at the bottom center.

3. Stretch the cloth to the left and right and staple it again. Continue to stretch and staple the cloth around the perimeter of the bulletin board.

4. When you are finished stapling, cut away the excess cloth with a utility knife. (For more details on covering a bulletin board with cloth or paper, see the section on bulletin boards, under ***Backdrops*** in chapter 5.)

5. Cut a length of craft yarn (off-white or tan) slightly longer than the perimeter of your bulletin board. Wrap a strip of transparent tape around one end of the yarn to keep it from unraveling. *Alternative: Use colored rope or strips of light-colored cloth instead of yarn. To keep the yarn from unraveling, brush it with clear nail polish or sew up the end with a needle and thread instead of wrapping it with tape.*

6. Using a transparent pushpin, tack the taped end of the yarn to the lower left-hand corner of the bulletin board. If there is a staple holding the burlap at the lower left-hand corner, the yarn should cover it. *Alternative: Staple the yarn instead of tacking it. To make the staples less obvious, place them parallel—not perpendicular—to the yarn.*

7. Stretch the yarn gently to the lower right-hand corner of the bulletin board, and tack it in place with a transparent pushpin. (Pull the yarn taut enough so that it does not droop, but leave it loose enough so that it does not pull against the first pushpin.) The yarn should cover the row of staples along the bottom of the bulletin board.

8. Repeat step 7 three more times, taking the yarn counterclockwise to the upper right-hand corner, the upper left-hand corner, and the lower left-hand corner. When you return to the lower left-hand corner, remove the original pushpin, hold the overlapping ends of the yarn in place with your fingers, and replace the pushpin so that it fastens both layers to the bulletin board.

9. Cut away the end of the yarn that extends beyond the pushpin. Remove the pushpin once more, tape the freshly cut end to keep it from unraveling, and replace the pushpin.

10. Use a ruler or tape measure to find the point along the left side of the bulletin board that is halfway between the top and bottom. Mark that point on the yarn with a pushpin.

11. Repeat step 10 to mark the halfway point on the right-hand side.

12. Wrap the end of another piece of yarn with transparent tape. Place the end at the halfway point you marked in step 10. Remove the pushpin that marked the spot, and replace it so that it penetrates both pieces of yarn—the newly taped end and the existing vertical border.

13. Stretch the yarn horizontally across the bulletin board to the other halfway mark. Tack the yarn in place with the pushpin and cut away the excess. Remove the pushpin, tape the end of the yarn, and replace the pushpin as you did in step 9.

14. Use a ruler or tape measure to find the halfway point along this new, horizontal piece of yarn. Mark it with a pushpin, and then mark the corresponding halfway point along the bottom of the bulletin board.

15. Repeat steps 12 and 13 to add a vertical piece of yarn between the 2 markers.

16. Cut 4 strips from a sheet of yellow tagboard. One strip should be at least as long as the bulletin board is wide; the others should be at least half that length. (For example, if your bulletin board is 36 inches wide, one strip should be at least 36 inches long; the others should be at least 18 inches long.) The width of the strips should be about one-twentieth the height of the bulletin board. (For example, if your bulletin board is 60 inches high, the strips should be about 3 inches wide.) *Alternative: Use cardboard of any color, and attach yellow paper to it with hot wax, rubber cement, or spray-on adhesive.*

17. With the strips horizontal (that is, in landscape orientation), draw 2 pencil guidelines along the length of each strip. One guideline should be near the top edge, the other near the bottom edge. The distance between the guidelines should be about two-thirds the

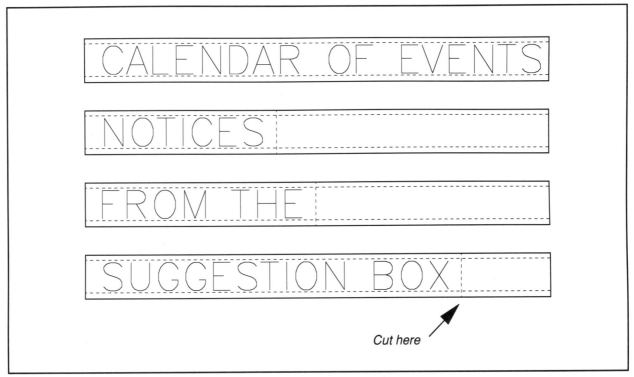

Figure 8.7 Text penciled on tagboard strips

width of the strip. (On a 3-inch-wide strip, for example, each guideline would be 1/2 inch from the edge, and the distance between the guidelines would be 2 inches.)

18. Lightly pencil in the text on the 4 strips. The first (and longest) strip should state CALENDAR OF EVENTS; the second, NOTICES; the third, FROM THE; and the fourth, SUGGESTION BOX. (Depending on the dimensions of your bulletin board, you may want to put FROM THE SUGGESTION BOX on 1 strip.) Leave a small amount of blank space before the first word on each strip, as shown in figure 8.7.

19. Finish the lettering on each strip with a red watercolor felt-tip marker, perhaps using the alphabet in figure 3.28 for reference. Then outline each letter with a black, fine-point, permanent felt-tip marker. *Alternatives: Use rub-on lettering or machine lettering or print computer-generated lettering onto yellow paper and mount the paper on strips of cardboard.*

20. Cut off the end of each strip, as indicated in figure 8.7. Leave as much blank space after the text as you left before the text.

21. Erase all visible pencil guidelines from the 4 strips and turn the strips face down.

22. Cut 4 pieces of cloth tape that are slightly shorter and narrower than the tagboard strips. With the sticky side facing you, push 2 thumbtacks through each piece of tape; then press the tape onto the back of each tagboard strip. (See figure 5.29 and the accompanying text on metal fasteners under *Fastening/Mounting* in chapter 5.)

23. Use a ruler to center each strip at the top of its proper section (figure 8.8).

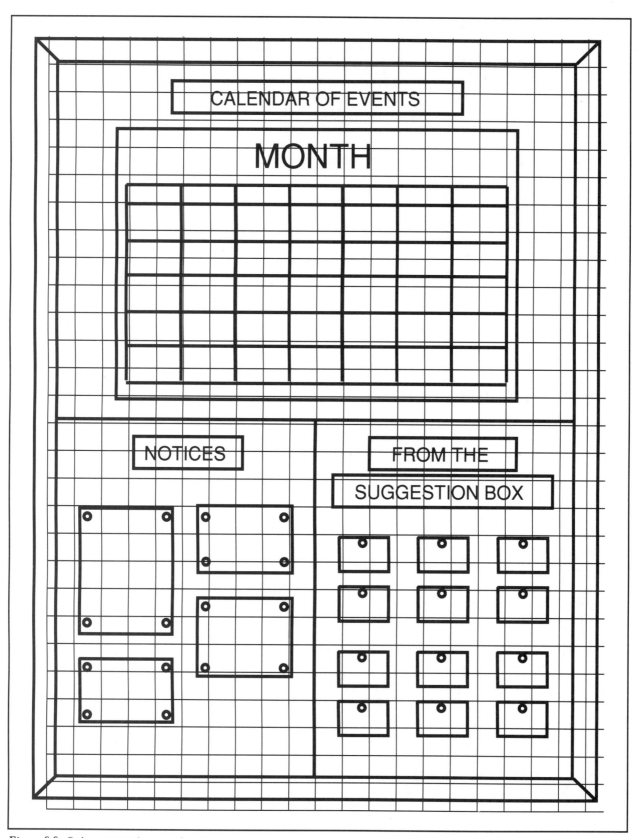

Figure 8.8 Strips centered at top of sections

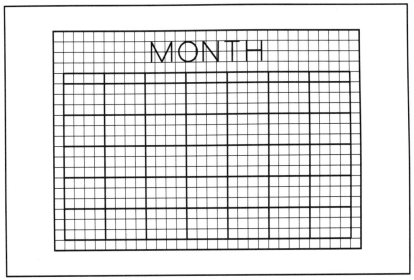

Figure 8.9 Calendar grid

When you are satisfied with the position of each strip, press its attached tacks into the bulletin board. *Alternative: Omit the thumbtacks and glue each strip directly to the cloth backing on the bulletin board. Hold the strips in place with pushpins until the glue dries.*

24. Cut a rectangle from a piece of white tagboard. The width of the rectangle should be about three-quarters the width of your bulletin board, and the height of the rectangle should be about one-third the height of your bulletin board. (If you have a 36-by-60-inch bulletin board, for example, the rectangle should be about 27 by 20 inches.) *Alternative: Use heavy white paper instead of tagboard.*

25. To begin making the rectangle into a calendar, draw a set of pencil guidelines as shown in figure 8.9. (The grid in figure 8.9 is to help you calculate the proper dimensions for your own calendar. There is no need to copy the grid onto the tagboard.)

26. Finish the calendar with a permanent, black felt-tip marker. If you wish, use colored felt-tip markers to add names and dates of events. (You can add more events after the calendar is hung.) *Alternatives: Sketch the calendar on a nonrepro blue grid, finish it with a black felt-tip marker, and photocopy it; computer-generate the calendar with a word processing or graphics program, print it on a laser printer, and enlarge it to the appropriate size by means of a photocopy or PMT; or use a page from a real, wall-sized calendar.*

27. Erase any visible pencil guidelines from the calendar.

28. Attach thumbtacks to the back of the calendar as you did in step 22. Use at least two tacks at the top and two at the bottom. (You may need additional tacks if the calendar is exceptionally large.)

29. Use a ruler to position the calendar within the top section of the bulletin board. When you are satisfied with the position, push in the tacks. *Alternative: Staple a strip of cardboard to the bulletin board,*

apply glue to the strip, and press the calendar onto it. Hold the calendar in place with pushpins until the glue dries.

30. Repeat steps 24 through 29 periodically to create a calendar for each new month. *Alternative: Make a mechanical of a basic calendar page and reproduce it by means of photocopies, PMTs, or silk screen. Then add each month's specific information (name, numbers, and events) with felt-tip markers.*

31. Use a typewriter to copy items from the suggestion box onto multicolored index cards. (If you wish, include replies to the suggestions.) *Alternative: Use a computer to print the suggestions onto multicolored pieces of paper and cut the paper down to index-card size.*

32. Arrange the suggestions neatly within the FROM THE SUGGESTION BOX section. (Arrange them symmetrically if they are all the same size; asymmetrically if they are not.) Fasten each card to the bulletin board by means of a colored pushpin. Replace the posted suggestions with new ones regularly. *Alternative: Fasten the cards with staples.*

33. Arrange fliers, memos, and schedules neatly in the NOTICES section, and fasten them to the bulletin board with pushpins. Replace them as necessary. *Alternative: For a more uniform appearance, use a typewriter or word processor to rewrite notices on full-sized or half-sized sheets of paper.*

CHAPTER 9

Exhibits

An exhibit is a way to bring abstract ideas to life by linking those ideas with concrete objects. It is one thing to encourage library users to read about modern sculpture or Greek mythology; it is quite another to pique their interest by displaying reproductions of sculptors' works or by creating a diorama to represent Mount Olympus.

Exhibit will be used in this chapter to refer to any display that includes freestanding, three-dimensional objects. Although most exhibits are designed to occupy glass-covered display cases, it is possible to set up an exhibit almost anywhere: on a tabletop, in a window, or against a portable backdrop. (For information on making freestanding panels and other kinds of temporary backdrops, see *Backdrops* in chapter 5.)

Like posters, exhibits can inform, educate, amuse, or inspire. They can be devoted to books on specific themes (for example, environmentalism, circuses, Shakespeare) or they can have no literary connection at all. An exhibit that is interesting to look at, even if it has no educational content, can give the library an air of fun, excitement, or mystery.

Exhibits can also be used as a form of advertising—a way to attract attention to the library. On a tabletop at a community fair, an exhibit can promote the library's services or announce upcoming events. In a display window outside the library, an exhibit can turn the heads of pedestrians and encourage them to come inside for a quick look around. Even inside the library, an exhibit can acquaint library users with unusual services (such as a coupon exchange or an art reproduction lending program) that they might not have taken advantage of otherwise.

As with bulletin boards, the design and construction of exhibits is often a matter of necessity rather than choice. Nearly every library has at least one built-in display case, and many libraries are equipped with large, exterior display windows as well. If these display areas are left empty or filled haphazardly, the library may look unfriendly or uncared for. Therefore, it pays to find ways to decorate these spaces attractively and creatively.

SOME PRACTICAL CONSIDERATIONS

Designing and producing an exhibit may take many hours of work. If your library contains several prominent display areas, keeping them up to date can easily become a full-time job. To cut the task down to manageable size, you might consider filling one or two display cases with permanent exhibits devoted to subjects of continuing relevance—for example, the history of your library (or community, or school), the significance of certain classic works and authors, or the art of book conservation. Other display areas, particularly exterior windows, can then be changed more frequently to keep up with current events and trends.

Books, by nature, are attractive and interesting three-dimensional objects; therefore, it is natural to want to include them in library displays. Unfortunately, a book that is on exhibit cannot be read or checked out. For this reason, you may prefer to display only a book's jacket and let the actual book stay on the shelf. By wrapping the jacket around a phony book (see the discussion of substitute book under **Boxes** in chapter 5)—or around a real, noncirculating book, such as a yard sale find—you can advertise a book and circulate it at the same time.

If you prefer to include real books in an exhibit, it is best to choose titles of which you have several copies. If that is not possible, keep a supply of "understudy" books—other books on the same theme—to replace any books you remove from the display.

While exhibits attract attention more effectively than other kinds of displays, they also tend to be more susceptible to vandalism. For safety's sake, it is best to place your exhibits in well-supervised parts of the library (for example, near the circulation desk or the reference desk). If you need to set up exhibits in remote parts of the library, put them in sturdy, locked display cases.

SAMPLE PROJECTS

The three sample projects in this chapter can be adapted to several kinds of display spaces. Each set of directions assumes the existence of a flat, horizontal surface (a table, a shelf, or the floor of an exhibit case) and a sturdy, vertical backdrop (the wall behind a table, a freestanding panel, or the back wall of an exhibit case). As in the preceding chapter on bulletin boards, the directions for these projects will not include specific measurements. Use the grids provided in the illustrations to work out the best proportions for your own display.

Familiar techniques (such as attaching hidden thumb tacks or making boxes) will not be described in as great detail as in previous chapters. If you need more information about a particular technique, check the alphabetical reference sections in chapters 3, 4, and 5.

SAMPLE PROJECT 1
EXHIBIT: THE 1980S: FROM HEADLINES TO HISTORY

Exhibit suitable for a tabletop, a window, or a wide exhibit case. (See plate 14.)
Supplies needed:
  Large black cloth
  Decorator thumbtacks with black heads
  Computer with banner-making program and dot-matrix printer
  Ordinary thumbtacks
  Cloth tape, any color
  Microfilm reader with photocopying capability
  Spray-on adhesive
  Large supply of sturdy cardboard, any color

White glue
Craft yarn, four different colors
Real or dummy books
Metal bookends

1. Use black thumbtacks or pushpins to attach a large piece of black cloth to the back wall of the exhibit space. Bring the bottom of the cloth forward so that it covers the floor of the exhibit space as well. Tack it in place. *Alternatives: Use ordinary metallic thumbtacks and paint the heads black with enamel or use black paper or paint instead of cloth.*

2. Use any banner-making program to print out three banners on a dot-matrix printer. The first banner should state THE 1980s:; the second, FROM HEADLINES; the third, TO HISTORY. If your software offers a choice of fonts, choose a serif typeface such as Times Roman. The point size will depend on the size of your display space. *Alternatives: Have the banners made by a commercial service bureau or hand letter the text on long strips of paper and finish with black marker or paint.*

3. (Optional) Use scissors or a knife to trim excess white space from the top and bottom of each banner.

4. Use cloth tape to attach thumbtacks to the back of each banner. (See chapter 8, sample project 2, step 22; see also figure 5.29 and the accompanying text on metal fasteners under ***Fastening/Mounting*** in chapter 5.) *Alternative: Mount the banners with staples or double-sided tape.*

5. Use a ruler or tape measure to center THE 1980s: banner at the top of the backdrop and press it into place. Then center the second banner below the first and press it into place. (For help with positioning, see figure 9.1.)

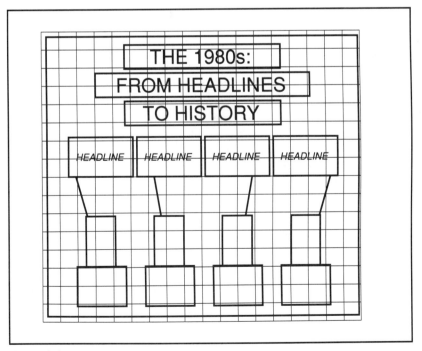

Figure 9.1 Centered banners

6. Find appropriate 1980s newspaper headlines on microfilm. Use the microfilm reader's built-in photocopier to make copies of the headlines. *Alternatives: Simulate newspaper headlines with rub-on lettering or computer-generated lettering.*

7. Use rubber cement or hot wax to mount the photocopied headlines on white cardboard. Touch up imperfections in the photocopies with a black felt-tip marker and white correction fluid.

8. "Blow up" the newspaper headlines by making enlarged PMTs of the touched-up photocopies. Keep in mind that you may have to wait twenty-four hours or more for a local print shop to make the PMTs. (Even if you do not need to enlarge the headlines, you may want to have PMTs made anyway. Photocopies from microfilm often have a gray, washed-out look. PMTs made from these photocopies will be significantly sharper and blacker. For more information, see **PMTs** in chapter 3.) *Alternative: Enlarge the headlines on a photocopying machine (not recommended unless budget considerations preclude the use of PMTs).*

9. Use spray-on adhesive or rubber cement to mount the PMTs on cardboard. If necessary, trim the mounted PMTs so that each headline is framed by a suitable amount of white space. *Alternatives: Use hot wax or rubber cement to mount the PMTs.*

10. Fasten thumbtacks to the back of each headline as you did in step 4. Position the headlines symmetrically on the backdrop, using the arrangement from figure 9.1 or your own arrangement. When you are satisfied with the location of each headline, press it into place. *Alternatives: Tape two safety pins to the back of each headline; then pin the headlines to the black cloth backdrop.*

11. Using a template similar to the one in figure 5.13, make 4 identical boxes out of cardboard and white glue. (These boxes will serve as pedestals for books.) The size of the boxes will depend on the size of your exhibit, but each box should be large enough to display at least 1 book. *Alternative: Use ready-made boxes of the appropriate size.*

12. Paint each box with black tempera paint. *Alternatives: Use spray paint, cover the boxes with black paper, or drape the boxes with black cloth.*

13. Arrange the boxes on the floor of the exhibit space. Place them in a single row as in figure 9.1, or stagger them if your exhibit space is narrow. Fasten each box securely to the floor with loops of cloth tape. *Alternative: If the height of your exhibit space is limited, omit the boxes entirely and stand the books on the floor.*

14. Cut a piece of brightly colored yarn that is long enough to reach from the first headline to the first box. Tape one end of the yarn to the back of the cardboard headline; pull the yarn taut and tape the other end to the back of the box. (Both pieces of tape should be out of sight.) *Alternatives: Use colored rope or strips of cloth or paper instead of yarn.*

15. Repeat step 14 for the other 3 headlines, using 3 different colors of yarn.

16. Gather the books that you plan to include in the exhibit, or prepare a set of dummy books with appropriate jackets.

17. Prepare a support for each book by bending a metal bookend as shown in figure 5.7. Slip the vertical portion of the bookend between the book and its jacket. (If you are using lightweight dummy books, tape each one to its stand with cloth tape and cover the tape with the book jacket.) *Alternatives: Make book supports out of wire hangers or boxes as described in chapter 5; open books slightly so they stand without book supports; lay the books flat with their covers facing up.*

18. Place the books and supports on their appropriate pedestals. For added stability, fasten each book support to the top of the pedestal with hidden loops of cloth tape.

SAMPLE PROJECT 2
EXHIBIT: READING IS IN FASHION!

Exhibit suitable for a tabletop, a window, or a vertical exhibit case with shelves. (See plate 15.)

Supplies needed:
> Purple cloth
> Red felt
> Pink felt
> White glue
> Strips of heavy cardboard, any color
> Thumbtacks
> Cloth tape, any color
> Many sheets of white tagboard
> Many clip-art books and magazines
> Rubber cement
> Three sturdy boxes (small, medium, large)
> Red cloth
> Real or dummy books

1. Cut a piece of purple cloth to a suitable size for the READING IS IN FASHION! banner. (See figure 9.2 for help in determining proper

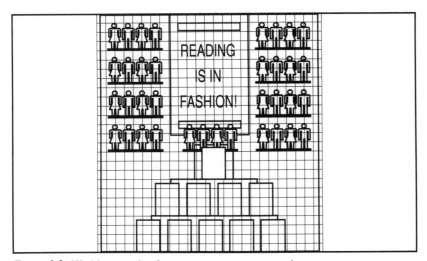

Figure 9.2 Working out size for READING IS IN FASHION! banner

147

size.) If you wish, give the banner a more finished look by folding back the edges of the cloth, sewing them or taping them in place, and ironing them flat. *Alternative: Use purple paper instead of cloth.*

2. Spread the purple cloth flat on your work table. Tack down the corners with pushpins so that the surface of the cloth is taut.

3. Cut a sheet of red felt into strips. The width of each strip should be equal to the height of the letters in READING IS IN FASHION! (Again, refer to figure 9.2 for help in determining a suitable height for the letters.) From these felt strips, cut out the letters and an exclamation point.

4. Cut two strips from a sheet of pink felt. The width of the strips should be about half the width of the red strips you cut in step 3. The length of the strips should be about 80 percent of the width of the banner.

5. With the aid of a ruler, arrange the letters and strips on the purple cloth as shown in figure 9.2. Make sure that each line of text is straight and properly centered. When you are satisfied with the positions of the cutouts, fasten them down with white glue. *Alternative: Instead of using cutouts, paint the letters and strips directly onto the cloth. Many art stores and hobby shops carry bright "special effects" paints, made especially for cloth, that dry with an embossed effect or a glittery appearance.*

6. Cut a narrow strip of cardboard to stiffen the top edge of the banner. The strip should be slightly longer than the banner is wide. Cover the strip with a zigzag line of white glue; then press the top edge of the banner onto it. Let the glue dry overnight.

7. Cut away the ends of the cardboard strip that extend past the edges of the banner. Attach hidden thumbtacks to the strip as described in sample project 1, step 4.

8. Center the banner on the back wall of the display and press it into place. *Alternative: If you are assembling the exhibit in a display case with built-in shelves, hang the banner in front of the shelves rather than on the back wall. Tape it to the front edge of the highest shelf or hang it from the ceiling of the display case. (See figure 9.3.)*

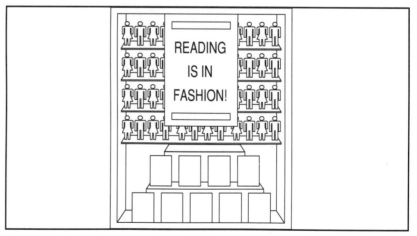

Figure 9.3 Banner hanging in front of display case

9. To make shelves, cut several sheets of white tagboard into 13-inch-wide strips. Determine the proper length of each strip by looking at the shelves in figure 9.2.

10. Draw guidelines along the length of each strip, using the measurements shown in figure 9.4. Fold each strip into a wedge-shaped shelf and glue it together. (For details on making wedge-shaped shelves, see figure 5.38 and its accompanying text.) *Alternatives: Make shelves from cardboard and tape (figure 5.36); use ready-made shelves in display case.*

11. Use a ruler or tape measure to arrange the shelves symmetrically on the back wall of the exhibit space. Indicate the proper position of each shelf with pencil marks.

12. Fasten each shelf in place with two thumbtacks. (Place the tacks inside the shelf as shown in figure 9.4.) *Alternative: Use double-sided tape.*

13. Search through magazines and clip-art books to find full-length human figures dressed in a variety of fashions—preferably from different cultures and historical periods. Cut out or photocopy each figure. (For now, just cut a rough rectangle around each illustration; do not cut along its outlines. Keep in mind that if you photocopy illustrations instead of cutting them out, you can enlarge or reduce them as necessary.) *Alternatives: Draw your own illustrations or have students draw them.*

14. Use a pencil and ruler to draw a horizontal line across the bottom of each illustration, just touching the human figure's feet (figure 9.5).

15. On a sheet of white tagboard, draw the set of guidelines shown in

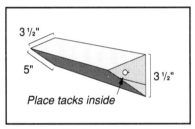

Figure 9.4 Tacks inside shelf

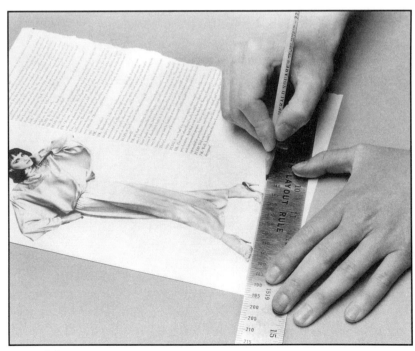

Figure 9.5 Drawing line on illustration

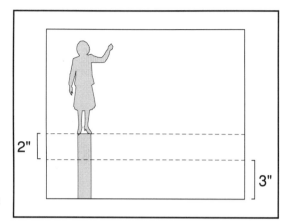

Figure 9.6 Guidelines on tagboard

figure 9.6. (If the illustrations you gathered in step 13 are especially large or numerous, you may have to do this on several sheets of tagboard.)

16. Arrange your illustrations side by side on the tagboard, so that the baselines you drew in step 14 align with the uppermost guideline on the tagboard. (See figure 9.6.) Apply rubber cement to the illustrations and fasten them in place. *Alternatives: Use spray-on adhesive or a glue stick.*

17. (Optional) If any of your illustrations are in black and white, use watercolor markers or paint to color them.

18. Use a ruler and pencil to draw a set of parallel vertical lines directly below each illustration. The distance between the lines should correspond to the size of the human figure's feet. (Once again, see figure 9.6.)

19. Carefully cut out each illustration along its outlines, leaving a tagboard "tail" at the bottom (figure 9.7).

20. Fold each "tail" into a wedge-shaped stand as shown in figure 9.8. Fasten it with glue or tape.

21. Arrange the cutout figures on the exhibit shelves, mixing colors, sizes, and styles on each shelf. When you are satisfied with the

Figure 9.7 Leaving tagboard "tail" on illustration

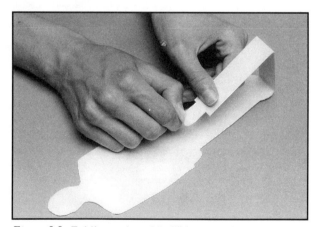

Figure 9.8 Folding tagboard "tail" into stand

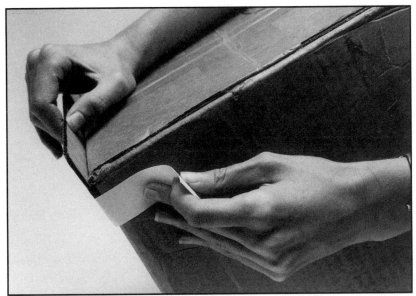

Figure 9.9 Fastening cardboard strip to make "lip"

arrangement, glue the figures in place. *Alternative: If you are using permanent shelves, anchor the cutouts with tape or tacks instead of glue.*

22. Stack 3 sturdy cardboard boxes, building a pyramid from widest to narrowest. (The height of each box should be about equal to the height of a book. If any of the boxes is too high, shorten it with scissors or a knife.) Fasten the boxes together securely with cloth tape. *Alternatives: Make your own boxes instead of using ready-made boxes. If vertical room is limited, use 2 boxes, 1 box, or none at all.*

23. Cut several strips of heavy cardboard, each about 2 inches wide. Use these strips to make a half-inch "lip" around the upper edge of the bottom box (figure 9.9). Fasten each strip in place with cloth tape. Do the same for the middle box (if there is one). It is not necessary to put a lip on the top box.

24. Put the stack of boxes on the floor of the exhibit space directly below the banner. Cover the boxes with a large piece of red cloth to form an attractive pedestal.

25. Place real or dummy books on the 2 lower levels of the pedestal. The bottom of each book should be held in place by the cardboard lip, and the top of each book should lean against the box behind it. (If you wish, place another book at the very top of the pedestal, using one of the book supports described in chapter 5.)

SAMPLE PROJECT 3
EXHIBIT: UNDERSEA TREASURE

Exhibit suitable for window or enclosed display case, but not for tabletop or portable exhibit. (See plate 16.)
Supplies needed:
 Round balloons
 Lots of old newspaper

Papier-mâché paste (wheat paste)
Transparent tape
Tempera paint, assorted colors
Large, rectangular cardboard carton
Black cloth tape
Black felt-tip marker, permanent
Aluminum foil
Large sheets of dark-blue paper
Sheet of light-blue tagboard
Thumbtacks
Assortment of student-made sea creatures
Blue or transparent thread
Scraps of cool-colored paper
Real or dummy books

1. Because the papier-mâché boulders are the most time-consuming part of this project, construct them first. Blow up a few party balloons (the round kind, not the long kind). These will be the armatures for the boulders. *Alternatives: Carve the boulders from blocks of Styrofoam instead of constructing them from papier-mâché; use real boulders; omit the boulders entirely.*

2. Tear several sheets of newspaper into strips. Dip the strips into papier-mâché paste and apply them to the surface of the first balloon. Keep going until the balloon is covered with four layers of paper strips; then repeat the process for the other balloons. Let the paste dry overnight. This is a messy process. The paste spatters, and the newsprint may come off on your hands and clothes. Protect your working surface and wear an apron or smock.

3. To create bumps and irregularities on the boulders, crumple pieces of newspaper into small balls and fasten them to the paper-covered balloons with transparent tape (figure 9.10). Cover these with a layer of paste-dipped paper strips.

Figure 9.10 Creating bumps on papier-mâché boulders

4. Cover each boulder with a few more layers of paper, smoothing out the areas where the bumps meet the boulders. Once again, let the paste dry overnight.

5. Paint the finished boulders with brown, green, and gray tempera paint (or choose colors of your own).

6. To make the treasure chest, find an appropriately shaped cardboard carton (such as a microwave oven box or a stereo speaker box) that has all 6 sides intact. Paint it, inside and out, with brown tempera paint. (If the box has markings on it, you may have to use several coats of paint to cover them. Be sure each coat of paint is dry before you apply another.) *Alternative: Make your own box from sturdy cardboard or use a real wooden chest.*

Figure 9.11 Painting box for wood-grain effect

7. Allow the brown paint to dry thoroughly. Then use a straightedge and a black marker to draw evenly spaced lines across each surface of the box to create the illusion of wooden slats. *Alternative: Use black paint and a narrow brush.*

8. (Optional) Dip a stiff brush in black paint and wipe the brush with a cloth until it is almost dry. Then stroke the brush along each surface of the box to create a wood-grain effect (figure 9.11). *Alternative: Draw the wood-grain lines individually with a fine marker or brush.*

9. Close the box and trim it with black cloth tape. Place strips of tape on every edge and seam, as shown in figure 9.12. To trim the ends of the box as neatly as possible, run a single strip of tape around all 4 sides of the box, with half the width of the tape hanging over the edge (figure 9.13). Make a slit in the tape whenever it turns a corner. Then, one side at a time, fold the tape down onto the box (figure 9.14).

10. Use a ruler to draw a horizontal line across the front and 2 sides of the box. The line should be about 25 percent of the way from the top to the bottom of the box. (For example, if your box is 2 feet high, the line should be about 6 inches from the top.)

11. Cut along the line with scissors or a knife; then fold the box back

Figure 9.12 Box trimmed with tape

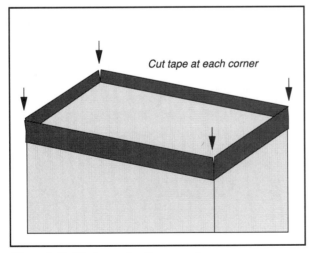

Cut tape at each corner

Figure 9.13 Taping ends of box: step 1

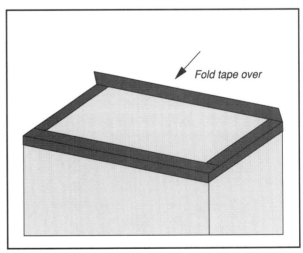

Fold tape over

Figure 9.14 Taping ends of box: step 2

Figure 9.15 Cut-open
box with taped edges

along the uncut side. Trim the newly exposed edges with black
cloth tape (figure 9.15).

12. Fill the box nearly to the top with crumpled newspaper; then put a
    layer of aluminum foil over the newspaper. *Alternatives: Use old
    clothes, discarded books, or a slightly smaller box instead of newspaper; use
    gold or silver metallic wrapping paper instead of foil.*

13. With the cooperation of an elementary grade art teacher, assemble
    a collection of student-made sea creatures. *Alternative: Make your
    own sea creatures from paper, cloth, cellophane, pipe cleaners, and so forth.*

14. Cover the back wall of the exhibit space with large sheets of
    dark-blue paper. Fasten the paper in place with staples, tacks, or
    tape. (To hide the fasteners, overlap the paper as described in the
    "Bulletin Boards" section of **Backdrops** in chapter 5.) *Alternatives:
    Use blue cloth or crepe paper streamers instead of paper.*

15. On a sheet of light-blue tagboard, draw the pencil guidelines shown
    in figure 9.16. (The size of the tagboard and the positions of the

Figure 9.16 Pencil guidelines

guidelines will depend on the size and proportions of your display space. Use the grid for assistance.) After you have drawn the guidelines, sketch in the text as shown.

16. Using a soft brush and black tempera paint, paint the words UNDER-SEA TREASURE onto the tagboard. *Alternatives: Use a jumbo felt-tip marker or cut out letters from black paper.*

17. Attach hidden tacks to the back of the UNDERSEA TREASURE sign (as described in sample project 1, step 4) and fasten the sign to the upper left corner of the backdrop. *Alternative: Glue the sign directly to the backdrop.*

18. Use blue or transparent thread to suspend the sea creatures invisibly. Depending on the nature of the sea creatures, you can attach a piece of thread with transparent tape or simply tie the thread around one of the creature's appendages. Tie the other end of the thread to a thumbtack or pushpin, and fasten it to the ceiling of the display case. Try to hang the sea creatures at different heights and depths. *Alternative: Tape the sea creatures to the backdrop and to the front window of the display case.*

19. Tear sheets of cool-colored paper (blue, green, and purple; perhaps brown, gray, and black as well) into small pieces. Spread them on the floor of the display case to represent the bottom of the sea. *Alternative: Place a variety of objects on the floor of the display case to create "rough terrain"; then cover them with a large blue, gray, or green cloth.*

20. Scatter the papier-mâché boulders around the sea floor. Place the treasure chest in the lower right-hand corner of the display.

21. Gather a number of real or dummy books relating to the sea, underwater exploration, and marine life. Place them face up in the treasure chest on top of the layer of aluminum foil.

CHAPTER 10

On Your Own

The preceding four chapters gave you a number of ready-made display ideas. Most of the design work was already done; all you had to do was to put the displays together.

In real life, however, there are generally no sets of instructions to guide you in creating displays. The ideas and themes have to come from your own imagination, and the final design must be reached through meticulous planning and much trial and error. You can, of course, find many more display ideas in books similar to this one (see Appendix C), but using other people's designs is no substitute for inventing your own. The best displays are those that grow from a unique set of circumstances: your library's distinctive personality, the needs of your community, and your own artistic strengths.

Therefore, the goal of this last chapter is to send you out on your own—to introduce you to the creative process, give you a few time-saving hints, and show you how to use your resources to their best advantage. When you begin to let your imagination run free, you will probably find that you have *too many* display ideas instead of too few.

STEPS FOR PLANNING DISPLAYS

Imagination does not work in a straight line. It darts off in many directions at once, wanders in circles, and takes unpredictable shortcuts. The best way to use your imagination is to give it the freedom to roam. If you restrict yourself to a linear way of doing things—do x, then do y, then do z—you will rarely achieve a creative result.

Therefore, the following series of steps for planning displays should be taken with a grain of salt. The purpose of this list is only to establish a framework—to define a standard set of tasks you will need to accomplish. In many cases, you are likely to find yourself completing these steps in a different order, redoing steps you have already done, or ignoring certain steps entirely. (For example, you may design an entire exhibit around a particular book; later, you may decide not to include that book in the exhibit after all. You may even decide you do not want *any* books in the exhibit.)

This list applies primarily to posters, bulletin boards, and exhibits. You may find it useful for signs as well, but steps 2 and 5 will generally not apply.

Step 1. Identify a Need   Every display should be designed with a specific goal in mind. Examples of possible goals might be:

- To highlight specific resources or services that library users are not taking advantage of

- To draw attention to books on a specific subject, or to particularly noteworthy titles
- To publicize an appearance by an author, lecturer, or other notable visitor
- To advertise activities sponsored by the library or by other community groups
- To increase awareness of important events (current or historical) and to encourage use of the library to find out more about those events
- To illustrate the history and background of the library, the community, or both
- To relate the library's resources to subjects that students are studying in class
- To explain the value and proper use of certain tools (for example, indexes, on-line services, vertical files)
- To introduce or explain library policies
- To encourage appreciation and respect for books as physical objects
- To help library users find their way around the library and locate the materials they need
- To make the library seem friendlier, more human, and more accessible
- To add color or visual interest to a certain part of the library, or simply to fill an obvious empty space
- To promote reading and other forms of intellectual inquiry
- To build awareness of and appreciation for the visual, creative, and performing arts
- To encourage support for important (but nonpolitical) causes, such as environmentalism or international understanding, even if they have no direct connection to the library

Step 2. Pick a Theme or a Specific Subject   This is simply a matter of narrowing and refining the goal you established in step 1. For example, if you want to design a bulletin board that relates to current events, you must decide which events to cover. If you need a sign that explains how to use the on-line catalog, you must decide what level of detail you want to include. If you plan an exhibit about Abraham Lincoln, you must decide which aspects to focus on. (His early life? His presidency? His speeches and writings? The real Lincoln versus the myth? The continuing, popular use of his face and image? His significance in American race relations?)

When you pick a specific subject for your display, you must also decide on a tone. For example, a poster promoting books about animals can be cute (with pictures of big-eyed puppies and kittens), analytical (with illustrations showing the great variety of the animal kingdom), philosophical (with thought-provoking questions about the rights of animals versus the rights of humans), stark (with graphic scenes illustrating the law of the jungle), or whimsical (with cartoon animals saying or doing humanlike things). In making decisions about tone, you will have to consider what sort of image you want your library to project and what kind of audience you are hoping to reach.

If you need a quick display idea and you cannot think of any suitable topics, the first places to look are your calendar and almanac. Are any holidays or special events approaching? Do the next few weeks include the birthdays of any famous people or anniversaries of any significant events? Are any interesting natural phenomena (an eclipse, a meteor shower, a comet) expected soon? For a list of calendar-related display ideas, see Appendix D.

The next places to look for inspiration are newspapers and magazines. What are the latest styles in music, art, speech, and dress? Are there any new trends in science, politics, or popular culture that you can tie into a display?

Finally, gather ideas from the people around you. Talk to library users (or listen to snatches of their conversations) to find out what is on their minds. If you work in a school library, ask teachers to tell you about their students' interests.

If none of these sources gives you the material you need, you can always turn to the old standby: the library's card catalog. Subjects such as history, travel, music, health, technology, careers, nature, food, fashion, and literature offer endless opportunities for displays. Through the use of humor, catch phrases, and appealing illustrations, you can make these perennial topics seem fresh and exciting.

Step 3. Find an Appropriate Space

Think, very generally, about what form your display should take. If you have a straightforward message to present, with few or no illustrations, you will probably want to create a sign or a flat poster. If you expect to include a number of small, lightweight, three-dimensional objects, you may want to think about a wall display, a tabletop exhibit, or even a mobile. If your topic lends itself to bulkier objects, or if you want to exhibit a number of books, you are best off with a large-scale exhibit in a window or a display case.

Once you know what kind of display you are planning, you can look for an appropriate spot in the library. A poster, for example, can be hung on a wall, taped to a window, tacked to a bulletin board, or placed on an easel. A sign can be placed on a wall or window, hung from the ceiling, or propped up on a table.

Your choice of location will often depend on the goal you established in step 1. If your primary purpose is to fill an empty wall, you will naturally want to put your display on that wall. If you want to convey an important message to all library users, you will need to put your display where everyone will see it—perhaps over the circulation desk or just inside the front door. If your display involves a particular category of books—biographies, for example—you may want to place the display where the biographies are shelved, or you may want to put it in a busier section of the library so that more people will be persuaded to visit the biography section. If you want to give the library a sense of playfulness or mystery, you can put displays in unexpected places—for example, hidden among stacks or in stairwells.

The location you select will have a significant influence on the design of your display. If you plan to hang a poster on a bulletin board, for example, you will have to make sure that it fits the bulletin board's dimensions and is light enough to be supported by tacks or staples. If you plan to put a sign on a table, you will have to design a sign that is small and sturdy. If you want to place a display in an isolated area, you will want to make sure it can be protected from vandalism.

Step 4. Write the Text of the Display
Decide exactly what message you want the display to convey, and then try to express that message in as few words as possible. PLEASE SPEAK SOFTLY is much more direct and effective than PLEASE BE CONSIDERATE OF YOUR FELLOW LIBRARY USERS BY REFRAINING FROM UNNECESSARY NOISE.

Nearly every poster, bulletin board, and exhibit has some sort of title or heading. In some cases, this heading is the only text to be found in the display; in others, it summarizes or identifies the more detailed text that follows. Headings are best when they are short and catchy. (For example, look at the sample displays in chapter 9. Imagine how much less appealing they would be if their titles were BOOKS ABOUT NEWS EVENTS THAT HAPPENED IN THE 1980s, CLOTHING IN MANY TIMES AND PLACES, and GOOD READING ABOUT LIFE UNDER THE SEA.) If you are stuck with a wordy heading, try dividing it into a snappy title and a somewhat longer subtitle. For example, WE NOW HAVE THE LATEST HORROR NOVELS FROM STEPHEN KING AND PETER STRAUB might work better as MORE HORROR! THE LATEST BOOKS FROM STEPHEN KING AND PETER STRAUB ARE HERE.

To avoid embarrassment, always double-check the spelling and syntax of your text before you incorporate it into a display. This is especially important if you are dealing with unusual authors' names or unfamiliar languages.

Step 5. Select Books that Tie in with the Display
If you plan to include books or book jackets in your display, it is best to gather them in advance. Knowing the number of books to be exhibited, along with their sizes, shapes, and weights, will help you design a display that can accommodate them comfortably and show them off properly. (For a discussion of the advantages and disadvantages of exhibiting books, see the section called "Some Practical Considerations" in chapter 9.)

Even if your display is not intended to include books, you may want to make up a list of titles anyway. If an exhibit about missions to the moon captures the interest of library users, some of them may ask you to recommend books about space or space travel. By giving these people specific titles instead of sending them to the card catalog, you increase the probability that they will follow through on your suggestions.

Step 6. Design and Produce the Display
The design process is discussed extensively in chapter 2, under "Practical Steps for Creating Designs." For production techniques, see chapters 3, 4, and 5.

Although design and production are the last steps in the creative process, they may also help to stimulate new display ideas. Suppose, for example, that when you tried the last sample project in chapter 9, you discovered that you enjoyed working with papier-mâché. You might look around for other papier-mâché projects to do and decide that you would like to try making papier-mâché masks. You might then try to come up with display topics for which papier-mâché masks would be suitable and finally arrive at the idea of Mardi Gras. This, of course, is a hypothetical example, but your own experience may take similarly unforeseeable turns.

SAVING TIME AND MONEY

Creating displays may not be your most important responsibility, but it can easily take up much of your time. Tools and materials for displays can also take a big bite out of your discretionary funds. Fortunately, there are a number of steps you can take to keep your display work load from overwhelming the other aspects of your job.

Keep Supplies on Hand   The best way to save time in producing displays is to have the necessary supplies available when you need them. The preceding chapters have mentioned a great variety of tools and materials, ranging from the cheap and familiar to the expensive and obscure. (See Appendix A for a complete list, including sources and prices.) You clearly cannot buy all of them—nor would you want to, even if you could. You know better than anyone which items you are likely to use and which you are not. If you are uncomfortable handling a paint brush, for example, there is no point in buying a set of acrylic paints.

At the same time, however, if you think you will have a need for acrylic paints, the time to shop for them is now. Do not wait until you begin work on a display. (At that point, if you cannot get the colors you need, or if you cannot find the paints at a reasonable price, you will end up doing time-consuming redesign work.)

If your budget for displays is tight, decide what tools and materials you can buy with the available funds. Then buy them. When it comes time to design your displays, you can tailor your ideas to use the supplies and equipment you have purchased.

There are certain items that everyone who produces displays should have on hand. These include tagboard and construction paper (in various colors), white liquid glue, rubber cement, cloth tape, thumbtacks, pencils, and an assortment of tempera paints, brushes, and felt-tip markers. In addition, you will need scissors, a ruler, a tape measure, a graphics knife, a heavy-duty utility knife, and a stapler. If your budget allows, you may also want to stock up on illustration board, nonrepro blue grids, and various sizes and styles of rub-on lettering.

Do Not Throw Anything Away   Keep a scrap box to store odd-shaped pieces of paper, cardboard, and cloth for future use. Never cut up a new piece of paper if you can use an old one instead.

Stash copies of old magazines wherever you have room; you can rely on them for numerous illustrations and display ideas.

If you have enough space, keep an "odds and ends" box as well. Use this box to store three-dimensional objects (toys, dolls, souvenirs, broken gadgets, and so forth) that may someday be useful for displays.

Look for Bargains   Whenever you shop or travel, keep your eye out for inexpensive items that you may be able to use in displays. If you find an interesting print, an unusual rubber stamp, a bolt of discounted cloth, or a cut-rate decorative shelf, buy it—even if you are not sure what you are going to do with it. A few months from now, you may find that it is just what you need to complete the display you are working on—or the item itself may inspire an entirely new display idea.

Carry a Notepad   Many writers keep journals to help them in their work. When they have an idea that seems funny or profound, or when they experience an event that seems unique or significant, they write down their thoughts in a journal entry. Months or even years later, they may return to that journal entry to get true-to-life material for a novel or a play.

You can use a simpler version of the same technique to help you develop ideas for library displays. Keep a little spiral-bound notepad with you wherever you go. When you see something that may provide a theme for a display—a news article, a museum exhibit, or even a display in another library—make a brief note of it.

Sometimes, a promising display idea may flit through your mind out of nowhere. It may seem quite vivid to you at the time, but, as you return your attention to whatever you were doing, you are likely to forget the idea within minutes. If you get into the habit of carrying a notepad, you can jot down the idea while it is still fresh in your mind.

Later, when you need to design a new display and you lack inspiration, you can flip through your notepad. Some of the ideas you jotted down may have lost their luster with the passage of time, but others may give you just the creative spark you were looking for.

REUSING AND RECYCLING

Reusing displays—or parts of displays—is more than a way to save time and money. It is an incentive to put extra care into each element of a display. You are unlikely to spend hours making a colorful map of the world, for example, if you know that the map will only be seen for a few weeks on a poster promoting travel books. But if you know that the map can be used a few months later in an exhibit about the United Nations, and then again a few months later on a sign announcing the library's new map collection, you are more likely to want to make your map as attractive and as accurate as possible.

Nearly every element of a display can be reused (used again in the same form) or recycled (turned into something else). Cloth backdrops can be cut into smaller pieces and used to drape pedestals; old papier-mâché objects can be cut apart and used as armatures for new papier-mâché objects. Even a piece of illustration board that has been written on can be recycled: you can use it as a stiff backing for a paper sign, cover it with cloth or paper and use it as part of a freestanding backdrop, or cut it up to make boxes or shelves.

The following are suggestions for reusing and recycling several kinds of display items. Keep in mind, however, that these suggestions are not exhaustive. As you use your imagination to come up with creative display ideas, you can doubtless come up with equally creative ways to give your displays a second life.

Illustrations   Never throw away a photograph, painting, cartoon, or drawing. As in the preceding example of the map, illustrations can be reused endlessly in different contexts. If necessary, you can cut apart an illustration and use parts of it separately. (For example, if you need a picture of an apple, you can cut it from a picture of a bowl of fruit.)

If an illustration has been mounted on cardboard with rubber cement or hot wax, you can usually peel the illustration off without harming it. If it has been permanently glued to a poster—or if it was drawn directly onto the poster with markers or paints—use a pencil and ruler to draw a neat rectangle around it; then cut it out with a sharp knife.

Illustrations should be stored flat, never rolled or folded. Protect each illustration by wrapping it separately in paper or putting it in an envelope. Stacks of illustrations (or of any flat items) can be stored easily even when space is tight. You can slide them under tables and shelves, wedge them behind pieces of furniture, or stand them against the inside walls of closets.

Human Figures   Human figures, whether flat or three-dimensional, are especially useful and versatile. You can change their clothing or even their faces to suit their roles in new displays. You can cut human figures out of illustrations (see "Illustrations," above) and place them in entirely different surroundings. A cartoon of a running man, for example, can become a jungle explorer running from a tiger, a baseball player running to first base, a policeman chasing a criminal, or a student hurrying to get to school in time.

Clip Art   Never cut a clip-art illustration from a book. Instead, photocopy it, trace it, or make a PMT. In this way, you can make the book last indefinitely.

Computer Files   If you use a computer graphics program to create a new illustration or to modify an old one, save your work to a disk file. (For added protection, make a backup copy on a separate floppy disk. You can use this backup copy if the original file is damaged or erased.) Later, if you want to reuse the illustration, you can retrieve the file into the graphics program, modify the illustration as necessary, and print out a fresh copy.

Boxes   Old boxes can be used for almost anything—see *Boxes* in chapter 5. When you are not using boxes in a display, you can nest them, smaller inside larger, for space-efficient storage. If you do not have room to store nests of boxes, unfold the boxes (carefully cutting apart glued tabs, if necessary) and store them flat.

Entire Displays   If you work in a school library, you can reuse a whole display whenever a new generation of students enters the school. (If yours is a four-year high school, for example, you can use the same display every four years without any student seeing it twice.) If you take care to keep the display in new condition, by touching up faded colors and mending ragged corners, it will seem as fresh to each new group of students as it did to the last.

Keep in mind, however, that styles change. A display that is repeated over too many years, even if it is well maintained, may begin to look old-fashioned. Each time you take the display out of storage and put it together again, try to look at it with a fresh eye. You may want to update it with a contemporary typeface or more timely illustrations, or you may decide to replace it with something entirely new.

GOING FURTHER

If you are good with gadgets, you may want to add a number of technological enhancements to your displays. You can try a variety of lighting effects, using spotlights, mirrored balls, or color wheels. You can find ways to incorporate audio, video, or slides into your exhibits. You can even use a computer to create desktop presentations—colorful, animated displays, with text, graphics, and optional music or sound effects—that play out automatically on your computer screen.

Further exploration of these techniques is beyond the scope of this book—it could, in fact, constitute an entire additional book—but, if you have an adventurous spirit, you might want to experiment with some of these ideas on your own.

It should be clear by now that the most important part of a library display is the personal touch that you bring to it. These ten chapters have shown you basic techniques for designing and producing displays, but those techniques are effective only when used in a spirit of caring, excitement, and fun. To return to an analogy from chapter 2, learning to think visually is like learning a language. Use this new language to express yourself creatively, and to share your love of books, reading, and knowledge with the people who enter your world.

Appendixes

APPENDIX A

Sources for Materials

Office supply stores and stationery stores carry most of the tools and materials referred to in this book.

Art supply stores offer broader variety and often better quality than office supply stores. They also carry items unlikely to be used in offices, such as silk screens and acrylic paints.

Toy and hobby stores are good places to find inexpensive craft items such as construction paper, glitter, stencils, colored clay, and pipe cleaners. They also sell miniatures and models (cars, appliances, animals, and so forth) that can be used in three-dimensional displays.

Hardware stores carry most of the wood and metal items you may need, such as clamps, dowel rods, hinges, hooks, shelves, and feet for freestanding panels.

Mail-order catalogs of art supplies, office supplies, and library supplies are excellent sources for the items mentioned in this book. Library-supply catalogs also offer ready-made displays and display elements (such as signs, banners, posters, mobiles, freestanding backdrops and shelves, and bulletin board kits) for those occasions when you lack the time or resources to make these things yourself. The following are some of the best known mail-order supply houses.

Arthur Brown & Bro., Inc. (art supplies)
58-95 Maurice Avenue, Maspeth, N.Y. 11378, (800)237-0619/
(718)628-0600

Brodart Co. (library supplies and furnishings)
1609 Memorial Avenue, Williamsport, Pa. 17705, (800)233-8959

Demco (supplies for libraries, schools, and offices)
Box 7488, Madison, Wis. 53707, (800)356-1200

Gaylord Bros. (library supplies and furnishings)
Box 4901, Syracuse, N.Y. 13221-4901, (800)448-6160

The Highsmith Co., Inc. (library and audiovisual equipment
 and supplies)
W5527 Highway 106, P.O. Box 800, Fort Atkinson, Wis. 53538,
(800)558-2110

University Products, Inc. (library and media center
 equipment and supplies)
517 Main Street, P.O. Box 101, Holyoke, Mass. 01041-0101,
(800)628-1912/(800)336-4847 (Massachusetts only)

Library journals often contain advertisements and listings of posters, books, catalogs, and other display-related materials. (See, for example, the section called "The Source" in the American Library Association's *American Libraries*.)

SOURCES FOR SPECIFIC ITEMS

The following list includes all of the tools and materials discussed in chapters 2 through 9, plus a few items not previously mentioned. Each item is followed by one or more sources, a few popular brand names, and an approximate price range. The brand names are offered for your convenience only; in no case should you infer that one listed brand is recommended over another (or over other brands not listed). The price ranges reflect approximate retail or catalog list prices as of early 1990.

Acetate
Sources: art stores, office supply stores
Brands: Grafix, Imagemaker
Price: $10–$30 per pack, depending on size and quantity

Acrylic Paint (see "Paint," below)

Adhesives (see "Glue," "Mounting Supplies," "Tape," "Waxers and Wax," below)

Airbrushes
Sources: art stores, hobby stores
Brands: Aztek, LetraJet, Paasche
Price: $60–$100

Backdrops (see "Fabric," "Paper and Cardboard," below)

Book Stands (see "Reading Stands," below)

Borders (See also "Clip Art," "Paper and Cardboard," "Yarn and Decorative Cord," below)
Craft Borders (ribbons, piping, and lace)
Source: sewing stores
Brands: Braid Winners, Conso, Offray
Price: $1–$5 per yard
Graphic Borders (self-adhesive tape or strips in various colors and patterns)
Source: art stores
Brands: Chartpak, Graphic Products Corp. (Formaline), Letraset (Letraline)
Price: $3–$5 per roll; $10–$15 per sheet
Border Boards (layout boards with imprinted borders)
Source: art stores
Brand: Graphic Products Corp.
Price: $2–$3 each

Boxes (Unused)
Sources: stationery stores, catalogs
Price: $5–$12

Brushes
Sources: art stores, hobby stores
Brands: Grumbacher, Langnickle, Windsor and Newton
Price: $1–$10, depending on size and quality

Burnishers
Sources: art stores, stationery stores, catalogs
Brands: Chartpak, Graphic Products Corp., Letraset, X-Acto
Price: $4–$7

Calligraphy Tools
Calligraphy Felt-Tip Markers
Sources: art stores, hobby stores, stationery stores, catalogs
Brands: Buffalo, Sanford, Speedball
Price: $1–$2
Calligraphy Pens and Nibs (See also "Ink and Ink Pads," below)
Sources: art stores, hobby stores, stationery stores
Brands: Osmiroid, Sheaffer, Speedball
Price: Pens, under $10; nibs, $7–$10; starter sets, $8–$10

Clip Art
Clip-Art Alphabets
Sources: libraries and general bookstores (limited selection), art
stores (broader selection)
Brands: Dover Pictorial Archive Series, Graphic Source Clip Art
Library (Graphic Products Corp.)
Price: $5–$10 per book
Clip-Art Illustrations
Sources: libraries and general bookstores (limited selection), art
stores (broader selection), catalogs
Brands: Clip Art and Dynamic Designs for Libraries and Media
Centers (Libraries Unlimited), Dover Pictorial Archive Series,
Graphic Source Clip Art Library (Graphic Productions Corp.)
Price: $5–$20 per book
Electronic Clip Art (see Appendix B)

Cloth (see "Fabric," below)

Cloth Paint (see "Paint," below)

Cloth Tape (see "Tape," below)

Colored Paper (see "Paper and Cardboard," below)

Computer Equipment (see "Printer and Typewriter Supplies," below)

Computer-Generated Lettering or Banners (see Appendix B)

Computer Graphics (see Appendix B)

Computer Paper (see "Paper and Cardboard," below)

Construction Paper (see "Paper and Cardboard," below)

Correction Fluid
Sources: office supply stores, stationery stores, catalogs
Brands: Liquid Paper, Wite-out
Price: about $1

Corrugated Paper (see "Paper and Cardboard," below)

Crayons
> Sources: art stores, hobby stores, stationery stores, toy stores, catalogs
> Brand: Crayola
> Price: $2–$3 for 64 colors

Cutting Mats (self-healing mats designed for use with graphics knives)
> Source: art stores
> Brands: Marvy Uchida, Pro Art
> Price: $8 and up

Dowel Rods
> Sources: art stores, hardware stores, hobby stores
> Price: less than $1 each

Electronic Clip Art (see Appendix B)

Erasers (see "Pencils and Erasers," below)

Fabric
> Sources: hobby stores, sewing stores
> Price: $2–$4 per yard

Fabric Paint (see "Paint," below)

Felt-Tip Markers (see "Markers," below)

Film, Self-Adhesive
> Sources: art stores, catalogs
> Brands: Graphic Products Corp. (FormX Film), Letraset (Letrafilm)
> Price: $5–$20 per sheet

Glitter
> *Liquid Glitter*
> Sources: art stores, craft stores, hobby stores, toy stores
> Brands: Tulip Production, Cres-Lite
> Price: $4 for 2 ounces
> *Loose Glitter*
> Sources: art stores, craft stores, hobby stores, stationery stores, toy stores
> Brands: Bemiss-Jason, Razzle Dazzle, Ross
> Price: $1–$2 per ounce

Glue
> *Glue Sticks*
> Sources: art stores, office supply stores, stationery stores
> Brands: Dennison, Pritt, Uhu Stic (standard quality); Jiffy, Pelikan (better quality)
> Price: Standard quality, $1–$2; better quality, $3
> *Rubber Cement*
> Sources: art stores, stationery stores, catalogs
> Brands: Best Test, Carter's, Sanford
> Price: $4 per pint

Spray on Adhesive
Sources: art stores, hobby stores, catalogs
Brands: Scotch SpraMent Adhesive, Seal Pro Bond Spray
Price: $9

Gold Leaf (comes in liquid or in sheets; silver, bronze, and copper also available)
Sources: art stores, craft stores
Brands: Easy Leaf, Sheffield, Cres-Lite
Price: $2 for 2 ounces, $10 for 25 sheets

Grids
Grids on Clear Plastic
Source: art stores
Brands: C-Thru, Grafix
Price: up to $4 each
Layout Grids (nonrepro blue grids on paper or cardboard)
Source: art stores
Brands: Bienfang, Graphic Products Corp., Morilla
Price: $10–$20 for packs of 20 boards

Illustration Board (see "Paper and Cardboard," below)

Ink and Ink Pads (for rubber stamps, calligraphy pens, or silk screens)
Sources: art stores, office supply stores, stationery stores
Brands: Carter's, Niji, Windsor and Newton
Price: $2 for pads; $2–$5 per bottle of ink; $3–$5 for silk screen ink

Knives (See also "Cutting Mats," above)
Graphics Knives (for fine work; also known as designer's knives, work knives, or X-Acto knives)
Sources: art stores, office supply stores, catalogs
Brands: Grifhold, Letraset, X-Acto
Price: $2–$3
Utility Knives (heavier-duty knives for cardboard and other thick materials)
Sources: art stores, hardware stores, catalogs
Brands: Ardell, Stanley, X-Acto
Price: $3–$7

Layout Grids (see "Grids," above)

Lettering (see "Calligraphy Tools," "Clip Art," above; "Lettering Devices," "Rub-on Lettering," "Stencils and Templates," "Stick-on Lettering," "Tack-Backed Lettering," below)

Lettering Devices
Alphaline Label System (consists of stencil guides mounted on a work base; allows lettering to be drawn on strips of tape)
Source: catalogs
Brand: Alphaline
Price: Starter kit (including base), letter guides, tape, and pens, is $85; extra letter guides are $8 each
Ellison Letter Machine (allows various styles and sizes of letters, shapes, and borders to be cut from paper, felt, or vinyl)

Source: Ellison Educational Equipment, Inc., P.O. Box 8209, Newport Beach, Calif. 92658-8209, (714)724-0555

Brand: Ellison

Price: Machine, $300; each set of alphabet dies, $500–$600; shape dies, $20–$60

LetraGraphix (consists of a workbase for specially designed sheets of rub-on lettering; allows lettering to be applied easily to full-sized sheets of paper)

Sources: art stores, catalogs

Brand: LetraGraphix

Price: Starter kit, $85; extra type sheets, $4 each

Lettering Machines (create lettering automatically on strips of transparent or colored tape)

Sources: office supply stores, catalogs (Leteron available only from Brodart catalog)

Brands: Kroy, Leteron

Price: Kroy, $150–$250; tape and additional fonts, $15–$20 each; Leteron starter kit, $500–$800

Scribers (consist of two pens mounted on a handheld device; allow letters of various styles and sizes to be drawn with liquid ink)

Source: Highsmith and other catalogs

Brands: Letterguide, Varigraph

Price: $100 for the Letterguide; $325 for the more sophisticated Varigraph

Signmaster Kit (works like Alphaline, but allows letters to be drawn directly on paper rather than on adhesive strips)

Source: Demco and other catalogs

Brand: Signmaster

Price: Starter kits, $85; extra letter guides, $8 each

Light Boxes (sometimes called tracing boxes)

Sources: art stores, catalogs, mail order from Testrite Instrument Corp., 135AA Monroe Street, Newark, N.J. 07105

Brands: Gradco, Mayline, Seerite (Testrite)

Price: $100 and up

NOTE: Do not confuse light boxes with slide viewers. Slide viewers cannot withstand the pressure of tracing and burnishing.

Markers

Paint Sticks/Markers (combine the ease of a marker with the look and feel of paint and a brush)

Sources: art stores, hobby stores, catalogs

Brands: Pentech, Shiva, UniPaint

Price: Pentech (water-based), $2 for set of 9; Shiva and UniPaint (oil-based), $1–$3 each

Permanent Felt-Tip Markers

Sources: art stores, hobby stores, office supply stores, stationery stores, catalogs

Brands: Boldline MarkMaster, Carter's, El Marko, Flair, Pilot. Midas Touch and Pilot Super Color Markers are available with gold or silver ink. In art stores, look for Berol, Chartpak, Eberhard Faber, or Pantone (Letraset).

Price: $1–$3, depending on tip width; less expensive in sets

Water-Soluble (Watercolor) Felt-Tip Markers
Sources: art stores, hobby stores, office supply stores, stationery
  stores, catalogs
Brands: Boldline SignMaster, Carter's, Crayola, El Marko, Flair,
  Paper Mate, Uniball
Price: $1–$3, depending on tip width; less expensive in sets

Mounting Squares and Strips (see "Mounting Supplies," below)

Mounting Supplies (See also "Tacks and Pushpins," "Tape," below)
Mounting Squares and Strips
Sources: art stores, hardware stores, office supply stores
Brand: Scotch
Price: $1–$2
Picture Hooks, Hangers, Wires
Sources: art stores, hardware stores, office supply stores, stationery
  stores
Brands: Anchor Brand, Bulldog, Homecraft, Moore
Price: less than $1 each
Putty (to hold up posters and boards temporarily)
Sources: art stores, office supply stores, stationery stores
Brands: Blu-Tack, Fun-Tak, Ross Tack Tabs
Price: $1–$2
Velcro (hooks and loops in various sizes and strengths, for hanging
  posters and signs)
Sources: art stores, hardware stores, office supply stores
Brand: Velcro
Price: $6

Nonrepro Blue Pencils and Pens (see "Pencils and Erasers," below)

Oaktag (see "Paper and Cardboard," below)

Origami Paper (see "Paper and Cardboard," below)

Paint (See also "Gold Leaf," above)
Acrylic Paint
Sources: art stores, hobby stores, toy stores
Brands: Binney and Smith, Palmer
Price: about $1 an ounce
Fabric Paint (can be used on cloth or paper)
Sources: art stores, craft stores, hobby stores
Brands: Deka, Scribbles, Tulip Production
Price: about $6 for 4 ounces
House Paint
Sources: hardware stores, paint stores
Price: $5 per quart
Spray Enamel
Sources: art stores, hardware stores
Brands: Krylon, Plastic-Kote
Price: $2 for 3 ounces
Tempera Paint
Sources: art stores, hobby stores, catalogs

Brands: Binney and Smith, Crayola, Kaylor, Leisuretone, Palmer, Prang, Ross
Price: up to $1 an ounce
Watercolor
Sources: art stores, hobby stores
Brands: Color Art, Crayola
Price: $2–$5 for kits of up to 24 colors

Paint Brushes (see "Brushes," above)

Pantographs
Source: art stores
Brand: Morilla
Price: $10–$40

Paper and Cardboard
Continuous-Feed Computer Paper (comes in various colors and weights)
Sources: office supply stores, stationery stores, catalogs
Brands: Century Pak, Paperland
Price: $8 and up per package
Corrugated Paper (comes in solid colors and patterns)
Sources: art stores, catalogs
Brands: Bordette makes narrow rolls of scalloped paper (for borders); Corrobuff makes wide rolls
Price: $2 for narrow scalloped rolls; $5 for wide rolls
Construction Paper, Stiff Paper, Illustration Board, Tagboard
Sources: art stores, stationery stores, toy stores, catalogs
Brands: Artmaster, Demco, Strathmore; most stores and catalogs carry their own brands
Price: Depends on size and weight; from a few pennies to $1 a sheet
Origami Paper
Sources: art stores, bookstores (usually sold with a book or as part of a kit), craft stores, hobby stores, stationery stores, toy stores
Brands: Harmony, Niji
Price: $3–$6 per package
Sheet-Feed Paper (for use with photocopying machines and laser printers; available in pastels and bold colors)
Sources: art stores, office supply stores, stationery stores, catalogs
Brands: Demco, Hammermill. Letraset makes Copy FX, copy paper with a graduated tint
Price: About a penny per sheet, sold in packages of 100–500; Copy FX is $10 for 25 sheets
Tracing Paper (available in rolls and pads)
Sources: art stores, stationery stores
Brands: Bienfang, Morilla
Price: $2–$6 per pad, depending on size; $3–$5 for rolls

Papier-Mâché Paste
Papier-Mâché Powder (alternative to wheat paste)
Source: art stores
Brand: Celluclay
Price: $11 for 5 pounds

Wheat Paste (wallpaper paste)
Sources: art stores, hardware stores
Brands: Metylan, Professional, Rex
Price: $2 per pound

Pencils and Erasers
Colored Pencils
Sources: art stores, hobby stores, stationery stores, catalogs
Brands: Crayola, Faber-Castell, Pedigree
Price: set of 12, $2
Kneaded Rubber Erasers
Sources: art stores, stationery stores
Brand: Eberhard Faber
Price: under $1
Nonrepro Blue Pencils and Pens
Sources: art stores, office supply stores, stationery stores
Brands: Berol, Staedtler
Price: pencils, up to $1 each; pens, up to $2 each

Picture Hooks, Hangers, Wires (see "Mounting Supplies," above)

Plastic Tape (see "Tape," below)

Posterboard (see "Paper and Cardboard," above)

Printer and Typewriter Supplies (See also "Paper and Cardboard," above)
Print Elements (daisy wheels or type balls)
Sources: office supply stores, typewriter stores, catalogs
Brands: Demco, IBM
Price: $20–$40
Ribbons (in black or colors)
Sources: computer suppliers, office supply stores, stationery stores, catalogs
Brands: Apple Dot Matrix Ribbon, Smith Corona Coronamatic
Price: $10–$15

Pushpins (see "Tacks and Pushpins," below)

Putty (see "Mounting Supplies," above)

Reading Stands (made of metal or clear lucite, to display an open book)
Sources: art stores, stationery stores, catalogs
Price: $1 metal; $2–$13 lucite

Rub-on Graphics (also called dry transfer sheets or pressure graphics)
Source: art stores
Brands: Chartpak, Graphic Products Corp., Letraset, Quiktype
Price: $10–$15 per sheet

Rub-on Lettering (also called dry transfer lettering)
Sources: art stores, office supply stores, stationery stores, catalogs
Brands: Avery, Chartpak, Geotype, Letraset, Quiktype
Price: $10–$15 per sheet

Rubber Cement (see "Glue," above)

Rubber Stamps (See also "Ink and Ink Pads," above)

Sources: art stores, card shops, hobby stores, toy stores; mail order from Inky Dinks, RD 1, Department 419SA, Montgomery, N.Y. 12549; KIDSTAMPS, Inc., P.O. Box 18699, Cleveland Heights, Ohio 44118, (800)727-5437; Teachers Stamp Company, 5407 Heathercrest, Houston, Tex. 77045, (713)434-0935

Brands: Small World Toys makes self-inking plastic stamps; Teachers Stamp Company specializes in holiday themes and animals; Stamptrax makes rolling stamps with running feet and paws; Yasutomo and All Night Media, Inc. offer a variety of wooden stamps with animals and characters; KIDSTAMPS offers whimsical letters and classic children's literature characters (Babar, Curious George, Peter Rabbit)

Price: Small World Toys, up to a few dollars; Teachers and Stamptrax, $2–$4; Yasutomo, All Night Media, and KIDSTAMPS, $10–$20

Self-Adhesive Film (see "Film, Self-Adhesive," above)

Self-Adhesive Letters (see "Stick-on Lettering," below)

Self-Adhesive Squares (see "Mounting Squares and Strips," above)

Silk Screen (See also "Ink and Ink Pads," above)

Professional Silk Screens
Source: art stores
Brands: Inko, Speedball
Price: $40–$100 for the printing unit
Starter Silk Screen Kits
Sources: art stores, hobby stores
Brand: Speedball
Price: $20–$35

Sparkles (see "Glitter," above)

Spray Paint (see "Paint," above)

Stencils and Templates

Stencils and Templates for Lettering (sometimes called lettering guides; available in sizes from 1/2 inch to 6 inches)
Sources: art stores, hardware stores, office supply stores
Brands: C-Thru, Mead, Presto (stencils); Avery, Helix, Pickett, Wrico (templates)
Price: $1–$4 per alphabet, depending on size and quality
Stencil and Template Graphics (animals, dinosaurs, and other illustrations)
Sources: hobby stores, toy stores
Brands: Galt Toys templates, Tuffy Learning Books stencils
Price: $8–$10
Stencil and Template Shapes (curves, circles, and other geometric shapes)
Sources: art stores, hardware stores, office supply stores
Brands: C-Thru, Helix, Pickett
Price: $1–$4

Stick-on Lettering (sign lettering)
 Sources: art stores, office supply stores, stationery stores, catalogs
 Brands: Avery, Chartpak, Letraset, Presto
 Price: Avery kits (approximately 100 letters and numbers), $3; Letraset kits (approximately 900 letters, 300 numbers), $90; individual letters, $2–$7 for 5 copies of one letter

Stickers (self-adhesive cutouts, often featuring holiday themes or animals)
 Sources: card shops, stationery stores, toy stores; stickers with library themes are available through catalogs and the ALA
 Brands: Dennison, Mrs. Grossman's Stickers by the Yard, Sandylion
 Price: up to $1 each

Stiff Paper (see "Paper and Cardboard," above)

Tack-Backed Lettering (for use on bulletin boards)
 Source: catalogs
 Brands: Brodart, Demco
 Price: $20–$30 per set

Tacks and Pushpins (available with plastic, metal, or wooden heads, in bright or natural colors)
 Sources: art stores, hardware stores, office supply stores, stationery stores, catalogs
 Price: $2–$5 per 100

Tagboard (see "Paper and Cardboard," above)

Tape (See also "Mounting Supplies," above)
 Colored Tape (Cloth and Plastic)
 Sources: art stores, hardware stores, office supply stores, stationery stores, catalogs
 Brands: Manco, Mystik, Scotch, Shurtape
 Price: $2–$3 per roll
 Other Tape
 Sources: art stores, hardware stores, office supply stores, stationery stores, catalogs
 Brand: Scotch offers virtually every kind of type, from masking tape to double-sided tape. Scotch Wallsaver removable poster tape is designed for hanging posters and light objects.
 Price: $2–$3 per roll

Tempera Paint (see "Paint," above)

Templates (see "Stencils and Templates," above)

Tracing Paper (see "Paper and Cardboard," above)

Transfer Letters (see "Rub-on Lettering," above)

Typewriter Equipment (see "Printer and Typewriter Supplies," above)

Utility Knives (see "Knives," above)

Velcro (see "Mounting Supplies," above)

Wallpaper Paste (see "Papier-Mâché Paste," above)

Water-Soluble (Watercolor) Markers (see "Markers," above)

Watercolor Paint (see "Paint," above)

Waxers and Wax
Source: art stores
Brands: Letrostik, Procote, Pyramid
Price: handheld waxers, $40–$70; wax, $1 per cake

Wheat Paste (see "Papier-Mâché Paste," above)

Yarn and Decorative Cord
Sources: hobby stores, card shops, sewing stores
Brands: Berwick, Cleo, Maxi-Cord, Yarn-it; some stores have their own brands
Price: Under $2 for 18 feet in card shops, $4 for 150 feet in hobby stores, $1–$5 per yard in sewing stores.

Suggested Computer Software

Programs for personal computers are generally divided into three different categories: commercial software, shareware (or user-supported software), and free software. These categories bear no relationship to the quality or reliability of a program; they merely describe how the program is distributed. A shareware program may be as good as, or better than, a comparable commercial program.

Commercial Software.   Commercial software is sold through traditional retail channels. It can be purchased from a store, from a mail-order distributor, or directly from the publisher. A commercial program typically comes in a shrink-wrapped package along with a manual, a warranty, and a registration card. The package may cost as little as $10 or as much as $800.

It is important to note that when you buy a commercial program, you are not buying the program itself. You are buying a license to use the program. Licenses vary, but the licenses issued by most software companies restrict the use of a program to one person or one computer. If you make copies of a program for use by other people, you are breaking the law. If anyone offers you a free copy of a commercial program, turn the offer down.

Most commercial software cannot be returned to the seller once it has been opened. Therefore, before you pay for an expensive program, be absolutely sure that it suits your needs and that it will run on your hardware. If you choose to buy from a retailer, find a store whose sales staff is willing to spend time with you and can answer your questions knowledgeably. Many computer stores keep demonstration copies of the programs they sell, so you can try out a program in the store before you decide to buy it.

If you want to pay the lowest possible price for a program, you might consider buying it through the mail. Mail-order distributors often sell programs for less than half the list price. The trade-off, of course, is that you must know exactly what you are buying: most mail-order houses cannot (or will not) answer your questions about software, and they will not allow you to try out a program and return it. Therefore, before you buy commercial software through the mail, do as much research as possible. Talk to people who have used the software, listen to the recommendations of local user groups, and read reviews of the software in computer magazines (or in consumer-oriented periodicals such as *Consumer Reports*). Then, when you have made the decision to buy, look around for the best price. Large-circulation computer magazines such as *PC Magazine, Mac World,* and *Computer Shopper* are jammed with ads for mail-order houses, each trying to undersell the others by a dollar or two.

Shareware.   Shareware, or user-supported software, is a distribution system that allows programmers to sell their products easily and inexpensively. Instead of relying on packagers and retailers to distribute their programs, shareware authors allow users to become the distributors.

Copying a commercial program for distributing to others is prohibited. Users of shareware programs, however, are encouraged to make copies and to give them to as many people as possible. Some users distribute shareware programs electronically, by uploading them to a computer bulletin board system (BBS) or by sending them over a computer network. In this way, a popular shareware program can make its way to users all over the world in a matter of days.

Shareware programs have fewer frills than commercial software. Because they are designed to be copied easily, shareware programs rarely have printed manuals; instead, they include documentation files that you can read on the screen or print out on your printer. Similarly, shareware programs do not come with postage-paid registration cards; many simply list the name and address of the author—and the price of the program—in an automatic "shareware message" (the text that first appears on the screen when you run the program).

Shareware is sold on a try-before-you-buy basis. If you obtain a copy of a shareware program, you are permitted to use the program for a limited period of time—generally thirty days—to see whether it suits your needs. If you continue to use the program after this trial period, you are expected to register the program—that is, to pay for a license to use the software. (The license fees for shareware programs are much lower than those for commercial programs, generally between $5 and $89.) If you do not register after a reasonable period of time, you are expected to destroy or give away your copy of the program.

Contrary to what you might have heard, the license fee for a shareware program is not a voluntary contribution; it is a legal requirement for using the software. The author of a program retains all rights under U.S. copyright law, and therefore has the right to restrict use of the program to those who have paid the fee.

Shareware is not available in retail stores. If you are interested in obtaining a shareware program, you can get it from one of the following sources.

- *User groups.* Computer enthusiasts in many communities have joined together to form user groups. Usually, each group is centered around a specific type of computer—for example, IBM PC users might belong to one group, Macintosh users to another. Joining a user group is an ideal way to learn more about computers and to try out a wide variety of programs.

  In some user groups, members swap shareware programs at meetings. Other groups maintain large shareware libraries to which members are allowed access. If you are unsure about what programs to try, or how to use a program you already have, fellow members of a user group will usually be able to answer your questions or give you advice.

- *Bulletin board systems.* If your computer has a modem—a device that allows it to communicate with other computers over telephone lines— you can use it to tap the resources of a local BBS. BBSs are run by individuals, by businesses, and by user groups; nearly every community has at least one or two. Access to some BBSs is restricted, but most are open to anyone who dials in.

Most BBSs have two sections: a message area or bulletin board where callers can communicate with each other, and a file area or library from which callers can download program files. (In this context, to *download* is to copy a file from the BBS to your own computer; to *upload* is to send a file from your computer to a BBS.) If you are looking for a particular shareware program, you can dial into the BBSs in your area and check their file lists to see whether the program is available. You can also browse the file lists to discover programs you may not have heard about before. When you find a program you want to try out, simply follow the BBS's directions for downloading the file.

Most BBSs are not advertised (except on other BBSs), so you may have trouble finding out the phone number of a BBS in your area. If you are interested, however, you may want to inquire with user groups, computer stores, or computer-using friends. Local computer magazines or newsletters also may include listings of BBSs.

- *National on-line services.* On-line services are similar to BBSs, but they operate on a much larger scale. The most popular on-line services have nationwide telephone networks that allow them to be reached from anywhere in the country, simply by dialing a local "node." When your computer is connected to an on-line service, you may have access to stock quotations, news wire services, airline reservation systems, and an electronic mail system. You may also have access to vast software libraries, with programs for almost any imaginable purpose.

  Unlike BBSs, which are usually free, on-line services can be an expensive resource. Users of on-line services must pay either a flat monthly membership fee, a per-minute on-line rate, or both. In exchange, however, members get access to expert technical advice, the best and most up-to-date software, and a chance to correspond with computer users around the country.

  If you are interested in joining an on-line service, you will probably want to look at CompuServe Information Service (CIS) and GEnie. CIS is the oldest and largest on-line service, especially since it absorbed its chief competitor, The Source, in 1989. GEnie, a creation of the General Electric corporation, offers fewer resources than CIS but is somewhat cheaper. For information about joining CompuServe, call (800)848-8199; for information about GEnie, call (800)638-9636. (A third popular on-line service, Prodigy, is run jointly by Sears and IBM. It does not yet allow downloading of program files, but it promises to do so in the future.)

- *Mail-order distributors.* A few catalog companies offer shareware by mail. These companies will send you the software of your choice for a modest charge of three to six dollars per disk. (Depending on the size of the programs you choose, you may be able to get ten or more on a single disk.) Be aware, however, that this charge covers only the distributor's services (processing your order, duplicating the software, and shipping the disks). It does *not* cover license fees for using the software. If you buy shareware by mail, you are still responsible for contacting each program's author and paying the registration fees. (Beware of misleading magazine ads that try to obscure this fact.)

The largest and most reputable distributor of shareware is the Public Software Library in Houston, Texas. PSL puts out a monthly magazine called *PSL News*, which reviews about 250 shareware programs in each issue. The cost for a year's subscription to *PSL News*, along with PSL's complete catalog, is eighteen dollars. [Write to P.O. Box 35705, Houston, Tex. 77235-5705, or call (800)2424-PSL.]

The following are names and addresses of other shareware distributors. Unless indicated, each offers software for IBM-compatible and Macintosh computers.

Gemini Marketing, Inc.
P.O. Box 640, Duvall, Wash. 98019-0640, (800)346-0139

Micro Star
1105 Second Street, Encinitas, Calif. 92024, (800)444-1343

Public Brand Software (IBM only)
P.O. Box 51315, Indianapolis, Ind. 46251, (800)426-DISK

Rainware (IBM only)
P.O. Box 1194, Mercer Island, Wash. 98040, (800)441-1458

Reasonable Solutions
2101 West Main Street, Medford, Oreg. 97501, (800)876-3475

Software Excitement!
P.O. Box 3097, 6475 Crater Lake, Central Point, Oreg. 97502, (800)444-5457

The Software Labs (TSL) (IBM only)
3767 Overland Avenue, #112, Los Angeles, Calif. 90034, (800)359-9998

Free Software.   Free software is similar to shareware, except that users of free programs are not required to pay a license fee. Many programmers distribute their more elaborate programs as shareware and their simpler programs as free software.

Although you do not have to pay to use free software, you may nevertheless be subject to certain restrictions. (Authors of free software retain their copyright, and they therefore have a right to set conditions for use of their programs.) Licenses for free software generally forbid users to modify a program or to resell it for a profit.

Occasionally, the author of a program may explicitly waive all rights and contribute the program to the public domain. Public domain programs are available for unrestricted use; they may be copied, modified, renamed, or resold by anyone for any reason. Because programmers have little to gain and much to lose by relinquishing their rights, true public domain programs have become increasingly rare. Most so-called public domain software is actually copyrighted free software. (Again, beware of misleading ads.)

Free software is available from the same sources as shareware: user groups, BBSs, on-line services, and mail-order distributors. Because free programs tend to be relatively unsophisticated, you will find few that are useful for producing displays; there are, however, a number of free banner-making programs and fonts available.

WARNING: Whenever you run a program from an unknown source, you take a risk. Shareware or free software has sometimes been known to contain "worms," "Trojan horses," "viruses," or other traps that are designed to damage your computer or your stored data. (Often these bits of hidden code are not part of the original programs, but were inserted later by malicious pranksters.) The chance of your encountering these problems is slight, but you can reduce the risk even further by using only programs that you have obtained from reliable sources. (CompuServe Information Service, for example, will not offer a program for download until it has been analyzed, checked, and certified "clean"; the Public Software Library has a similar policy.) Before you download a program from a local BBS, find out who uploaded the program and where it came from originally. If someone gives you a program on a disk, do not run the program unless you know that others have tried it first.

GENERAL DESCRIPTIONS

Many kinds of software are useful for library displays. What follows is a list of the types of software you might use for different tasks, with a brief description of the capabilities you can expect from each type.

To Do Lettering

- *Banner programs* are among the simplest and cheapest programs available. A banner program may be all that you need if you want to make banners, cards, signs, or posters. The least expensive programs work only with text; others let you add pictures from a supplied library or from separately purchased clip-art collections.

- A *font* is a series of bitmaps (dot patterns) representing a particular typeface in a particular size. Fonts may be installed in a printer in either of two ways: *soft fonts* are loaded into a printer's memory; *font cartridges* are plugged directly into the printer. Rather than buy a collection of different-sized fonts representing a single typeface, you may choose to buy a font outline (a generalized description of a typeface) and use a font generator to produce multiple fonts from the outline.

- *Word processing programs* are designed specifically to handle text. Any word processing program can produce a neat, typewritten-looking page; the more sophisticated programs, which can take advantage of fonts installed in a printer, can be used to produce large and attractive lettering for signs, posters, and exhibits.

- *Graphics programs* are intended primarily to create illustrations, but they are quite useful for text as well. Most graphics programs have built-in fonts or font outlines; they therefore handle lettering with greater flexibility than word processing programs. Some graphics programs allow letters to be arranged in a circle, reversed into a mirror image, squeezed, stretched, or given a three-dimensional look.

- *Printer utilities* can be used to enhance the text-printing abilities of a laser or dot-matrix printer. They manipulate files produced by ordinary word processing or graphics programs, to improve the appearance of the printed output.

To Do Graphics

- *Graphics programs* (draw or paint programs) allow you to draw freehand or to manipulate lines, boxes, shapes, and patterns. Even the simplest graphics programs handle text as well as graphics, so they can be used to make finished, illustrated signs, cards, banners, or posters. Full-featured graphics programs allow more sophisticated editing of images—drawings can be cropped, bent, rotated, or flipped.

- *Clip art* is included with most graphics programs; it is also sold separately. There is an extensive variety of clip art on the market: most clip-art publishers offer at least a general collection, a business collection, and a school collection. Before purchasing a clip-art package, ask to see what the art looks like, as the quality of clip-art images varies considerably.

To Do Page Layout

- *Desktop publishing programs* are intended primarily to lay out books, newsletters, brochures, and other printed documents. They can also be used, however, to create sophisticated signs and posters. The simplest and cheapest desktop publishing programs combine text produced by a word processing program with graphics produced by a draw or paint program. Higher-end systems have sophisticated word processing and graphics functions built in.

- *Word processing programs* have come to include a growing number of desktop publishing capabilities. Full-featured word processing programs can import and edit graphic images, create lines, boxes, tables, and shaded areas, handle multicolumn formats, and position elements on a page to a tolerance of thousandths of an inch. They are ideal for producing signs, posters, brochures, and newsletters.

SPECIFIC PROGRAMS

The following is a list of recommended programs for the IBM PC (and PC-compatibles), the Apple Macintosh, and several other personal computers. This list is in no way exhaustive; it is limited to programs that are suitable for library displays and that, in the judgment of the author, are inexpensive, easy to use, and easy to learn. Programs that require unusual hardware configurations (such as expanded or extended memory) or unusual operating environments (such as Microsoft Windows) have been excluded.

Keep in mind that most programs are enhanced and improved regularly. Each major improvement is reflected by a new version number, and each registered user is given the opportunity to upgrade to the latest version for a modest fee. When the name of a program on the following list is accompanied by a version number, the features described for the program apply to the specified version. While later versions (higher numbers) will have those features, earlier versions may not.

The prices given for commercial programs are manufacturers' suggested list prices as of early 1990. Very few retailers charge the full list price for software; with some shopping around, you should be able to find discounts of 25 to 50 percent or even more.

Commercial Software for IBM PCs and Compatibles

Banner Programs

BannerMania ($35) by Broderbund Software, Inc.
17 Paul Drive, San Rafael, Calif. 94903
(800)521-6263/(415)492-3200
Makes banners only. Includes some special effects.

PCBanner ($30) by Sourceview Software International
P.O.Box 578, Concord, Calif. 94522-0578
(415)685-3635
Makes 6 1/2-inch character banners only.

Print Power ($20) by Hi Tech Expressions
584 Broadway, Suite 509, New York, N.Y. 10012
(212)941-1224
Makes cards and banners up to 8 inches high.

Twist & Shout ($80) by The Software Toolworks
19808 Nordoff Place, Chatsworth, Calif. 91311
(800)223-8665/(818)885-9000
Makes banners up to 1 foot high, with four different typefaces and a
    variety of symbols. Also works as a printer utility to print text files
    sideways (in landscape mode) on dot-matrix printers.

Clip Art   This list covers the most popular general packages. Specialized packages (for example, for businesses or schools) are also available from the same manufacturers, but the only one listed here is The Print Shop Graphics for Libraries. The prices are per package; each package may contain from 50 to 200 images.

Art Gallery Series ($40) by Unison World
1321 Harbor Bay Parkway, Alameda, Calif. 94501
(800)444-7553/(415)748-6938
For PrintMaster and NewsMaster, over 100 pieces of art in each package.
    Packages include general, fantasy (trolls, dragons, wizards), fonts, and
    borders.

ClickArt ($70; $130 for PostScript version) by T/Maker Company
1390 Villa Street, Mountain View, Calif. 94041
(415)962-0195
Includes several collections of alphabets and graphics.

DeskTop Art ($75) by Dynamic Graphics, Inc.
6000 N. Forest Park Drive, P.O. Box 1901, Peoria, Ill. 61656
(800)255-8800
Available in PC Paintbrush or in PostScript format; each package contains 200 illustrations. Packages include sports, business, four seasons, education, health care.

Harvard Graphics Accessories ($100) by Software
Publishing Corporation
1901 Landings Drive, P.O. Box 7210, Mountain View, Calif. 94039
(415)962-8910
For use with Harvard Graphics only; an extensive collection. A set of maps ($150) is also available.

Images With Impact ($120) by 3G Graphics
11140 NE 124th Street, Suite 6155, Kirkland, Wash. 98034
(800)456-0234/(206)823-8198
In PostScript format; each package includes 70 to 100 images.

The Print Shop Graphics for Libraries ($25) by Broderbund
Software, Inc.
17 Paul Drive, San Rafael, Calif. 94903
(800)521-6263/(415)492-3200
For use with The New Print Shop. Two different packages, including library signs, books, readers, literary images, and holiday illustrations.

The Print Shop Graphics Library ($40) by Broderbund
Software, Inc.
17 Paul Drive, San Rafael, Calif. 94903
(800)521-6263/(415)492-3200
For use with The New Print Shop. Several packages of 120 pictures each: school, business, holidays, general.

Desktop Publishing Programs

Byline ($250) by Ashton-Tate Corporation
20101 Hamilton Avenue, Torrance, Calif. 90502-1319
(213)329-8000
A sophisticated desktop publishing program, with built-in word processing functions (such as spell checking). It cannot create graphics, but it can manipulate imported graphics and scanned images.

NewsMaster II ($80) by Unison World
1321 Harbor Bay Parkway, Alameda, Calif. 94501
(800)444-7553/(415)748-6938
A simple and inexpensive program that can achieve professional-looking results. Includes some clip art and fonts.

PFS: First Publisher ($130) by Software Publishing Corporation
1901 Landings Drive, P.O. Box 7210, Mountain View, Calif. 94039
(415)962-8910
A very popular entry-level program. Includes some clip art and fonts.

Fonts   Each package includes one or more typefaces in roman, bold, italic, and bold italic varieties. You can use these packages to generate fonts of any size.

Adobe Type Library ($100–$400) by Adobe Software
P.O. Box 7900, Mountain View, Calif. 94039
(800)344-8335/(415)961-4400
For PostScript-compatible laser printers.

Fancy Fonts ($180) by SoftCraft, Inc.
16 N. Carroll, Suite 500, Madison, Wis. 53703
(800)351-0500
For dot-matrix printers or HP-compatible laser printers.

Fluent Laser Fonts ($90) by Casady & Greene, Inc.
P.O. Box 223779, Carmel, Calif. 93922
(800)359-4920/(408)624-8716
For PostScript-compatible laser printers.

Fontware ($200) by Bitstream, Inc.
Athenaeum House, 215 First Street, Cambridge, Mass. 01242
(617)497-6222
For HP-compatible or PostScript-compatible laser printers.

Glyphix ($100) by SWFTE International, Ltd.
P.O. Box 219, Rockland, Del. 19732
(800)237-9383
For HP-compatible laser printers.

Graphics (Low-End)

The New Print Shop ($60) by Broderbund Software, Inc.
17 Paul Drive, San Rafael, Calif. 94903
(800)521-6263/(415)492-3200
The most popular simple graphics program. Does not allow the creation of original graphics, but includes many low-resolution clip-art images. Additional clip-art packages are also available.

Print Magic ($60) by Epyx, Inc.
600 Galveston Drive, Redwood City, Calif. 94063
(415)368-3200
An easy-to-use program. Permits manipulation of text and graphics. Includes paint functions and clip art (graphics and borders).

PrintMaster Plus ($60) by Unison World
1321 Harbor Bay Parkway, Alameda, Calif. 94501
(800)444-7553/(415)748-6938
Allows creation and editing of simple bitmapped graphics. Comes with a good-sized collection of pictures, patterns, borders, and fonts.

Graphics (Paint Programs)   All of the following are full-featured paint programs. The three ZSoft programs (PC Paintbrush IV, PC Paintbrush IV Plus, and Publisher's Paintbrush) offer increased levels of sophistication that correlate with their prices.

DeluxePaint II ($100) by Electronic Arts
1820 Gateway Drive, San Mateo, Calif. 94404
(415)571-7171

PC Paintbrush IV ($100), *PC Paintbrush IV Plus* ($200), and *Publisher's Paintbrush* ($300) by ZSoft Corporation
450 Franklin Road, #100, Marietta, Ga. 30067
(404)428-0008

Graphics (Draw Programs)

All of the following are popular business presentation programs with sophisticated drawing and charting capabilities. Each includes an extensive clip-art library and a variety of built-in font outlines.

Applause II ($500) by Ashton-Tate Corporation
20101 Hamilton Avenue, Torrance, Calif. 90502-1319
(213)329-8000

DrawPerfect ($500) by WordPerfect Corporation
1555 North Technology Way, Orem, Utah 84057
(800)321-4566/(801)225-5000

Harvard Graphics ($500) by Software Publishing Corporation
1901 Landings Drive, P.O. Box 7210, Mountain View, Calif. 94039
(415)962-8910

Lotus Freelance Plus ($500) by Lotus Development Corporation
55 Cambridge Parkway, Cambridge, Mass. 02142
(617)577-8500/(800)345-1043

Graphics (Paint and Draw Programs)

Dr. Halo ($140) by Media Cybernetics, Inc.
8484 Georgia Avenue, Silver Spring, Md. 20910
(800)992-HALO(992-4256)/(301)495-3305
The only program available for the PC that combines drawing and painting capabilities in a single package.

Printer Utilities

These three programs allow dot-matrix and HP-compatible laser printers to emulate PostScript printers. They operate slowly (printing a complex page may take as long as fifteen minutes), but they are an inexpensive alternative to buying a PostScript-compatible printer.

GoScript ($200 with 13 fonts, $400 with 35 fonts) by LaserGo, Inc.
9369 Carroll Park Drive, Suite A, San Diego, Calif. 92121
(800)451-0088/(619)450-4600

PreScript ($200 with 13 fonts, $400 with 35 fonts) by POC
44 Route 46, Pine Brook, N.J. 07058
(201)808-1900

Freedom of Press ($500, includes 35 fonts) by Custom
    Applications, Inc.
900 Technology Park Drive, Building 8, Billerica, Mass. 01821
(800)873-4367/(508)667-8585

Word Processing Programs   All of the following are high-end
word processing programs. They allow use of a wide variety of fonts, and
they are able to integrate graphics with text. Lotus Manuscript and
Wordstar 2000 Plus are slightly less sophisticated than the others, but they
may be easier to learn for people who have used Lotus 1-2-3 or earlier
versions of Wordstar.

Lotus Manuscript ($500) by Lotus Development Corporation
55 Cambridge Parkway, Cambridge, Mass. 02142
(617)577-8500/(800)345-1043

Microsoft Word ($450) by Microsoft Corporation
1 Microsoft Way, Redmond, Wash. 98052-6399
(800)426-9400/(206)882-8088

WordPerfect (version 5.0 or higher, $500) by WordPerfect Corporation
1555 North Technology Way, Orem, Utah 84057
(800)321-4566/(801)225-5000

Wordstar 2000 Plus ($500) by MicroPro International Corporation
33 San Pablo Avenue, San Rafael, Calif. 94903
(800)227-5609/(415)499-1200

Shareware and Free Software for IBM PCs and Compatibles

Banner Programs   A great variety of banner-making programs
are in circulation; many are in the public domain, and most use the name
BANNER.COM. Some of these programs are limited to specific
programs; some work only in character mode; others offer a variety of
typefaces. Your best bet is to try out a number of banner programs until
you find one you like. (Many mail-order distributors will send you a
collection of banner programs for the price of a single program.)

Clip Art   Virtually every BBS offers a great selection of clip-art
images, some created by artistically inclined users of the BBS. Every
mail-order distributor also has compilations of clip art, often sold in
thematically linked packages (for example, logos, cartoons, animals).
Most clip art is free or in the public domain, but some artists require a
one-time registration fee for unlimited use of their collections.

When you acquire clip art, be sure that it will work with your
graphics software. There is free clip art available for every major program, most notably Print Shop, Printmaster, PC Paintbrush, and Word-
Perfect.

Desktop Publishing Programs

City Desk (version 7 or higher; shareware)
Handles basic page layout; works with two or three columns, allows
   integration of text and graphics.

Fonts

Bradford (version 2 or higher; shareware)
For dot-matrix printers. 27 typefaces in 62 varieties; includes foreign
   language characters.

Fonts for PFS: First Publisher by Scandalous Technology
   (shareware)
Includes script typefaces, ornate letters, and more.

Glyphix by SWFTE International (free)
Several commercial Glyphix fonts are available from BBSs and on-line
   services, but you may not be able to use them unless you have
   SWFTE's font-handling software.

Graphics Programs

PC Finger Paint (version 2 or higher; shareware)
A full-featured program for creating and editing graphics. Includes six
   fonts.

PC Key Draw (version 3 or higher; shareware)
A powerful draw program that comes with an extensive collection of clip
   art.

Picture This (shareware)
Creates and edits EPS (Postscript-format) graphics.

Word Processing Programs

Black Magic (version 1.3 or higher; shareware)
Works with text and graphics, but supports a limited number of printers.

Galaxy (version 2 or higher; shareware)
Easy to learn and to use, a good first word processing program.

New York Word (version 2.3 or higher; shareware)
Easy to use; supports many printers.

PC Write (version 3 or higher; shareware)
Works with most printers; handles proportional spacing and multiple
   columns.

Commercial Software for Apple Macintosh

Clip Art Many of the following packages are available in Post-Script format at a slightly higher price.

Art à la Mac ($40) by Springboard Software, Inc.
7808 Creekridge Circle, Minneapolis, Minn. 55435
(800)445-4780

ClickArt ($60) by T/Maker Company
1390 Villa Street, Mountain View, Calif. 94041
(415)962-0195

Image Club Graphics ($100) by Image Club Graphics
Suite 51902, 11th Street SE, Calgary, Alberta, T2G3G2, Canada
(403)262-8008/(800)661-9410

Images With Impact! (PostScript format only; $120) by 3G Graphics
11410 N.E. 124th Street, Suite 6155, Kirkland, Wash. 98034
(800)456-0234/(206)823-8198

Mac the Knife ($80) by Miles Computing, Inc.
7741 Alabama Avenue, #2, Canoga Park, Calif. 91304-4946
(818)341-1411

Post-Art (PostScript format only; $100) by Olduvai Corporation
7520 Red Road, Suite A, South Miami, Fla. 33143
(800)822-0772/(305)665-4665
A "fine art" collection including highly detailed, signed works.

The Print Shop Graphics for Libraries ($25) by Broderbund
  Software, Inc.
17 Paul Drive, San Rafael, Calif. 94903
(800)521-6263/(415)492-3200

The Print Shop Graphics Library ($35) by Broderbund Software, Inc.
17 Paul Drive, San Rafael, Calif. 94903
(800)521-6263/(415)492-3200

WetPaint ($50) by Dubl-Click Software
9316 Deering Avenue, Chatsworth, Calif. 91311
(818)349-2758

Works of Art ($60) by Springboard Software, Inc.
7808 Creekridge Circle, Minneapolis, Minn. 55435
(800)445-4780

Desktop Publishing Programs (Low-End) Both of the
following programs include paint functions and import graphics.

Publish It! ($400) by Timeworks, Inc.
444 Lake Cook Road, Deerfield, Ill. 60015-4919
(312)948-9200

Springboard Publisher ($200) by Springboard Software, Inc.
7808 Creekridge Circle, Minneapolis, Minn. 55435
(800)445-4780

Desktop Publishing Programs (High-End)
All of the following programs offer complete page-layout features. Their differences are minor: Ready, Set, Go! and QuarkXPress have spell checkers; QuarkXPress has the most flexible font handling; PageMaker has simple graphics creation ability and imports scanned images.

PageMaker (version 3 or higher; $600) by Aldus Corporation
411 First Avenue South, Suite 200, Seattle, Wash. 98104
(206)628-2320

QuarkXPress (version 2.1 or higher; $800) by Quark, Inc.
300 South Jackson, Suite 100, Denver, Colo. 80209
(800)356-9363/(303)934-2211

Ready, Set, Go! (version 4.5 or higher; $500) by Letraset USA
40 Eisenhower Drive, Paramus, N.J. 07653
(201)845-6100

Fonts

Adobe Type Library ($100–$400) by Adobe Systems, Incorporated
P.O. Box 7900, Mountain View, Calif. 94039
(800)344-8335/(415)961-4400
For PostScript-compatible laser printers only.

Fluent Fonts ($50; $90 for PostScript version) by
  Casady & Greene, Inc.
P.O. Box 223779, Carmel, Calif. 93922
(800)359-4920/(408)624-8716
For dot-matrix printers or PostScript-compatible laser printers.

World Class Fonts ($85) by Dubl-Click Software
9316 Deering Avenue, Chatsworth, Calif. 91311
(818)349-2758
For dot-matrix printers or PostScript-compatible laser printers.

Graphics (Low-End)

The Print Shop ($60) by Broderbund Software, Inc.
17 Paul Drive, San Rafael, Calif. 94903
(800)521-6263/(415)492-3200
The most popular program for making signs and banners; very easy to
  use. Comes with 140 clip-art images and 12 fonts. Additional clip-art
  packages are available.

Graphics (Paint Programs)
All of the following are full-featured paint programs. The most sophisticated are PixelPaint and Studio/8, with access to millions of colors and extremely flexible editing capabilities.

Cricket Paint ($200) by Cricket Software
40 Valley Stream Parkway, Malvern, Pa. 19355
(215)251-9890

Fullpaint ($100) by Ashton-Tate Corporation
20101 Hamilton Avenue, Torrance, Calif. 90502-1319
(213)329-8000

MacPaint ($125) by Claris Corporation
5201 Patrick Henry Drive, Santa Clara, Calif. 95052
(408)727-8207

PixelPaint ($400) by Supermac Technology
485 Potrero Avenue, Sunnyvale, Calif. 94086
(408)245-2202

Studio/8 ($500) by Electronic Arts
1820 Gateway Drive, San Mateo, Calif. 94404
(415)571-7171

Graphics (Draw Programs)   All of the following are full- featured draw programs. Aldus FreeHand and Illustrator 88 are more sophisticated than the others; all but MacDraw require PostScript-compatible laser printers.

Aldus FreeHand ($500) by Aldus Corporation
411 First Avenue South, Suite 200, Seattle, Wash. 98104
(206)628-2320

Cricket Draw ($300) by Cricket Software
40 Valley Stream Parkway, Malvern, Pa. 19355
(215)251-9890

Illustrator 88 ($500) by Adobe Systems, Incorporated
P.O. Box 7900, Mountain View, Calif. 94039
(800)344-8335/(415)961-4400

MacDraw II ($400) by Claris Corporation
5201 Patrick Henry Drive, Santa Clara, Calif. 95052
(408)727-8207

Graphics (Paint and Draw Programs)   The following programs combine drawing and painting capabilities in a single reasonably priced package.

Canvas ($300) by Deneba Software
3305 Northwest 74th Avenue, Miami, Fla. 33122
(800)6-CANVAS(622-6827)/(305)594-6965

DeskPaint & DeskDraw (one package; $150) by Zedcor, Inc.
4500 East Speedway, Suite 22, Tucson, Ariz. 85712
(800)482-4567/(602)881-8101

SuperPaint ($200) by Silicon Beach Software
P.O. Box 261430, San Diego, Calif. 92126
(619)695-6956

Printer Utilities

Click Art Effects ($50) by T/Maker Company
1390 Villa Street, Mountain View, Calif. 94041
(415)962-0195
Manipulates MacPaint-format files. Allows text and images to be
   rotated, slanted, and stretched.

Freedom of Press ($500, includes 35 fonts) by Custom
Applications, Inc.
900 Technology Park Drive, Building 8, Billerica, Mass. 01821
(800)873-4367/(508)667-8585
For the Mac II only. Permits inexpensive dot-matrix and laser printers
   to emulate PostScript printers.

Word Processing Programs   The following programs offer
full PostScript font support and sophisticated page-layout functions.
Each includes some degree of graphics capability as well.

FullWrite Professional ($400) by Ashton-Tate Corporation
20101 Hamilton Avenue, Torrance, Calif. 90502-1319
(213)329-8000
Includes a simple draw program; imports and edits images created in
   paint programs.

MacWrite (version 5 or higher: $250) by Claris Corporation
5201 Patrick Henry Drive, Santa Clara, Calif. 95052
(408)727-8207
Allows sizing and cropping of imported images.

Microsoft Word ($400) by Microsoft Corporation
1 Microsoft Way, Redmond, Wash. 98052-6399
(800)426-9400/(206)882-8088
Includes a copy of Microsoft's SuperPaint to create and edit graphic
   images.

WriteNow (version 2 or higher: $200) by T/Maker Company
1390 Villa Street, Mountain View, Calif. 94041
(415)962-0195
Can import and resize graphic images.

Shareware and Free Software for Apple Macintosh

Clip Art   An enormous variety of clip art can be found on Macintosh BBSs: cartoons, holiday figures, science fiction and fantasy, and many
other genres. There are also numerous MacDraw maps of countries,
states, counties, and even highway systems. Mail-order distributors also
carry huge collections of clip art for the Mac.

Fonts   Numerous free fonts for the Macintosh (including IE Fonts
and Laser Fonts) are available on BBSs and from mail-order distributors;
in addition, there are shareware font editors such as the following.

Retouch (shareware)
Creates special effects (such as shadowed and shaded text); scales and rotates fonts and graphics.

Size2Fit .2 (shareware)
Resizes lines of text to fit specific spaces; for use only with PostScript-compatible printers.

Graphics   Look for shareware graphics programs such as Nupaint, Scribbler 3, and XTV-Draw. In addition, you may find the following specialized programs useful.

Blow Up (shareware)
Allows an ordinary graphic to be enlarged to poster size.

Pattern Maker (free)
A small, simple program to create patterns that can later be added to graphics.

Commercial Software for Apple II Series Computers

Banner Programs

Print Power ($20) by Hi Tech Expressions
584 Broadway, Suite 509, New York, N.Y. 10012
(212)941-1224
A simple program that makes cards and banners up to 8 inches high.

Professional Sign Maker ($60) by Sunburst Communication
101 Castleton Street, Pleasantville, N.Y. 10570
(800)431-1934
Makes signs and banners 1, 2, 4, or 8 inches high.

Desktop Publishing Programs

Personal Newsletter ($60) by Softsync
162 Madison Avenue, New York, N.Y. 10016
(212)685-2080
Can create as well as import graphics.

Publish It! ($100) by Timeworks, Inc.
444 Lake Cook Road, Deerfield, Ill. 60015
(312)948-9200
Does not edit graphics, but can crop them.

Springboard Publisher ($200) by Springboard Software, Inc.
7808 Creekridge Circle, Minneapolis, Minn. 55435
(800)445-4780
Can edit, crop, and resize graphics.

Graphics Programs

DeluxePaint II ($140) by Electronic Arts
1820 Gateway Drive, San Mateo, Calif. 94404
(415)571-7171
A full-featured paint program; allows creation and editing of images.

Print Magic ($60) by Epyx, Inc.
600 Galveston Drive, Redwood City, Calif. 94063
(415)368-3200
Permits manipulation of text and graphics. Includes paint functions and
    clip art (graphics and borders).

The Print Shop ($60) by Broderbund Software, Inc.
17 Paul Drive, San Rafael, Calif. 94903
(800)521-6263/(415)492-3200
For making signs and banners. Comes with 140 clip-art images and 12
    fonts; very simple to use.

Commercial Software for Atari Computers

Banner Programs

Print Power ($20) by Hi Tech Expressions
584 Broadway, Suite 509, New York, N.Y. 10012
(212)941-1224
A simple program that makes cards and banners up to 8 inches high.

Graphics Programs

Easy Draw ($150) by Migraph, Inc.
200 S. 333d Street, Suite 220, Federal Way, Wash. 98003
(206)838-4677
A simple drawing program.

PrintMaster Plus ($50) by Unison World
1321 Harbor Bay Parkway, Alameda, Calif. 94501
(800)444-7553/(415)748-6938
Allows creation and editing of simple bitmapped graphics. Comes with
    a good-sized collection of pictures, patterns, borders, and fonts.

The Print Shop ($60) by Broderbund Software, Inc.
17 Paul Drive, San Rafael, Calif. 94903
(800)521-6263/(415)492-3200
Comes with 140 graphics and 12 fonts; very simple to use.

Word Processing Programs

WordPerfect (version 5.0 or higher: $500) by WordPerfect Corporation
1555 North Technology Way, Orem, Utah 84057
(800)321-4566/(801)225-5000
Allows use of a wide variety of fonts; can integrate graphics with text.

Commercial Software for Commodore Computers

Banner Programs

Print Power ($20) by Hi Tech Expressions
584 Broadway, Suite 509, New York, N.Y. 10012
(212)941-1224
A simple program that makes cards and banners up to 8 inches high.

Desktop Publishing Programs

Geopublish ($100) by Berkeley Softworks
2150 Shattuck Avenue, Penthouse, Berkeley, Calif. 94704
(415)644-0883
Does page layout and banners; able to import graphics.

Personal Newsletter ($60) by Softsync
162 Madison Avenue, New York, N.Y. 10016
(212)685-2080
Can create and import graphics.

Graphics Programs

Billboard Maker ($40) by Software Link
281 Mamaroneck Avenue, White Plains, N.Y. 10605
(914)683-5158
Makes posters up to 4 by 3 feet, with graphics and text.

DeluxePaint II ($100) by Electronic Arts
1820 Gateway Drive, San Mateo, Calif. 94404
(415)571-7171
A full-featured paint program; allows creation and editing of images.

PrintMaster Plus ($50) by Unison World
1321 Harbor Bay Parkway, Alameda, Calif. 94501
(800)444-7553/(415)748-6938
Allows creation and editing of simple bitmapped graphics. Comes with
a good-sized collection of pictures, patterns, borders, and fonts.

The Print Shop ($60) by Broderbund Software, Inc.
17 Paul Drive, San Rafael, Calif. 94903
(800)521-6263/(415)492-3200
For making signs and banners; comes with 140 graphics and twelve fonts.

Suggested Reading

The books in this appendix are divided into twelve subject categories: calligraphy, computer graphics and desktop publishing, design, drawing, library displays, library public relations, miscellaneous, origami and paper sculpture, painting, papier-mâché, printing and typography, and silk screening. Within each category, books are listed alphabetically by author.

All of the books listed here are suitable for beginners. The criteria for selection were purely subjective: in the author's judgment, these books are easy to use and are appropriate to the subject of library displays. You will no doubt find many more helpful books in your library or your local bookstore.

CALLIGRAPHY

These books teach the art of drawing letters by hand. No experience is required to use these books, but good hand-eye coordination is certainly helpful.

Biegeleisen, J. I. *The ABC of Lettering,* 5th ed. Cincinnati: ST Publications, 1986. 255 pages. A volume of alphabets, with an introduction to the basics of strokes and spacing.

Douglass, Ralph. *Calligraphic Lettering with Wide Pen and Brush*, 3d ed. New York: Watson-Guptill Publications, 1967. 88 pages. A more advanced text; includes a detailed discussion of pens and lettering styles, with extensive illustrations.

Metcalf, Eugene. *Calligraphy and Lettering Design.* Tustin, Calif.: Walter Foster Publishing, Inc., 1986. 64 pages. Part of the Artist's Library series, a collection of short handbooks for amateur and professional artists.

Shepard, Margaret. *Basics of Left-Handed Calligraphy.* Englewood Cliffs, N.J.: Prentice-Hall, Inc. 1988. 143 pages. Suggests five positions for left-handed people learning calligraphy.

Shepard, Margaret. *Learning Calligraphy.* New York: The Macmillan Company, 1978. 121 pages. Moves quickly through several alphabets and designs: for the beginner with some artistic talent.

Shepard, Margaret. *Modern Calligraphy Made Easy.* New York: The Putnam Publishing Group, 1988. 63 pages. A basic workbook for simple calligraphic lettering; offers letter-by-letter instruction for one modern alphabet.

COMPUTER GRAPHICS AND DESKTOP PUBLISHING

Some of these books cover general desktop publishing techniques; others deal with specific word processing and graphics programs.

Anzovin, Steve. *Using Deluxe Paint*. Greensboro, N.C.: Compute! Books, 1989. 262 pages.

Benton, Randi, and Mary Schenck Balcer. *The Official Print Shop Handbook*. New York: Bantam Books, 1987. 291 pages.

Bove, Tony, Cheryl Rhodes, and Wes Thomas. *The Art of Desktop Publishing: Using Personal Computers to Publish It Yourself,* 2d ed. Toronto: Bantam Books, 1987. 296 pages.

Collier, David, and Kay Floyd. *Ready-to-Use Layouts for Desktop Design*. London: Quarto Publishing, 1989. 143 pages.

Field, Tim. *Using MacWrite and MacPaint*. Berkeley, Calif.: Osborne McGraw-Hill, 1984. 200 pages.

Kater, David A. *Mastering Ready, Set, Go!* San Francisco: Sybex, 1988. 482 pages.

Larson, Glenn H. *Mastering Harvard Graphics*. San Francisco: Sybex, 1989. 323 pages.

McClelland, Deke. *Painting on the Macintosh: A Non-Artist's Drawing Guide to MacPaint, SuperPaint, Pixel Paint, Hypercard and Many More*. Homewood, Ill.: Dow Jones-Irwin Desktop Publishing Library, 1989. 250 pages.

McClelland, Deke. *Painting on the PC*. Homewood, Ill.: Dow Jones-Irwin Desktop Publishing Library, 1989. 250 pages.

DESIGN

These books introduce basic design concepts and techniques to the general reader. They are not intended specifically for librarians.

Gill, Bob. *Forget All the Rules You Ever Learned about Graphic Design. Including the Ones in This Book*. New York: Watson-Guptill Publications, 1981. 168 pages. Illustrates some bold and unconventional design ideas.

Heller, Steve, and Seymour Chwast. *Sourcebook of Visual Ideas*. New York: Van Nostrand Reinhold Company, 1989. 159 pages. A collection of striking magazine covers, posters, and album covers—on topics from aging to war—that demonstrate how graphics can convey messages effectively.

Mulvey, Frank. *Graphic Perception of Space*. New York: Reinhold Book Corporation, 1969. 96 pages. Illustrates how changes in background, size, shade, pattern, and position of elements can affect an overall design.

Powell, William F. *Color and How to Use It.* Tustin, Calif.: Walter Foster Publishing, Inc., 1984. 64 pages. Part of the Artist's Library series.

Roth, Laszlo. *Display Design.* Englewood Cliffs, N.J.: Prentice-Hall, Inc., 1983. 168 pages. Geared to professional store window dressers, this book is rich with discussions of equipment, tools, props, and philosophies for window displays. Includes professional tips for simple or elaborate window displays, plus a glossary of display terms.

DRAWING

Intended for nonartists, these books range from gentle confidence boosters to straightforward technical guides.

Anderson, Doug. *How to Draw with the Light Touch.* New York: Sterling Publishing, Inc., 1954. 80 pages. Explains how to turn your doodles into presentable cartoons and images, and how to combine drawings and pictures into collages.

Blake, Wendon. *Starting to Draw.* New York: Watson-Guptill Publications, 1981. 80 pages. Guides the novice slowly from shapes to figures, and finally to landscapes.

Brookes, Mona. *Drawing with Children.* Los Angeles: Jeremy P. Tarcher, Inc., 1986. 211 pages. A step-by-step guide—for adults as well as children—to overcoming fear of drawing. Teaches simple and advanced animals, still lifes, and landscapes.

Edwards, Betty. *Drawing on the Right Side of the Brain.* Los Angeles: Jeremy P. Tarcher, Inc., 1989. 254 pages. Tackles fear of drawing by teaching a new way of seeing and thinking. Shows how to handle space, shadows, proportions, and perspectives.

Franks, Gene. *Pencil Drawing.* Tustin, Calif.: Walter Foster Publishing, Inc., 1988. 64 pages. Part of the Artist's Library series.

Glassford, Carl. *Pen and Ink.* Tustin, Calif.: Walter Foster Publishing, Inc., 1985. 64 pages. Part of the Artist's Library series.

Hamm, Jack. *Drawing the Head and Figure.* New York: The Putnam Publishing Group, 1963. 120 pages. Traditional techniques for drawing human body positions and facial expressions.

Powell, William F. *Perspective.* Tustin, Calif.: Walter Foster Publishing, Inc., 1989. 64 pages. Part of the Artist's Library series.

Tolluson, Hal. *Cartooning.* Tustin, Calif.: Walter Foster Publishing, Inc., 1989. 64 pages. Part of the Artist's Library series.

Wang, Thomas C. *Sketching with Markers.* New York: Van Nostrand Reinhold Company, 1981. 104 pages. Includes techniques for achieving varied textures and tones, particularly in landscapes.

Wise, Morrell. *Drawing with Colored Pencils.* Tustin, Calif.: Walter Foster Publishing, Inc., 1985. 64 pages. Part of the Artist's Library series.

LIBRARY DISPLAYS

These are how-to books, written specifically for librarians, on the design and production of signs, posters, bulletin boards, and exhibits. The Horn and Garvey books emphasize techniques; the others are strong on ideas and themes for displays.

Coplan, Kate. *Effective Library Exhibits: How to Prepare and Promote Good Displays.* Dobbs Ferry, N.Y.: Oceana Publications, Inc., 1974. 176 pages. Extensively illustrated; includes basic production techniques and sources for inexpensive display materials.

Franklin, Linda Campbell. *Display and Publicity Ideas for Libraries.* Jefferson, N.C.: McFarland & Company, 1985. 264 pages. Offers numerous display themes, including month-by-month topics; includes complete display designs; shows how to use clip art.

Franklin, Linda Campbell. *Library Display Ideas.* Jefferson, N.C.: McFarland & Company, 1980. 230 pages. Offers dozens of display ideas and designs to be used as-is or adapted for your own needs.

Garvey, Mona. *Library Displays: Their Purpose, Construction, and Use.* New York: The H. W. Wilson Company, 1969. 88 pages. Includes solid discussion of design, planning, lettering, and illustration; explains how displays enhance use of the library.

Gomberg, Karen Cornell. *Books Appeal: Get Teenagers into the School Library.* Jefferson, N.C.: McFarland & Company, 1987. 129 pages. Full of ideas for school bulletin boards and related activities.

Horn, George F. *How to Prepare Visual Materials for School Use.* Worcester, Mass.: Davis Publications, Inc., 1963. 73 pages. Offers simple instructions and ideas for making displays and panoramas from such varied materials as cardboard tubes and window shades. Discusses lettering, color, shapes.

Kohn, Rita. *Experiencing Displays.* Metuchen, N.J.: The Scarecrow Press, Inc., 1982. 220 pages. Offers a variety of creative ideas and simple ways to achieve them; includes a glossary of display terms.

Marshall, Karen K. *Back to Books: 200 Library Activities to Encourage Reading.* Jefferson, N.C.: McFarland & Company, 1983. 138 pages. Designed to encourage children's use of libraries; offers many innovative ideas for tying in games and activities with exhibits and bulletin boards.

Wallick, Clair H. *Looking for Ideas? A Display Manual for Libraries and Bookstores.* Metuchen, N.J.: The Scarecrow Press, Inc., 1970. 104 pages. Ideas to incorporate into your library displays.

LIBRARY PUBLIC RELATIONS

These books offer general ideas about what public relations can accomplish, along with specific tips on media presentations, classes, book talks, special events, fund raisers, outreach programs, and displays.

Baeckler, Virginia. *PR for Pennies: Low-Cost Library Public Relations.* Hopewell, N.J.: Sources, 1978. 89 pages.

Edsall, Marian S. *Library Promotion Handbook.* Phoenix, Ariz.: The Oryx Press, 1980. 244 pages.

Ford, Gary T., ed. *Marketing and the Library.* New York: The Haworth Press, Inc., 1984. 80 pages.

Kohn, Rita, and Krysta Tepper. *You Can Do It: A PR Skills Manual for Librarians.* Metuchen, N.J.: The Scarecrow Press, Inc., 1981. 232 pages.

LiBretto, Ellen V., ed. *New Directions for Young Adult Services.* New York: R. R. Bowker Company, 1983. 225 pages. Contains a chapter on the merchandizing of collections and services, including an innovative library training program developed by the B. Dalton bookstore chain.

Usherwood, Bob. *Practical PR for Public Libraries.* London: Library Associates Publishing, Ltd., 1981. 207 pages.

MISCELLANEOUS

This category includes general reference books on arts and crafts, as well as books on specific techniques outside the other major categories.

Biegeleisen, J. I. *Design and Print Your Own Posters.* New York: Watson-Guptill Publications, 1976. 168 pages. A valuable guide to making posters. Discusses design, tools, several methods of lettering, color, making three-dimensional displays, printing, silk-screening, stencils, ink.

Daniels, George. *Home and Workshop Guide to Glues and Adhesives.* New York: Harper & Row, 1984. 120 pages. Includes drying times, clamping techniques, and suggestions for planning projects.

Firpo, Patrick, Lester Alexander, and Claudia Katayanagi. *Copy Art: The First Complete Guide to the Copy Machine.* New York: Richard Marek Publishers, 1978. 157 pages. Introduction to creative and bizarre effects that can be achieved with a copy machine.

Giles, Carl and Barbara. *Glue It!* Blue Ridge Summit, Pa.: TAB Books, Inc., 1979. 103 pages. Guide to glues and adhesives.

Jarvey, Paulette S. *You Can Dough It!* Canby, Oreg.: Hot Off the Press Publishing, 1980. 96 pages. A manual for creating baked art; includes a section on letters.

Laury, Jean Ray, and Joyce Aiken. *The Pantyhose Craft Book*. New York: Taplinger Publishing Company, 1978. 159 pages. Clever techniques for making objects from pantyhose.

Mayer, Ralph. *The Artist's Handbook of Materials and Techniques*, 4th ed. New York: Viking Penguin Inc., 1981. 733 pages. Discusses all kinds of art materials, from paints to glues; includes extensive glossaries and a list of distributors.

Rome, Carol Cheney, and Reidy Orr. *Needlepoint Letters and Numbers*. Garden City, N.Y.: Doubleday & Company, Inc., 1977. 159 pages. An unusual way of lettering. Includes several alphabets and a variety of symbols.

Rushton, Dorgan. *Dorgan Rushton's Collages*. London: Pelham Books Ltd., 1984. 110 pages. Shows how to create basic collages from paper and fabric.

Snook, Barbara. *Making Birds, Beasts, and Insects*. New York: Charles Scribner's Sons, 1974. 96 pages. Explains how to make a variety of figures from wood scraps, ping pong balls, pipe cleaners, sponges, bottle tops, nutshells, and other household objects.

Vero, Radu. *Airbrush: The Complete Studio Handbook*. New York: Watson-Guptill Publications, 1983. 190 pages. A guide to airbrush use, from basic skills to advanced techniques.

Wankleman, Willard F., and Philip Wigg. *A Handbook of Arts and Crafts*, 6th ed. Dubuque, Iowa: Wm. C. Brown Publishers, 1985. 348 pages. A basic reference book on arts and crafts. Includes techniques for ceramics, chalk, paper, papier-mâché, stencils, printing, and textiles, as well as general design tips.

West, Peter. *Step-by-Step Airbrushing*. Tustin, Calif.: Walter Foster Publishing, Inc., 1986. 64 pages. Part of the Artist's Library series.

Wickers, David, and Sharon Finmark. *How to Make Your Own Kinetics*. New York: Van Nostrand Reinhold Company, 1972. 68 pages. Describes how to make moving art from household items; includes instructions for making kinetoscopes, paper wind socks, and mobiles.

Williams, Guy R. *Making Mobiles*. New York: Emerson Books, Inc., 1969. 94 pages. Shows how to make mobiles—hanging or standing—from paper, string, and wire.

ORIGAMI AND PAPER SCULPTURE

Some of these books cover traditional Japanese origami techniques; others describe more unusual ways to cut and fold paper for many different purposes.

Antique Paper Dolls: The Edwardian Era. New York: Dover Publications, 1975. 16 pages. Includes full-color cutouts and instructions for making dolls and clothing.

Becker, Edith C. *Adventures with Scissors and Paper.* Scranton, Pa.: International Textbook Company, 1959. 116 pages. Shows how to use paper and paper products—such as cardboard tubes, egg cartons, and paper bags—to make simple paper sculptures, bas reliefs, and mobiles.

Carlis, John. *How to Make Your Own Greeting Cards.* New York: Watson-Guptill Publications, 1968. 142 pages. Offers clever techniques that can be used for many projects other than greeting cards. Discusses types of paper, pop-up folds, tracing, rubbing, and blotting; includes chapters on stencils, silk screening, and collage.

Hawcock, David. *Paper Dinosaurs.* New York: Sterling Publishing Co., Inc., 1988. 144 pages. Directions for making twenty different dinosaurs using only paper, scissors, glue, and paint.

Johnson, Pauline. *Creating with Paper.* Seattle: University of Washington Press, 1958. 207 pages. Includes directions for making paper lanterns, chains of dolls, and numerous human and animal figures.

Kasahara, Kunihiko. *Origami Made Easy.* Tokyo: Japan Publications, Inc., 1973. 128 pages. Includes directions for sixty-two figures, from simple to complex.

Kenneway, Eric. *Complete Origami.* New York: St. Martin's Press, Inc., 1987. 192 pages. Detailed directions for sophisticated paper figures.

Kenneway, Eric. *Origami, Paper Folding for Fun.* New York: Gallery Books, 1984. 77 pages. A good, basic selection of origami figures.

Rubi, Christian. *Cut Paper, Silhouettes and Stencils: An Instruction Book.* New York: Van Nostrand Reinhold Company, 1970. 177 pages. A guide to paper cutting, silhouettes, and stencil painting; moves quickly from simple to ornate.

Scheele, Zulal Ayture. *The Great Origami Book.* New York: Sterling Publishing Company, 1987. 80 pages. Step-by-step instructions for traditional origami figures.

Slade, Richard. *Paper Airplanes.* London: Faber and Faber Limited, 1970. 94 pages. Directions for making a Sopwith Camel, a Messerschmitt 109, and eighteen other classic airplanes from paper.

PAINTING

These books assume some familiarity with drawing and design. They explain how to achieve a variety of effects (light, texture, depth) with colored media.

DeMille, Leslie B. *Painting with Pastels.* Tustin, Calif.: Walter Foster Publishing, Inc., 1985. 64 pages. Part of the Artist's Library series.

Franks, Gene. *Drybrush Watercolor.* Tustin, Calif.: Walter Foster Publishing, Inc., 1988. 64 pages. Part of the Artist's Library series.

Hill, Tom. *Color for the Watercolor Painter.* New York: Watson-Guptill Publications, 1975. 159 pages. Complete introduction to watercolor painting, with discussion of tools, techniques, planning, and execution. Also includes a detailed section on color and mixing colors.

Johnson, R. Bradford. *Acrylics.* Tustin, Calif.: Walter Foster Publishing, Inc., 1984. 64 pages. Part of the Artist's Library series.

Light, Duane R. *Watercolor.* Tustin, Calif.: Walter Foster Publishing, Inc., 1984. 64 pages. Part of the Artist's Library series.

Palluth, William. *Painting in Oils.* Tustin, Calif.: Walter Foster Publishing, Inc., 1984. 64 pages. Part of the Artist's Library series.

PAPIER-MÂCHÉ

Dawson, Robert and Joan. *Sculpture with Simple Materials.* Menlo Park, Calif.: Lane Books, 1972. 96 pages. The "simple materials" include papier-mâché, clay, wire, and cloth.

Kenny, Carla and John B. *The Art of Papier Mâché.* Philadelphia: Chilton Book Company, 1968. 144 pages. Discusses basic techniques and includes directions for making specific items.

Rush, Peter. *Papier Mâché.* New York: Farrar Straus Giroux, 1980. 103 pages. Shows how to make heads, human figures, and animals.

PRINTING AND TYPOGRAPHY

These books cover traditional typographic techniques, including design, layout, pasteup, and marking copy. For computer techniques, see "Computer Graphics and Desktop Publishing," above.

Alphabet Thesaurus: A Treasury of Letter Designs. New York: Reinhold Publishing Corporation, 1960. 740 pages. A collection of over 3,000 typefaces, from Abbate Aqua to Zudeck Primer.

Craig, James. *Phototypesetting: A Design Manual.* New York: Watson-Guptill Publications, 1978. 223 pages. Includes an extensive glossary of typesetting terms.

Hutchins, Michael. *Typographics: A Designer's Handbook of Printing Techniques.* New York: Reinhold Book Corporation, 1969. 96 pages.

Skillin, Marjorie. *Words into Type.* Englewood Cliffs, N.J.: Prentice-Hall, Inc., 1974. 585 pages. The classic guide to preparing a manuscript for printing; includes directions for marking copy for a typesetter.

van Uchelen, Rod. *Paste Up: Production Techniques and New Applications.* New York: Van Nostrand Reinhold Company, 1976. 132 pages.

Watson, Jack. *Basic Graphic Design and Paste-Up.* Cincinnati: North Light Publishers, 1985. 95 pages.

White, Jan V. *Mastering Graphics*. New York: R. R. Bowker Company, 1983. 180 pages.

SILK SCREENING

These books describe the mechanics of using a silk screen, including creating appropriate designs, making stencils, and printing.

Biegeleisen, J. I. *Screen-Printing*. New York: Watson-Guptill Publications, 1971. 159 pages.

Biegeleisen, J. I. *Silk Screen Techniques*. New York: Dover Publications, Inc., 1958. 185 pages.

Gardner, Andrew B. *The Artist's Silkscreen Manual*. New York: The Putnam Publishing Group, 1976. 160 pages.

An Almanac of Displays

The following list of annual events may help you develop ideas for displays. It is organized by month. Each month's long-term events (such as Fire Prevention Week) and events whose dates vary (such as the Chinese New Year) are listed first. The remaining events for each month are listed in chronological order.

The name and date of each event are followed by one or more display suggestions. In most cases, these suggestions consist of book genres that suit the topic of the display; occasionally, you will also find suggestions about how the display might be designed. (For example, the listing for Election Day suggests that book titles be arranged in the form of a ballot.) You are, of course, encouraged to ignore these suggestions and come up with creative ideas of your own.

This list has been limited to events that happen every year to keep it from going out of date quickly. As a result, it consists largely of holidays, anniversaries of historic events, and birthdays of well-known people. Unfortunately, many picturesque events—such as National Soup Month or Pet Owners' Liberation Day—have had to be excluded, since the businesses and organizations that sponsor these events tend to do so only for a specific year.

If you want to find out the names and dates of currently sponsored events, the best source is a book called *Chase's Annual Events.* A new edition is published each year. If your library's reference department does not have *Chase's,* you can order it from Contemporary Books, Inc., Department C, 180 North Michigan Avenue, Chicago, Illinois 60601.

As you go through this appendix, you will find that many of the listed events fall into predictable categories. There are, for example, fifty suggested displays devoted to state history (on the day each state was admitted to the Union), and many displays devoted to the history and culture of other countries (on the day each country holds its national celebration). There are also a great many display suggestions tied to birthdays of famous authors, artists, and composers. (For help in designing these displays, see the templates in Appendix E.)

Once you have designed one display in a particular category, you will find it easy to design the others—but it is doubtful that you will want to do all of them. (For example, one or two displays devoted to composers can be interesting, but a new composer each month may become boring.) Therefore, it is a good idea to plan ahead. If you decide to celebrate Pierre Auguste Renoir's birthday (February 25) by devoting a display to his paintings, be aware that you will probably have to ignore Vincent Van Gogh's birthday (March 30).

Though most of the events in this appendix are one-day events, displays commemorating them obviously can last much longer. A display with a Valentine's Day theme, for example, can be put up several weeks before February 14. Once the holiday has passed, however, you will want to take down the display relatively quickly. As a general rule, no poster or exhibit should be on display for more than a month.

A final note: the events listed here have been selected arbitrarily, largely according to one person's judgment. There are doubtless many items on this list that you will feel are inappropriate for library displays; at the same time, there are holidays and anniversaries that you may feel have been unjustly omitted. Fortunately, this list is not engraved in stone—feel free to make your own additions and emendations. You, more than anyone, are familiar with the interests and tastes of the people who use your library.

JANUARY

Martin Luther King Day (celebrated on the Monday closest to January 15). *Biographies of King or general works on the history of the civil rights movement.*

Super Bowl Sunday (date varies). *Biographies and autobiographies of football players, surrounded by pennants, popcorn, an easy chair, and a (real or cardboard) television set.*

Chinese New Year (date varies according to Chinese calendar; late January or early February). *WHAT'S YOUR SIGN?: illustration of Chinese horoscope accompanied by books on Chinese folklore and astrology.*

New Year's Day (January 1). *Streamers, glitter, noisemakers, and champagne glasses in combination with self-improvement books such as* How to Be Slimmer in Sixty Days, Quit Smoking Now, *job hunters' manuals, and manuals on tax-return preparation.*

Haiti Independence Day (January 1). *Books on the history and culture of Haiti or on travel to Haiti.*

Birthday of Paul Revere, American silversmith and patriot (January 1, 1735). *Display of decorative metal items (such as mugs, bowls, and candlesticks), promoting books on metalworking.*

Birthday of Betsy Ross, who is said to have made the first American flag (January 1, 1752). *Books on sewing and needlework or on the history of the American flag.*

Birthday of J. D. Salinger, novelist (January 1, 1919). *Books by Salinger and other books for young adults.*

Georgia becomes the fourth state (January 2, 1788). *Books on the history of Georgia and the southern states or on travel to Georgia and the South.*

Birthday of Isaac Asimov, writer (January 2, 1920). *An exhibit called SCIENCE FICTION: FAST BECOMING SCIENCE FACT, with selected books of both types by Asimov and others.*

March of Dimes founded (January 3, 1938). *Books on charities and other nonprofit organizations, along with a display on such organizations in your community.*

Alaska becomes the forty-ninth state (January 3, 1959). *Books on the history of Alaska or on travel to Alaska.*

Birthday of Jacob Grimm, coauthor with brother Wilhelm of *Grimm's Fairy Tales* (January 4, 1785). *Exhibit publicizing the library's services for children and the most popular children's books and tapes.*

Birthday of Louis Braille, inventor of the Braille alphabet for the blind (January 4, 1809). *Exhibit of inventions for the blind, a poster explaining the Braille system, or a display promoting the library's services for the blind.*

Utah becomes the forty-fifth state (January 4, 1896). *Books on the history of Utah or on travel to Utah and the western states.*

Anniversary of the death of George Washington Carver, chemist (January 5, 1943). *Books on the life and work of Carver, as well as a poster showing examples of his work with peanuts.*

Birthday of Carl Sandburg, poet (January 6, 1878). *Books by Sandburg, along with works by other American poets.*

New Mexico becomes the forty-seventh state (January 6, 1912). *Books on the history of New Mexico or on travel to New Mexico and the Southwest.*

Birthday of E. L. Doctorow, writer (January 6, 1931). *Books by Doctorow, along with works by other contemporary American novelists.*

Birthday of Elvis Presley, singer (January 8, 1935). *Biographies of Elvis Presley, or a display promoting your library's collection of rock 'n' roll records, tapes, and CDs.*

Connecticut becomes the fifth state (January 9, 1788). *Books on the history of Connecticut or on travel to Connecticut and New England.*

Birthday of Richard Nixon, thirty-seventh president (January 9, 1913). *Books on the Nixon era and Watergate.*

Birthday of Ethan Allen, American patriot and soldier (January 10, 1738). *Biographies of Allen and other military heroes, or books on the American Revolution.*

Birthday of Alexander Hamilton, statesman (January 11, 1755 or 1757). *Books on the adoption of the U.S. Constitution, on the Federalist papers, or on the history of the U.S. banking system.*

Birthday of Jack London, author (January 12, 1876). *Books by Jack London, along with works by other adventure novelists.*

France: Molière Day (January 15). *Plays by Molière, along with works by other French playwrights.*

Birthday of Benjamin Franklin, printer, diplomat, inventor (January 17, 1706). *Biographies of Franklin.*

Birthday of Peter Roget, scholar (January 18, 1779). *Exhibit or poster encouraging the use of the thesaurus, perhaps including word games that require a thesaurus.*

Birthday of A. A. Milne, author of Winnie the Pooh series (January 18, 1882). *Display of Pooh books or exhibit introducing Milne's lesser-known works for adults.*

Birthday of James Watt, inventor who perfected the steam engine (January 19, 1736). *Display celebrating great inventions, with books on the industrial revolution or how-to books for inventors and tinkerers.*

Birthday of Robert E. Lee, general (January 19, 1807). *Biographies of Lee and general books on the Civil War.*

Birthday of Edgar Allan Poe, writer (January 19, 1809). *Books by Poe, along with works by other mystery and horror writers.*

Inauguration Day (January 20). *Biographies of American presidents, perhaps surrounded by red, white, and blue bunting.*

National Handwriting Day, in celebration of John Hancock's birthday (January 23, 1737). *Books on improving handwriting or books that teach calligraphy.*

Gold discovered in California (January 24, 1848). *Books about the gold rush and how it affected U.S. history.*

Birthday of W. Somerset Maugham, writer (January 25, 1874). *Novels and short stories by Maugham.*

India: Republic Day (January 26). *Books on the history and culture of India, great Indian leaders, or travel to India; or cookbooks of Indian food.*

Michigan becomes the twenty-sixth state (January 26, 1837). *Books on the history of Michigan, or on travel to Michigan.*

Birthday of Wolfgang Amadeus Mozart, composer (January 27, 1756). *Biographies of Mozart or a display promoting your library's collection of classical recordings and sheet music.*

Birthday of Lewis Carroll, writer (Charles L. Dodgson, January 27, 1832). *A WONDERLAND OF CHILDREN'S CLASSICS: an exhibit of classic books for children, perhaps accompanied by drawings of well-known Lewis Carroll characters.*

Kansas becomes the thirty-fourth state (January 29, 1861). *Books on the history of Kansas or on travel to Kansas and the Midwest.*

Birthday of Franklin Delano Roosevelt, thirty-second president (January 30, 1882). *Biographies of Roosevelt and of other American presidents, or histories of the New Deal and World War II.*

FEBRUARY

American Heart Month. *Exhibit promoting the work of the American Heart Association, poster presenting a health awareness quiz, or a display of healthy-food cookbooks.*

Black History Month. *Books on the black experience in America, black contributions to American culture, and the history of the civil rights movement.*

Pre-Lent festivals and feasts, including Mardi Gras (New Orleans), Carnival (Brazil and elsewhere), Pancake Tuesday, Bun Day (Iceland), Feast of Fools (Germany and Austria). (Dates of these festivals vary, but they usually take place in mid to late February.) *Exhibit of carnival costumes, gaily painted masks, confetti, and balloons surrounding recordings of New Orleans music or books on international festivals.*

Presidents' Day, formerly George Washington's Birthday (celebrated on the Monday closest to February 22). *Books about George Washington, the American Revolution, and the earliest days of the United States. (Presidents' Day has become a joint celebration of Washington's and Abraham Lincoln's birthdays, so you may want to include books about Lincoln as well. If Lincoln's birthday is celebrated separately in your state [generally on February 12], you may want to devote a separate display to Lincoln. See "Birthday of Abraham Lincoln," below.)*

Winter Olympic games (February, every fourth year). *Books on the Olympics, great athletes, or winter sports.*

National Freedom Day, commemorating the Thirteenth Amendment, outlawing slavery in the United States (February 1, 1865). *Books on American black slavery, the Civil War, or the history of the civil rights movement.*

Groundhog Day (February 2). *A display divided into two sections: books on indoor activities (crafts, cooking, music) in the event of six more weeks of winter; books on outdoor activities (gardening, sports) in the event of an early spring.*

Birthday of Elizabeth Blackwell, first female physician (February 3, 1821). *Books by and about women leaders, books about the history of medicine, or study aids for pre-med students.*

Birthday of Gertrude Stein, poet (February 3, 1874). *Books of Stein's poetry, along with works by other Lost Generation writers.*

Birthday of Norman Rockwell, American painter (February 3, 1894). *Books of Rockwell's work, art technique books, or an exhibit promoting your library's poster rental collection.*

Birthday of James Michener, novelist (February 3, 1907). *Novels by Michener, along with other books (fiction and nonfiction) describing the places Michener writes about.*

Boy Scouts are founded (February 4, 1910). *Books on scouting, perhaps accompanied by an exhibit of scouting-related items (uniforms, badges, awards, crafts) lent by a local Boy Scout troop.*

Birthday of Betty Friedan, author and feminist (February 4, 1921). *Books by Friedan, along with works by other feminist authors and books on the women's movement.*

Massachusetts becomes the sixth state (February 6, 1788). *Books on the history of Massachusetts or on travel to Massachusetts and New England.*

Birthday of George Herman "Babe" Ruth, baseball player (February 6, 1895). *Biographies and autobiographies of baseball players, perhaps arranged in the form of a baseball diamond.*

Birthday of Ronald Reagan, fortieth president (February 6, 1911). *Books by and about Ronald and Nancy Reagan.*

Birthday of Charles Dickens, novelist (February 7, 1812). *Novels by Dickens, perhaps accompanied by reproductions of Victorian-era illustrations.*

Birthday of Sinclair Lewis, novelist (February 7, 1885). *Novels by Lewis, along with works by other social satirists.*

Birthday of Jules Verne, novelist (February 8, 1828). *Display promoting early science fiction books or films based on Verne's novels.*

Japan Empire Day, commemorating the founding of Japan (February 11, 660 B.C.). *Books on the history and culture of Japan, on travel to Japan, or on notable Japanese Americans.*

Birthday of Thomas Alva Edison, inventor (February 11, 1847). INVENTIONS THAT CHANGED THE WORLD: *an exhibit of commonly used inventions by Edison and others, perhaps illuminated by a bare light bulb.*

Birthday of Charles Darwin, naturalist (February 12, 1809). *Books by Darwin and other books on natural science or evolution.*

Birthday of Abraham Lincoln, sixteenth president (February 12, 1809). *Books about Lincoln and the Civil War.*

Birthday of Judy Blume, author (February 12, 1938). *Books by Blume and other recommended books for young adults.*

The *American Magazine,* **America's first magazine, is published** (February 13, 1741). *Exhibit or poster promoting your library's periodical collection.*

Valentine's Day (February 14). *Display promoting romance novels or great romance movies available on videocassette, perhaps surrounded by children's valentine cards.*

Oregon becomes the thirty-third state (February 14, 1859). *Books on the history of Oregon or on travel to Oregon and the Pacific Northwest.*

Arizona becomes the forty-eighth state (February 14, 1912). *Books on the history of Arizona or on travel to Arizona and the Southwest.*

Birthday of Susan B. Anthony, early leader of the women's rights movement (February 15, 1820). *Books on Anthony and other champions of women's rights.*

National PTA (Parent-Teacher Association) Founder's Day (February 17, 1897). *Books on education and the state of our schools, or posters promoting PTA membership.*

Birthday of Nicolaus Copernicus, astronomer who determined that the planets revolve around the sun (February 19, 1473). *Books on astronomy, perhaps arranged around a glowing sun.*

The *New Yorker* **publishes its first issue** (February 20, 1925). *Display of classic* New Yorker *covers, perhaps tied in with a cartooning or short-story-writing contest.*

John Glenn, Jr., is the first American in space (February 20, 1962). *Books on the history and future of the U.S. space program.*

Birthday of W. H. Auden, poet (February 21, 1907). *Books of Auden's poetry, along with works by other twentieth-century poets.*

Birthday of George Frederick Handel, composer (February 23, 1685). *Biographies of Handel, or a display promoting your library's collection of classical recordings and sheet music.*

Birthday of Pierre Auguste Renoir, artist (February 25, 1841). *Books about Renoir and other Impressionists, books on painting techniques, or an exhibit promoting your library's poster rental collection.*

Birthday of Victor Hugo, novelist and dramatist (February 26, 1826). *Biographies of Hugo, as well as his novels,* Les Miserables, *and* The Hunchback of Notre Dame.

Grand Canyon National Park is established in Arizona (February 26, 1919). *Books on the Grand Canyon and other natural wonders.*

Birthday of Henry Wadsworth Longfellow, poet (February 27, 1807). *Books of Longfellow's poetry, along with works by other early American poets.*

Leap Day (occurs every four years on February 29). *Books of leisure activities, to occupy an extra day of spare time.*

MARCH

Red Cross Month. *Books on the Red Cross and on first aid techniques, a quiz on first aid techniques, or a poster listing local classes on first aid.*

Spring cleaning. *Poster urging return of long-overdue library books, exhibit of books on housecleaning (perhaps surrounded by cleaning supplies), exhibit promoting charitable organizations that accept donations of unwanted clothing.*

Academy Awards presented (March or April, date varies). *Books on the Oscars and on actors, actresses, and directors who have won the award.*

Save Your Vision Week (first week in March). *Display of eyeglasses, with a donation box to collect patron's old glasses for charity; or a display promoting the library's collection of large-print books.*

Girl Scout Week (second week of March). *Exhibit of Girl Scout badges and books that may help to earn those badges.*

National Poison Prevention Week (third week of March). *Exhibit or poster on poison prevention, with prominently posted poison hotline number.*

Town Meeting Day, Vermont (first Tuesday in March). *Books on the history of New England and on the democratic process.*

Diabetes Awareness Day (third Tuesday in March). *Display of healthy-food cookbooks.*

Cherry blossom festival (late March or early April, in Japan, Washington, D.C., and elsewhere). *Books on plants, gardening, traditional Japanese gardening.*

Ohio becomes the seventeenth state (March 1, 1803). *Books on the history of Ohio or on travel to Ohio and the Midwest.*

Nebraska becomes the thirty-seventh state (March 1, 1867). *Books on the history of Nebraska or on travel to Nebraska and the Midwest.*

Birthday of Glenn Miller, orchestra leader (March 1, 1904). *Books about Miller, the big bands, and the swing era, or an exhibit promoting swing-era recordings and sheet music.*

U.S. Peace Corps begins (March 1, 1961). *Books on the Peace Corps or a poster on how to join the Peace Corps.*

Birthday of Theodore Seuss Geisel (Dr. Seuss), writer (March 2, 1904). *Exhibit of Dr. Seuss books, surrounded by children's drawings of favorite Dr. Seuss characters.*

Birthday of John Irving, novelist (March 2, 1942). *Books by John Irving, along with works by other contemporary novelists.*

Florida becomes the twenty-seventh state (March 3, 1845). *Books on the history of Florida or on travel to Florida.*

National Anthem Day: President Hoover signs a bill making "The Star Spangled Banner" the U.S. national anthem (March 3, 1931). *Display of books and recordings of patriotic music, perhaps tied in with a contest to write a new city anthem or school song.*

Vermont becomes the fourteenth state (March 4, 1791). *Books on the history of Vermont or on travel to Vermont and New England.*

Alamo Day (March 6). *Books about the history of Texas, the Battle of the Alamo, and such heroes as William Barrett Travis, James Bowie, and David Crockett.*

Birthday of Michelangelo, artist (March 6, 1475). *Books about Michelangelo and his works, books on painting and sculpture techniques, or an exhibit promoting your library's poster rental collection.*

Birthday of Elizabeth Barrett Browning, poet (March 6, 1806). *Books of poetry by Elizabeth Barrett Browning and Robert Browning, along with works by other nineteenth-century British poets.*

International Women's Day (March 8). *Books on great women of all times and places.*

Birthday of Amerigo Vespucci, explorer (March 9, 1451). *Books on explorers, past and present.*

Birthday of Harriet Tubman, founder of the Underground Railroad (March 10, 1820). *Books on Tubman, the antislavery movement, and the Underground Railroad.*

Alexander Graham Bell makes first telephone transmission (March 10, 1876). *Exhibit or poster promoting your library's information-by-phone services.*

U.S. Salvation Army is founded (March 10, 1880). *Display promoting American charities and charitable work.*

Birthday of Edward Albee, playwright (March 12, 1928). *Plays by Albee, along with works of other twentieth-century American playwrights.*

Birthday of Albert Einstein, physicist (March 14, 1879). *Biographies of Einstein and other great scientists, or books about modern physics.*

Julius Caesar is assassinated (the ides of March—March 15—in the year 44 B.C.). *Histories of ancient Rome.*

Maine becomes the twenty-third state (March 15, 1820). *Books on the history of Maine or on travel to Maine and New England.*

St. Patrick's Day, a national holiday in Ireland (March 17). *Books on Irish history and culture, travel to Ireland, or Irish legends; books by and about Irish writers; or books about notable Irish Americans.*

First day of spring (March 21). *Books on springtime activities (for example, books on biking and walking trails, gardening manuals, and kite-flying books), perhaps displayed on a picnic blanket in a simulated outdoor setting.*

Birthday of Johann Sebastian Bach, composer (March 21, 1685). *Biographies of Bach, or a display promoting your library's collection of classical recordings and sheet music.*

Birthday of Stephen Sondheim, composer (March 22, 1930). *Books about Sondheim and other Broadway composers, or a display promoting your library's collection of Broadway show recordings and sheet music.*

Birthday of Harry Houdini, magician and escape artist (March 24, 1874). READING: THE GREAT ESCAPE: *books about Houdini, magic, and the occult.*

Greek Independence Day (March 25, 1821). *Books on the history and culture of Greece, books on travel to Greece, or Greek cookbooks.*

Fire at Triangle Shirtwaist factory in New York calls attention to hazardous work conditions in sweatshops (March 25, 1911). *Books on the history of unions and union activists.*

Birthday of Robert Frost, poet (March 26, 1874). *Books of Frost's poetry, along with works by other American poets.*

Birthday of Sandra Day O'Connor, first female Supreme Court justice (March 26, 1930). *Books about O'Connor, the American legal system, the Supreme Court, and controversial decisions the current Court faces.*

Three Mile Island nuclear power plant accident (March 28, 1979). *Books on Three Mile Island, the history of nuclear power, and alternative energy sources.*

Birthday of Vincent Van Gogh, artist (March 30, 1853). *Books about Van Gogh and his works, books on painting techniques, or an exhibit promoting your library's poster rental collection.*

Birthday of Franz Joseph Haydn, composer (March 31, 1732). *Biographies of Haydn, or a display promoting your library's collection of classical recordings and sheet music.*

The Eiffel Tower opens in Paris to celebrate the centennial of the French Revolution (March 31, 1889). *A model or drawing of the Eiffel Tower, surrounded by travel books on Paris and France.*

APRIL

Cancer Control Month. *Exhibit on the warning signs of cancer, incorporating posters and brochures available from the American Cancer Society.*

Older Americans' Month. *Exhibit promoting healthy and active living for the elderly, using materials available from the American Association of Retired Persons.*

Diet season begins. *Guides to weight loss, exercise, and fitness, for those who want to prepare for approaching bathing-suit weather.*

Daylight Savings Time (starts first Sunday in April). *Books on gardening, biking, and other outdoor activities that can make good use of the extra hour of sunlight.*

Arbor Day (last Friday in April). *Books on trees, gardening, nature, and hiking.*

Good Friday and Easter Sunday (dates vary, usually in mid-April). *Books about Easter traditions around the world, or exhibit of Easter crafts (bonnets, eggs, and baskets) accompanied by books that explain how to make them.*

Israeli Independence Day (date varies according to Hebrew calendar; usually falls in April). *Books on the history and culture of Israel or on travel to Israel and the Middle East.*

Passover (date varies according to Hebrew calendar; usually begins in April). *Books about the history and meaning of Passover, or Passover cookbooks.*

College selection time for many high school students. *Books and guides on colleges and universities, along with books on higher education.*

April Fools Day (April 1). *Books of riddles, jokes, games, and puzzles, or biographies of famous clowns.*

U.S. mint opens (April 2, 1792). *Exhibit on coin collecting, or display called MAKING MONEY, with books on the stock market or investments in real estate.*

Birthday of Hans Christian Andersen, Danish author of fairy tales (April 2, 1805). *Books of fairy tales and children's tales by Andersen and others.*

Birthday of Maya Angelou, writer (April 4, 1928). *Books by Angelou, along with works by other contemporary black women.*

Birthday of Raphael, Renaissance painter (April 6, 1483). *Books about Raphael and his works, books on painting techniques, or an exhibit promoting your library's poster rental collection.*

Mormon church is founded (April 6, 1830). *Books on the history, beliefs, and practice of Mormonism.*

Robert E. Peary and his team reach the North Pole (April 6, 1909). *Books about Peary's expeditions, as well as other books on Arctic exploration.*

World Health Day (April 7, 1948). *Display of health information, including books on exercise, nutrition, and home health care.*

Birthday of Buddha (approximately April 8, c. 560 B.C.). *Books on Buddhism, Buddhist festivals, and countries where Buddhism is prominent.*

Jackie Robinson, first black player enters Major League baseball (April 11, 1947). *Books on the Negro leagues and on black baseball greats.*

Salk polio vaccine is announced effective (April 12, 1955). *Books on strides in medicine.*

Pan-American Day (April 14). *Books on Latin and North American cultures and contributions, or histories of the two continents.*

Income Tax Day (April 15). *HOW TO SPEND YOUR TAX REFUND, with books on weekend escapes, home improvement and decorating, local restaurants, and other nonnecessities.*

Birthday of Henry James, novelist and critic (April 15, 1843). *Books by James, such as* Washington Square, Portrait of a Lady, *and* The American, *as well as criticisms of his works.*

Sinking of the *Titanic* (April 15, 1912). *Books on the* Titanic *and other great ships, or adventure novels set on the ocean.*

Birthday of Charlie Chaplin, silent film actor (April 16, 1889). *Books about Chaplin and other early film comedians, or a display promoting your library's film series or videotape collection.*

Verrazano Day (April 17). *Books about Giovanni de Verrazano's exploration, as well as on other noted explorers.*

Great San Francisco earthquake (April 18, 1906). *Books on earthquakes and natural disasters, or (in earthquake-prone areas) earthquake-preparedness information.*

Birthday of Clarence Darrow, lawyer (April 18, 1932). *Biographies of Darrow and other well-known lawyers, books about the Scopes trial and other great American legal cases, or test-preparation books for the LSAT.*

Birthday of Charlotte Brontë, novelist (April 21, 1816). *Books by the Brontë sisters, along with works by other Victorian authors.*

Birthday of John Muir, naturalist (April 21, 1838). *Books on national parks (such as Yosemite and Yellowstone), camping, and natural wonders, perhaps displayed under a tent.*

Earth Day (April 22). *Books and displays focusing on environmental issues such as recycling, efforts to control air and water pollution, and environmentally responsible corporations.*

Birthday of William Shakespeare, dramatist (April 23, 1564). *Collections of Shakespeare's plays and poetry, or a display promoting your library's audio collection.*

Spain: Book Day, commemorating the death of Cervantes (April 23, 1714). *Books by Cervantes and other Spanish authors.*

Library of Congress is established (April 24, 1800). *Poster explaining the Library of Congress classification system or the Library of Congress Cataloging-in-Publication data.*

Birthday of John James Audubon, ornithologist and artist (April 26, 1785). *Books about Audubon and about birds and bird watching.*

Death of Magellan, explorer (April 27, 1521; his birthdate is unknown). *Books about explorers, past and present.*

Birthday of Ulysses S. Grant, eighteenth president (April 27, 1822). *Books about the Civil War and great military leaders.*

Maryland becomes the seventh state (April 28, 1788). *Books on the history of Maryland or on travel to Maryland and the mid-Atlantic states.*

Louisiana becomes the eighteenth state (April 30, 1812). *Books on the history of Louisiana or on travel to Louisiana.*

MAY

Pulitzer prizes are announced (date varies). *Books on Joseph Pulitzer, the history of the prize, and books that have been awarded the prize in past years.*

Asian/Pacific American Heritage Week (first full week in May). *Books by and about Asian Americans.*

Be Kind to Animals Week or National Pet Week (first full week in May). *Display of animal adoption information from local animal shelter, along with books on dogs, cats, and other pets.*

National Police Week (week of May 15). *Display on crime prevention or books by and about police officers.*

Kentucky Derby (first Saturday in May). *Books on the Kentucky Derby or on famous racehorses.*

Mother's Day (second Sunday in May). *Books on motherhood and mother-child relations, or cookbooks for children (so mothers can take the day off).*

Armed Forces Day (third Saturday in May). *Books on the army, navy, and air force, as well as on notable military leaders.*

Memorial Day (last Monday in May). *PLANS FOR THE BIG WEEKEND: a display of barbecue cookbooks, weekend getaways, and books on making kites or paper boats.*

Indianapolis 500 (Memorial Day weekend). *Books on the Indianapolis 500, great racers, or the history of auto racing.*

Law Day (May 1). *Books about the American legal system, or law books for nonlawyers (for example, books on writing contracts or preparing wills), perhaps displayed on large, cardboard scales of justice.*

May Day (USSR International Labor Day, May 1). *Books on marxism, communism, and the history of the Soviet Union.*

Empire State Building is opened (May 1, 1931). *Books about architectural landmarks or other tourist attractions in New York City.*

Death of Leonardo da Vinci, artist and scientist (May 2, 1519; his birthdate is unknown). *Books about Leonardo and his works, books on painting and drafting techniques, or an exhibit promoting your library's poster rental collection.*

Birthday of Dr. Benjamin Spock, writer on child care (May 2, 1903). *Books on child care by Dr. Spock and others.*

Cinco de Mayo (May 5), Mexican national holiday. *Books on Mexican history and cultural contributions.*

Birthday of Karl Marx, German philosopher (May 5, 1818). *Books by and about Marx, or books about communism and communist countries.*

Hindenburg explodes (May 6, 1937). *Books on the history of aviation, or on aviation disasters.*

Birthday of Harry S Truman, thirty-third president (May 8, 1884). *Books about Truman and the era during which he was president.*

V-E (Victory in Europe) Day (May 8, 1945). *Books about the European campaign during World War II.*

European Economic Community is founded (May 9, 1950). *Books on the European Economic Community (focusing particularly on the changes expected in 1992), or books on economics in general, under an array of European flags.*

The Golden Spike is put in place, completing the transcontinental railroad (May 10, 1869). *Novels and nonfiction books about trains and rail travel.*

Minnesota becomes the thirty-second state (May 11, 1858). *Books on the history of Minnesota or on travel to Minnesota and the northern states.*

Limerick Day, in honor of birthday of Edward Lear, poet (May 12, 1812). *Display of limericks contributed by students or other library users.*

Birthday of Florence Nightingale (May 12, 1820). *Books about Nightingale and other nurses, or books about nursing and medicine.*

Lewis and Clark expedition begins (May 14, 1804). *Books about their exploration of the American West.*

New York Stock Exchange is opened (May 17, 1792). *Books on the history and mechanics of the stock market, or how-to books for investors.*

Supreme Court rules school segregation unconstitutional (May 17, 1954). *Books on* Brown v. Board of Education *and the history of desegregation.*

Birthday of Pope John Paul II (May 18, 1920). *Biographies of John Paul and other Catholic leaders, or books on the history, beliefs, and practice of Catholicism.*

Mount St. Helens erupts in Washington state (May 18, 1980). *Books about geology, natural disasters, and volcanoes.*

Charles Lindbergh departs on first nonstop transatlantic flight (May 20, 1927). *Books by Charles Lindbergh* (The Spirit of St. Louis) *and Anne Lindbergh* (North to the Orient *and* Listen! The Wind), *as well as on the history of aviation.*

Victoria Day, birthday of Queen Victoria (May 21, 1819). *Biographies of Victoria and other British monarchs, or novels set in Victorian England.*

National Maritime Day (May 22). *Books about the* Savannah, *the first steam vessel to cross the Atlantic, and the history of commercial shipping.*

Birthday of Sir Arthur Conan Doyle (May 22, 1859). *Sherlock Holmes books, along with other popular mystery novels.*

South Carolina becomes the eighth state (May 23, 1788). *Books on the history of South Carolina or on travel to the Carolinas.*

Brooklyn Bridge is dedicated (May 24, 1883). *Books on the Brooklyn Bridge and other engineering masterpieces, perhaps surrounded by blueprints and working drawings.*

African Freedom Day in Chad, Zambia, and other African states (May 25). *Books on the history of the African continent, books on the history and culture of individual African countries, or books on travel to Africa.*

Birthday of Dorothea Lange, photographer (May 26, 1895). *Books of Lange's photography, as well as books on the depression era she photographed.*

Birthday of Rachel Louise Carson, biologist (May 27, 1907). *Include copies of Carson's book* Silent Spring, *as well as other books about environmental pollution.*

Birthday of Dionne quintuplets (May 28, 1934). *Name-your-baby books and books on baby and child care, perhaps arranged in groups of five.*

Rhode Island becomes the thirteenth state (May 29, 1790). *Books on the history of Rhode Island, or on travel to Rhode Island and New England.*

Wisconsin becomes the thirtieth state (May 29, 1848). *Books on the history of Wisconsin or on travel to Wisconsin and the Midwest.*

Birthday of Walt Whitman, poet (May 31, 1819). *Books of Whitman's poetry, along with works by other nineteenth-century American poets.*

JUNE

World Cup (date varies). *Books about the game of soccer, its rules, and notable players worldwide.*

Black Music Month. *Display promoting recordings of classical, ragtime, jazz, folk, country, soul, rhythm and blues, rock, and rap music by black musicians, perhaps accompanied by books about some of these musicians.*

Dairy Month. *Books about the dairy industry, or vegetarian and dairy cookbooks.*

Television rerun season begins (date varies). *Display suggesting summer reading and other activities to occupy television addicts until the new season begins.*

National Safe Boating Week (first full week in June). *Books on ships and boats, or posters offering boating safety tips.*

Father's Day (third Sunday in June). *Books on fatherhood and child care, perhaps accompanied by Father's Day cards made by local children.*

Graduation Day (date varies according to school, but usually in June). *Guides to college selection, job hunting, and résumé writing.*

Kentucky becomes the fifteenth state (June 1, 1792). *Books on the history of Kentucky or on travel to Kentucky.*

Tennessee becomes the sixteenth state (June 1, 1796). *Books on the history of Tennessee or on travel to Tennessee.*

Italy: Republic Day, on which the country chose republic status instead of return to monarchy (June 2, 1946). *Books on the history and culture of Italy or on travel to Italy.*

"Casey at the Bat" is first printed in the *San Francisco Examiner* (June 3, 1888). *Books on baseball and baseball players, accompanied by a reproduction of the Casey poem.*

Death of Muhammad (June 8, 632). *Books about Islam, the life of Muhammad, and Moslem countries.*

Birthday of Frank Lloyd Wright, architect (June 8, 1867). *Biographies of Wright and other architects, or books on architecture.*

Birthday of Maurice Sendak, children's author and illustrator (June 10, 1928). *Books by Sendak or exhibit promoting the library's services for children.*

Alcoholics Anonymous is founded (June 10, 1935). *Books on Alcoholics Anonymous and similar twelve-step programs, perhaps accompanied by information on where alcoholics can find help in your area.*

Philippines Independence Day (June 12, 1898). *Books on the history and culture of the Philippines or on travel to the Philippines.*

Birthday of George Bush, forty-first president (June 12, 1924). *Books on Bush or on the American presidency.*

Birthday of William Butler Yeats, poet (June 13, 1865). *Books of Yeats's poetry, along with works by other early twentieth-century poets.*

Birthday of Jon Bartlett, editor of Bartlett's Quotations (June 14, 1820). *Display of quotes from* Bartlett's Quotations, *along with the books that these quotes were originally drawn from.*

First commercial computer (Univac I) is demonstrated (June 14, 1951). *Books about computers, languages, and computer programming, as well as a display pointing out your library's computer facilities.*

Magna Carta is signed (June 15, 1215). *Books on English history or on the evolution of democratic government.*

Arkansas becomes the twenty-fifth state (June 15, 1836). *Books on the history of Arkansas or on travel to Arkansas.*

Bloomsday (June 16). *A display devoted to the life and works of James Joyce, or a display centered on* Ulysses *and the controversy surrounding its publication in the United States.*

Birthday of Igor Stravinsky, composer (June 17, 1882). *Biographies of Stravinsky or a display promoting your library's collection of classical recordings and sheet music.*

West Virginia becomes the thirty-fifth state (June 20, 1863). *Books on the history of West Virginia or on travel to West Virginia.*

First day of summer (June 21). *Exhibit introducing new titles for summer reading or poster kicking off summer reading program.*

New Hampshire becomes the ninth state (June 21, 1788). *Books on the history of New Hampshire or on travel to New Hampshire and New England.*

First reported sighting of flying saucers (June 24, 1947). *Books on UFOs and unexplained phenomena, or pulp science fiction novels.*

Virginia becomes the tenth state (June 25, 1788). *Books on the history of Virginia or on travel to Virginia and the southern states.*

Custer's Last Stand at the Battle of Little Big Horn (June 25, 1876). *Books on the battle and the Indian wars, as well as on the history of westward expansion in the United States.*

Birthday of George Orwell, novelist and social critic (June 25, 1903). *Books by Orwell, or display of anti-utopian novels such as Orwell's* 1984, *Huxley's* Brave New World, *and Burgess's* A Clockwork Orange.

Birthday of Pearl S. Buck, author (June 26, 1892). *Books by Buck, including* The Good Earth, Sons, *and* A House Divided.

James Smithson, founder of Smithsonian Institution, dies (June 27, 1829). *Books about the Smithsonian museums or on travel to Washington, D.C.*

Birthday of Helen Adams Keller, author and lecturer (June 27, 1880). *Books by Keller, including* The Story of My Life *and* Helen Keller's Journal, *as well as books about her achievements.*

First Newbery medal is awarded (June 27, 1922). *Newbery medal–winning books such as* The Twenty-One Balloons, A Wrinkle in Time, *and* Bridge to Terabithia.

Beginning of World War I (Archduke Ferdinand and wife assassinated, June 28, 1914), **and end of World War I** (Treaty of Versailles signed, June 28, 1919). *Books on World War I or on twentieth-century European history.*

Pure Food and Drug Act and Meat Inspection Act are passed (June 30, 1906). *Books on social reform by muckrakers such as Upton Sinclair, Ida Tarbell, and Lincoln Steffens.*

JULY

Canada Day (July 1). *Books on the history and culture of Canada or on travel to Canada.*

Halfway point of the year (July 1). *TIME TO REVIEW YOUR NEW YEAR'S RESOLUTIONS: display of self-help books on such subjects as dieting, curing procrastination, and quitting smoking.*

Medicare program is started (July 1, 1966). *Books on the American health care system or on personal health and fitness.*

Civil Rights Act of 1964 is signed by President Lyndon B. Johnson (July 2, 1964). *Books on the history of the civil rights movement and its leaders, as well as books on present-day civil rights activism.*

Dog days of summer (July 3 through August 15). *READING TO KEEP YOU COOL, with books on topics such as Alaska, ice cream, and skiing.*

Idaho becomes the forty-third state (July 3, 1890). *Books on the history of Idaho or on travel to Idaho and the Northwest.*

Birthday of Louis Armstrong, musician (July 4, 1900). *Biographies of Armstrong and other jazz musicians, or a display promoting your library's collection of jazz records, tapes, and CDs.*

Birthday of Neil Simon, playwright (July 4, 1927). *Books of Simon's plays, along with comic plays by other contemporary playwrights.*

Independence Day (July 4). *Display of American history books, books on the history of fireworks, barbecue cookbooks, or recordings of John Phillip Sousa marches.*

Wyoming becomes the forty-fourth state (July 10, 1890). *Books on the history of Wyoming or on travel to Wyoming and the western states.*

Birthday of E. B. White, author, essayist (July 11, 1899). *Include his books for children (Charlotte's Web, Stuart Little) and his collected essays for the New Yorker.*

Birthday of Bill Cosby, actor and comedian (July 12, 1938). *Books and records by Cosby, or a poster promoting your library's collection of comedy recordings.*

France: Bastille Day (July 14). *Books on the history and culture of France, travel to France, or the French language.*

Birthday of Henry David Thoreau, author (July 14, 1817). *Include his classic books Walden, On the Duty of Civil Disobedience, and Excursions.*

Birthday of Gerald R. Ford, thirty-eighth president (July 14, 1913). *Books on Ford's presidency in the post-Watergate years.*

District of Columbia becomes U.S. capital (July 16, 1790). *Books on travel to Washington, D.C.*

Birthday of Nelson Mandela, South African civil rights leader (July 17, 1918). *Biographies of Mandela or books on the history and politics of South Africa.*

Birthday of Edgar Degas, painter (July 19, 1834). *Books about Degas and his works, books on painting techniques, or an exhibit promoting your library's poster rental collection.*

Neil Armstrong becomes the first man on the moon (July 20, 1969). *Biographies of astronauts or books on NASA and space travel.*

Birthday of Ernest Hemingway, author (July 21, 1899). *Books by Hemingway, along with works by other Lost Generation authors.*

Birthday of Isaac Stern, violinist (July 21, 1920). *Biographies of Stern and other classical musicians, or a display promoting your library's collection of classical recordings and sheet music.*

Poland: National Liberation Day (July 22). *Books on the history and culture of Poland, books on travel to Poland and eastern Europe, or books about notable Polish Americans.*

Birthday of Amelia Earhart, aviator (July 24, 1898). *Biographies of Earhart and other early aviators, or books on the history of air travel.*

John T. Scopes is found guilty of teaching evolution in school (July 24, 1925). *Books on the Scopes trial, as well as on the evolution-creationism debate and the conflicts between church and state.*

Birthday of Louise Brown, first test-tube baby (July 25, 1978). *Books on medical science, infertility, or medical ethics.*

New York becomes the eleventh state (July 26, 1788). *Books on the history of New York or on travel to New York.*

Birthday of George Bernard Shaw, playwright (July 26, 1856). *Books by Shaw, along with works by other Irish playwrights and authors.*

First permanent transatlantic cable is completed (July 27, 1866). *Books on the history of communications as well as on new telecommunications technology.*

Birthday of Beatrix Potter, children's author (July 28, 1866). *Include some of her best-loved books, such as* The Tale of Peter Rabbit *and* Mr. Jeremy Fisher.

Birthday of Henry Ford, inventor (July 30, 1863). *Books about the inventor and his contributions to the automobile industry and manufacturing.*

AUGUST

Birthday of Herman Melville, author (August 1, 1819). *Books by Melville, along with recommended adventure books by other authors.*

Birthday of Ernie Pyle, journalist (August 3, 1900). *Include books of his collected columns:* Ernie Pyle in England, Here Is Your War, *and* Brave Men.

John Peter Zenger is acquitted of libel (August 4, 1735). *Books on the history of journalism and on freedom of the press.*

Colorado becomes the thirty-eighth state (August 6, 1876). *Books on the history of Colorado or on travel to Colorado and the western states.*

Japan Peace Festival, in commemoration of the first atomic bomb being dropped on Hiroshima (August 6, 1945). *Books on the history of atomic weapons and on the peace movement.*

Birthday of Herbert Hoover, thirty-first president (August 10, 1874). *Books on the Great Depression and the Hoover era.*

Missouri becomes the twenty-fourth state (August 10, 1921). *Books on the history of Missouri or on travel to Missouri and the Midwest.*

Birthday of Alex Haley, author of *Roots* (August 11, 1921). *Books by Alex Haley, or exhibit on tracing one's family history.*

Birthday of Alfred Hitchcock, movie director (August 13, 1899). *Books about Hitchcock and his films, or a display promoting your library's film series or videotape collection.*

Social Security Act is passed (August 14, 1935). *Books on social programs in the United States.*

V-J (Victory over Japan) Day (August 14, 1945). *Books on the Pacific campaign during World War II.*

Anniversary of Woodstock festival (August 15, 1969). *Colorful, 1960s-style display featuring recordings by musicians who performed at Woodstock, or books about the music of the 1960s.*

Robert Fulton's steamboat first sails (August 17, 1807). *Books on the history of steam power and its commercial use.*

Birthday of Virginia Dare, first European born in America (August 18, 1587). *Books on early history of the American colonies.*

National Aviation Day (August 19). *Books on aircraft, history of flight, and model airplane building.*

Birthday of Ogden Nash, poet (August 19, 1902). *Books of poetry by Nash, along with works by other humorous poets.*

Hawaii becomes the fiftieth state (August 21, 1959). *Books on the history and culture of Hawaii or on travel to Hawaii.*

Birthday of Claude Debussy, composer (August 22, 1862). *Biographies of Debussy and other French composers, or a display promoting your library's collection of classical recordings and sheet music.*

Vesuvius erupts (August 24, in the year 79). *Books about Vesuvius and other volcanos, or about the ancient cities of Pompeii and Herculaneum.*

Birthday of Leonard Bernstein, composer and conductor (August 25, 1918). *Biographies of Bernstein, or a display promoting your library's recordings of classical music and Broadway scores.*

Women's Equality Day (August 26). *Exhibit about career choices open to women, with biographies of women in science, medicine, politics, academics, and other traditionally male-dominated fields.*

Birthday of Geraldine Ferraro, politician (August 26, 1935). *Biographies of women in politics or books about the 1984 presidential election campaign.*

Birthday of Lyndon B. Johnson, thirty-sixth president (August 27, 1908). *Biographies of Johnson and other American presidents, or books about the Vietnam War.*

Birthday of Mother Theresa, humanitarian (August 27, 1910). *A display on volunteerism, suggesting local organizations to which library users can volunteer their time and talents.*

Birthday of Oliver Wendell Holmes, Supreme Court justice (August 29, 1809). *Books on the history of the American legal system or on controversial legal issues.*

SEPTEMBER

School opens (date varies; usually first week in September). *Poster or exhibit introducing your library's reference services—what reference aids are available and how to use them.*

Labor Day (first Monday in September). *Books about the history of the American labor movement or biographies of labor leaders.*

American Indian Day (fourth Friday in September). *Books on Native American history, culture, and beliefs.*

Rosh Hashanah (Jewish New Year; date varies according to Hebrew calendar, but usually falls in September). *Books about the history, beliefs, and practice of Judaism.*

Birthday of Confucius, philosopher (date varies according to Chinese calendar, 551 B.C.). *Biographies of philosophers, ancient and modern.*

Henry Hudson enters New York harbor (September 3, 1609). *Books on Hudson and the exploration of North America.*

First meeting of the Continental Congress (September 5, 1774). *Books on the early history of the United States, as well as on the early struggle for independence from Britain.*

Birthday of Jane Addams, social leader (September 6, 1860). *Books on her life as well as on the founding of Hull House in Chicago.*

California becomes the thirty-first state (September 9, 1850). *Books on the history of California or on travel to California.*

Ellis Island reopens as a museum (September 9, 1990). *Books on European immigration and Ellis Island, perhaps accompanied by a model of the Statue of Liberty.*

Birthday of O. Henry (William Sydney Porter), writer (September 11, 1862). *Anthologies containing O. Henry stories and short stories by other writers.*

Birthday of Jesse Owens, Olympic gold medalist (September 12, 1913). GOLD MEDAL READING: *Biographies of Olympic athletes.*

Birthday of Agatha Christie, mystery writer (September 15, 1890). *Books by Christie, along with works by other mystery writers.*

Pilgrims leave Plymouth, England, for the New World (September 16, 1620). *Books on the first English settlers in America and the early colonies.*

U.S. Constitution signed (September 17, 1787). *Books on the framing of the Constitution or on constitutional law.*

Autumn begins (September 21). *Books on fall fashions, indoor sports, travel to New England, or knitting.*

Birthday of H. G. Wells, writer (September 21, 1866). *Books by Wells and other early science fiction writers, perhaps in a "time machine" setting.*

Birthday of Stephen King, novelist (September 21, 1947). *Books by King and other modern horror writers, or a poster promoting the library's collection of recorded books by King and others.*

Office of Postmaster General instituted (September 22, 1789). *Books on stamps and stamp collecting.*

Ice cream cone patented (September 22, 1903). *Display of dessert cookbooks containing recipes for cakes, pies, chocolate, and ice cream.*

Birthday of Ray Charles, musician (September 23, 1930). *Biographies of Charles and other rhythm-and-blues artists, or a display promoting your library's collection of rhythm-and-blues records, tapes, and CDs.*

Birthday of Jim Henson, puppeteer (September 24, 1936). *Books about puppets and puppet-making, or Sesame Street books featuring Henson's Muppet characters.*

Birthday of William Faulkner, writer (September 25, 1897). *Books by Faulkner, including* As I Lay Dying, The Sound and the Fury, *and* Go Down, Moses. *Include criticisms of his work and biographies of the author.*

Birthday of T. S. Eliot, poet (September 26, 1888). *Books of Eliot's poems, along with works by other twentieth-century poets.*

Birthday of George Gershwin, composer (September 26, 1898). *Books about Gershwin and other Broadway composers, or a display promoting your library's collection of Broadway show recordings and sheet music.*

Birthday of Enrico Fermi, physicist (September 29, 1901). *Books about Fermi and his studies in nuclear physics.*

OCTOBER

Columbus Day (second Monday in October). *Books on Columbus and other explorers, or on notable Italian Americans.*

Fire Prevention Week (second week in October). *Exhibit on fire prevention, using materials provided by your local fire department.*

World Series (date varies). *Books on the history of baseball, biographies of great players, and books of statistics.*

Nobel prizes are announced (date varies). *Books about and by winners of Nobel prizes for literature, peace, chemistry, physics, economics, and medicine.*

Supreme Court convenes (date varies). *Books about the U.S. judicial system and its history, law, and landmark cases.*

Germany: Oktoberfest (date varies). *Books on the history and culture of Germany, on travel to Germany, or on brewing beer.*

Standard Time resumes (last Sunday in October). *BOOKS FOR THOSE DARK NIGHTS, featuring thrillers and adventure stories.*

United Nations Universal Children's Day (first Monday in October). *A display decorated by local children, featuring folktales from around the world.*

Birthday of Jimmy Carter, thirty-ninth president (October 1, 1924). *Books by Carter* (Keeping the Faith: Memoirs of a President *and* The Blood of Abraham); *books about the Carter years.*

Gandhi Jayanti: birthday of Mohandas K. Gandhi, Indian political leader (October 2, 1869). *Books on his life and teachings.*

Korean National Day, Tangun Day (October 3). *Books on the history and culture of Korea or on travel to Korea.*

10-4 day for radio operators (October 4). *Books on ham radio, citizen's band radio, and other radio-related hobbies.*

America Library Association founded (October 6, 1876). *Poster or exhibit on the history of the ALA.*

Birthday of Yo Yo Ma, cellist (October 7, 1955). *Biographies of Ma and other classical musicians, or a display promoting your library's collection of classical recordings and sheet music.*

Birthday of Jesse Jackson, politician (October 8, 1941). *Biographies of Jackson and other black civil rights leaders.*

Leif Erikson Day, celebrating Erikson's discovery of North America (October 9, 1000). *Books on Scandinavia, on the Vikings, or on ancient explorers.*

Birthday of Giuseppe Verdi, composer (October 10, 1813). *Biographies of Verdi and other opera composers, or a display promoting your library's collection of opera recordings and sheet music.*

Birthday of Harold Pinter, playwright (October 10, 1930). *Plays by Pinter, along with works by other British playwrights.*

Birthday of Martina Navratilova, tennis star (October 10, 1956). *Biographies and autobiographies of tennis players.*

Pulaski Memorial Day (October 11). *Books about General Casimir Pulaski and his role during the American Revolution, as well as books on other distinguished Polish Americans.*

Birthday of Eleanor Roosevelt, humanitarian and United Nations delegate (October 11, 1884). *Include her books, such as* This Is My Story, This I Remember, *and* On My Own.

Dia de la Raza (October 12). *Books about Mexico and Latin America, as well as books on contributions of Spanish civilization to the American continent.*

Birthday of Dwight D. Eisenhower, thirty-fourth president (October 14, 1890). *Books about Eisenhower and his years as president, including his book* The White House Years.

World Poetry Day (October 15). *Include books of poetry around the world.*

Birthday of Friedrich Wilhelm Nietzsche, philosopher (October 15, 1844). *Books by Nietzsche and other German philosophers.*

Birthday of Lee Iacocca, businessman (October 15, 1924). *Biographies and autobiographies of contemporary business leaders.*

Birthday of Noah Webster, lexicographer (October 16, 1758). *Exhibit introducing the variety of dictionaries available in the library (for example, etymological dictionaries, dictionaries of slang, dictionaries in specific fields, foreign language dictionaries).*

Black Poetry Day (October 17). *Books of poetry by, and biographies of, black poets.*

Birthday of Arthur Miller, playwright (October 17, 1915). *Books of Miller's plays, along with works by other contemporary playwrights.*

Birthday of John Le Carré, novelist (October 19, 1931). *Books by Le Carré and other spy and adventure novelists, or a poster promoting the library's collection of recorded books by Le Carré and others.*

Birthday of Christopher Wren, architect (October 20, 1632). *Biographies of Wren and other architects, or books on architecture.*

Thomas Edison lights first incandescent bulb (October 21, 1879). *Books about Edison and other inventors whose discoveries changed the world.*

Birthday of Sarah Josepha Hale, author and editor (October 24, 1788). *Books by and about Hale, as well as copies (or facsimiles) of* Godey's Lady's Book.

United Nations Day, celebrating the founding of the United Nations (October 24, 1945). *Books on the history of the United Nations.*

Geoffrey Chaucer, English poet, dies (October 25, 1400). *Books on the history of the English language.*

Birthday of Pablo Picasso, artist (October 25, 1881). *Books about Picasso and his works, books on painting techniques, or an exhibit promoting your library's poster rental collection.*

Erie Canal opens (October 26, 1825). *Books on the Erie Canal and its impact on U.S. transportation.*

Birthday of Dylan Thomas, poet (October 27, 1914). *Books of Thomas's poetry, along with works by other twentieth-century British poets.*

Harvard University is founded (October 28, 1636). *Books on the university and its distinguished alumni, and books on higher education in the United States.*

Statue of Liberty dedicated (October 28, 1886). *Books by and about immigrant Americans.*

Stock market crash (October 29, 1929). *Books on the stock market and the Great Depression.*

Orson Welles frightens America with *War of the Worlds* **broadcast** (October 30, 1938). *Display promoting your library's collection of spoken word recordings.*

Halloween (October 31). *Horror novels, mystery books, books on the occult and witchcraft, or books on making masks and costumes.*

Nevada becomes the thirty-sixth state (October 31, 1864). *Books on the history of Nevada or on travel to Nevada and the southwestern states.*

NOVEMBER

Election Day (first Tuesday after the first Monday in November). *Books on the political process, political participation, the American presidency, or political parties, perhaps with names of recommended books arranged on a "ballot."*

Sadie Hawkins Day (first Saturday in November). *Books on sexual mores, past and present.*

Thanksgiving (last Thursday in November.) *Cookbooks.*

Birthday of Daniel Boone, frontiersman (November 2, 1734). *Fiction and nonfiction books about life on the frontier.*

North Dakota becomes the thirty-ninth state; South Dakota becomes the fortieth state (November 2, 1889). *Books on the history of the Dakotas, or on travel to the Dakotas and the northern states.*

King Tutankhamen's tomb is discovered (November 4, 1922). *Books on ancient Egyptian civilization or on archaeology, perhaps displayed as treasures in an Egyptian burial chamber.*

Birthday of Adolphe Sax, inventor of the saxophone (November 5, 1814). *Books on the history of musical instruments, or music instruction books.*

Birthday of John Philip Sousa, composer (November 5, 1854). *Biographies of Sousa, or a display promoting your library's collection of march recordings and sheet music.*

Soviet Revolution Day (November 7). *Books on Russian and Soviet history, culture, and political change.*

Birthday of Marie Curie, chemist and physicist (November 7, 1867). *Biographies of Curie and of other Nobel prize–winning scientists.*

Montana becomes the forty-first state (November 8, 1889). *Books on the history of Montana or books on travel to Montana and the western states.*

X-Ray Discovery Day (November 8, 1895). *Books on medical science, past and present.*

Birthday of Carl Sagan, astronomer (November 8, 1934). *Books by Sagan, perhaps accompanied by other books about space and astronomy.*

Crystal Night (November 9). *Books on the original* Krystallnacht *riots in 1938 and on Jewish life under the Nazi regime.*

Birthday of Martin Luther, religious leader (November 10, 1483). *Books on the history, beliefs, and practices of the protestant religions.*

Veterans' Day (November 11). *Display honoring American veterans or poster offering information on veterans' benefits.*

Birthday of Fyodor Dostoyevsky, novelist (November 11, 1821). *Books by Dostoyevsky, along with works by other nineteenth-century Russian authors.*

Washington becomes the forty-second state (November 11, 1889). *Books on the history of Washington State or on travel to Washington and the Pacific Northwest.*

Birthday of Auguste Rodin, sculptor (November 12, 1840). *Books about Rodin and his works or books on sculpture techniques.*

Vietnam War Memorial is dedicated (November 13, 1982). *Books about the Vietnam War, veterans, and novels about the Vietnam experience.*

Birthday of Claude Monet, painter (November 14, 1840). *Books about Monet and other Impressionists, books on painting techniques, or an exhibit promoting your library's poster rental collection.*

Great American Smokeout (November 15). *Books on how to quit smoking, accompanied by posters from the American Heart Association, the American Lung Association, or the American Cancer Society.*

Oklahoma becomes the forty-sixth state (November 16, 1907). *Books on the history of Oklahoma or on travel to Oklahoma and the Midwest.*

Canal treaty is signed by Panama and the United States (November 18, 1903). *Books on the Panama Canal and on shipping.*

Mickey Mouse first appears, in *Steamboat Willie* (November 18, 1928). *Books on the life and work of Walt Disney, along with other books on cartoons and cartooning.*

Lincoln's Gettysburg Address (November 19, 1863). *Books of historic speeches or books on public speaking.*

North Carolina becomes the twelfth state (November 21, 1789). *Books on the history of North Carolina or on travel to the Carolinas.*

John F. Kennedy is assassinated (November 22, 1963). *Books about Kennedy's presidency or the latest speculative accounts of his assassination.*

Birthday of Billy the Kid, legendary outlaw (November 23, 1859). *Fiction and nonfiction books about life in the "wild west."*

Sojourner Truth Day (in anniversary of her death, November 26, 1883). *Books about Truth and her struggle for abolition and for women's rights.*

Birthday of Charles Schulz, cartoonist (November 26, 1922). *"Peanuts" books by Schulz, along with books about Schulz and other cartoonists.*

Birthday of Louisa May Alcott, novelist (November 29, 1832). *Books by Alcott, along with other classics for young adults.*

Birthday of Mark Twain (Samuel Clemens), author (November 30, 1835). *Books by Mark Twain, along with other adventure novels for young readers.*

DECEMBER

Army-Navy football game (second Saturday in December). *Books about football and football players.*

Hanukkah (date varies according to the Hebrew calendar). *Books about Hanukkah and Judaism, surrounded by traditional symbols of the season (a menorah, a dreidel, gifts).*

Rosa Parks Day, commemorating Parks's refusal to give up her seat on a public bus (December 1, 1955). *Books on the civil rights movement.*

Illinois becomes the twenty-first state (December 3, 1818). *Books on the history of Illinois or on travel to Illinois and the Midwest.*

Prohibition is repealed (December 5, 1933). *Bartending guides and books of drink recipes in a barroom setting, perhaps accompanied by a poster on drunk driving.*

AFL-CIO is formed by merger (December 5, 1955). *Books about the history of the American labor movement, or biographies of labor leaders.*

Delaware is the first state to sign the Constitution (December 7, 1787). *Books on the history of Delaware or on travel to Delaware and the mid-Atlantic states.*

Pearl Harbor Day (December 7, 1941). *Books on World War II or on the Japanese internment camps.*

Birthday of Clarence Birdseye, who perfected the deep-freeze method of preserving food (December 9, 1925). *Books on the technology of food processing, or cookbooks containing frozen-food recipes.*

Human Rights Day (December 10). *Books on international human rights, the United Nations, or Amnesty International.*

Birthday of Thomas Gallaudet, founder of Gallaudet University for the deaf (December 10, 1787). *Books about signing for the deaf, or biographies of people with hearing impairments and other disabilities.*

Mississippi becomes the twentieth state (December 10, 1817). *Books on the history of Mississippi or on travel to Mississippi and the southern states.*

Birthday of Emily Dickinson, poet (December 10, 1830). *Books of Dickinson's poetry, along with works by other American female poets.*

Indiana becomes the nineteenth state (December 11, 1816). *Books on the history of Indiana or on travel to Indiana.*

Birthday of Aleksandr I. Solzhenitsyn, author (December 11, 1918). *Books by Solzhenitsyn, along with other works by Russian and Soviet writers.*

Pennsylvania becomes the second state (December 12, 1787). *Books on the history of Pennsylvania or on travel to Pennsylvania and the mid-Atlantic states.*

Guglielmo Marconi sends first radio transmission (December 12, 1901). *Books on Marconi, the history of radio, and on building shortwave radios.*

Alabama becomes the twenty-second state (December 14, 1819). *Books on the history of Alabama or on travel to Alabama and the southern states.*

Roald Amundsen and his team reach the South Pole (December 14, 1911). *Books on Amundsen, Antarctica, and polar exploration.*

Bill of Rights Day (December 15). *Books dealing with civil rights, censorship, church-state conflicts, and other First Amendment issues.*

Birthday of Ludwig van Beethoven, composer (December 16, 1770). *Biographies of Beethoven, or a display promoting your library's collection of classical recordings and sheet music.*

Boston Tea Party (December 16, 1773). *Books on the American Revolution, or books on the history and customs surrounding tea (for example, cookbooks containing recipes for teas, iced teas, and tea cakes).*

Birthday of Margaret Mead, anthropologist (December 16, 1901). *Books by and about Mead and other anthropologists, or general books about anthropology.*

Wright Brothers' first flight (December 17, 1903). *Books on the history and principles of aviation or on famous inventors.*

New Jersey becomes the third state (December 18, 1787). *Books on the history of New Jersey or on travel to New Jersey and the mid-Atlantic states.*

Birthday of Ty Cobb, baseball player (December 18, 1886). *Biographies and autobiographies of baseball players.*

Louisiana Purchase (December 20, 1803). *Books about the Purchase, as well as books on the exploration of and expansion into the western United States.*

Winter begins (December 21). *Recommendations for reading by the fire: new titles and classics.*

Christmas (December 25). *Cookbooks for Christmas dinner, craft books for making Christmas gifts, or books on Christmas observances around the world.*

Kwanzaa, a family observance in recognition of traditional African harvest festivals (December 26 through January 1). *Books that celebrate African and African American culture.*

Birthday of Louis Pasteur, chemist (December 27, 1822). *Books on Pasteur, microbiology, and preventive medicine.*

Iowa becomes the twenty-ninth state (December 28, 1846). *Books on the history of Iowa or on travel to Iowa and the Midwest.*

Texas becomes the twenty-eighth state (December 29, 1845). *Books on the history of Texas or on travel to Texas.*

Generic Display Templates

The following pages contain models, or templates, for the kinds of displays listed most frequently in appendix D: geographical displays, biographical displays, and displays that commemorate a historical event. By referring to these templates, you can design your own displays much more quickly.

Each template uses general phrases as placeholders for specific names and dates. Template 3, for example, says HAPPY BIRTHDAY, PERSON'S NAME. You, of course, will want to substitute an actual name for the phrase PERSON'S NAME. Similarly, the phrase MONTH DAY, YEAR is used in all the templates to show where a date—such as JULY 4, 1776—should be inserted.

Each template also includes several white numerals in black circles. These numerals are not part of the design; they refer to notes in the text that accompanies each template.

Because these templates are intended to work for many possible displays in a single, broad category, they are, of necessity, less exciting than custom-made designs. Template 1, for example, is suitable for a display about the state of Washington, but you can probably come up with other ideas (such as designs that incorporate lumber or models of totem poles) that would be much more interesting. For this reason, these templates are recommended only as a last resort—for those occasions when you are in a hurry and your imagination has run dry.

When you do use the templates, feel free to use them creatively. Template 1, for example, though intended for a state, can easily be used for a foreign country; similarly, template 2 can be adapted for a state. Template 3 can be used to draw attention to places and things as well as to people. Template 4 can present virtually any sort of information, not just historical events.

Keep in mind that the sample projects in chapters 6 through 9 also can be used as templates for displays on a variety of topics.

TEMPLATE 1
POSTER: STATE ADMISSION DAY

This display can be produced on any scale, from notebook-size to wall-size, using materials that you probably already have on hand. The most time-consuming part of the project will be research, as you look for the most interesting details about each state.

Notes

1. The heading for the display can be produced any way you like. For small displays, you will probably want to use felt-tip markers or rub-on lettering. For larger displays, you might prefer to use paint, stick-on lettering, or cutout lettering.

2. You may want to use a different color for the state name than for the rest of the heading. For states with long names (such as New Hampshire), you will have to use smaller lettering or break the name into two lines.

3. These two lines can be omitted if the date of the display does not coincide with the state's admission day.

4. The outline of the state can be photocopied from a map, then traced onto a sheet of colored paper. If you wish, mount the state on cardboard and make it pop out from the display by means of a hidden cardboard support.

5. Each sheet of paper surrounding the state map should have a heading similar to those shown in the template. (The topics shown are only suggestions; you may prefer other headings such as PRODUCTS AND INDUSTRIES or FAMOUS PEOPLE FROM [NAME].) The space below the headings may be used for lists, illustrations, or both.

Depending on the shape of the state, you may need to change the number, shapes, and arrangement of the pieces of paper.

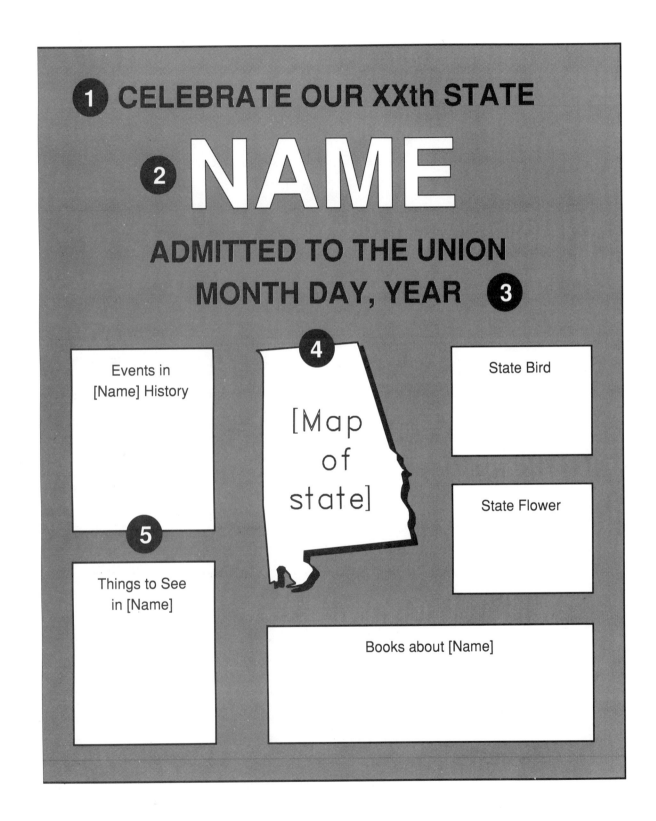

TEMPLATE 2
EXHIBIT: COUNTRY NATIONAL DAY

This design takes advantage of the three-dimensional space that an enclosed case provides. If you do not have a display case, you may be able to adapt this design to a wall display with pop-outs.

Notes

1. The heading is lettered on a cloth or paper banner that spans the width of the display case. The banner may be mounted on the back wall or suspended from the ceiling.

   You can use paint or cutout lettering for the text of the banner. You can also print the banner with a computer and printer. (If you use a computer and printer, however, you may have to redesign the banner; most banner software does not allow two lines to be printed on one banner.)

2. Use a wall-size world map (available from most stationery stores), or copy a smaller map onto a larger sheet of paper. (If you wish, use a map of the appropriate continent rather than a map of the world.)

   The arrow that points out the country should be made of stiff cardboard. Glue a triangular wedge underneath the arrow so that its tail stands out from the map.

3. You can use pictures, book jackets, or both to decorate the sides of the display. The pictures may be hand-drawn, cut from magazines, or enlarged from clip art; the book jackets may be real or hand-drawn imitations.

   The pictures or book jackets should be mounted on stiff cardboard, then taped to lengths of string or wire and suspended from the ceiling of the display case.

4. The books are displayed in an open suitcase. You may want to use a real suitcase, or else make a fake one from an appropriately shaped cardboard box. The books may be displayed lying down (as if packed), or else propped up on stands.

   If you do not want the display to have a travel theme, place the books on pedestals or omit them entirely.

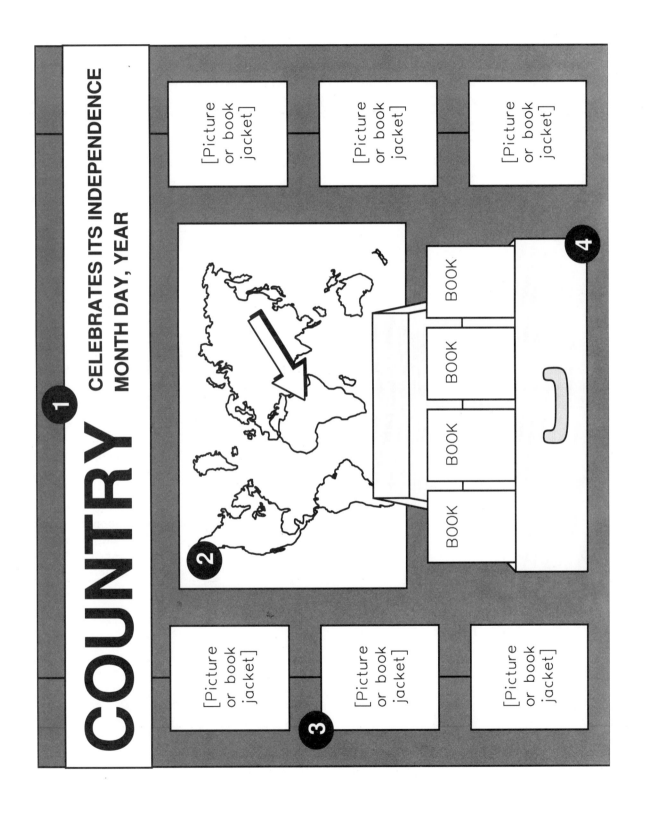

TEMPLATE 3
TABLETOP DISPLAY: NOTABLE PERSON'S BIRTHDAY

This display works best propped up on a table, with a selection of books in front of it. Mount the display on stiff cardboard, and use a sign support to hold it upright. If that is not practical, mount the cardboard on the wall and push the table (with books on it) against the wall.

Notes

1. If the event being commemorated is a death rather than a birth, you will need to replace this line with IN REMEMBRANCE OF, or else omit it entirely.

    See template 1, note 1, for suggestions about how to do the lettering.

2. You may want to experiment with different styles of lettering for different people's names—for example, glue lettering (with sparkles or sequins) for a movie star, or flowery script for a poet.

3. You may want to omit the title or profession for someone who is very well known (such as George Washington).

4. The picture may be hand-drawn or copied from a book. If you cannot get a picture of the person you are commemorating, use another appropriate picture—for example, a picture of a white whale for Herman Melville or a picture of a cane for Charlie Chaplin.

5. The symbols next to the picture should give some idea of what the person is famous for. For example, the pencil (on the left) might indicate a writer; the musical note (on the right) might indicate a musician. Other possibilities include a paintbrush for an artist, a bat for a baseball player, or a strip of film for a movie actor.

6. The books are displayed in front of the poster, propped up between bookends. If this arrangement is not practical, attach book jackets directly to the poster, or display a list of books instead of the books themselves.

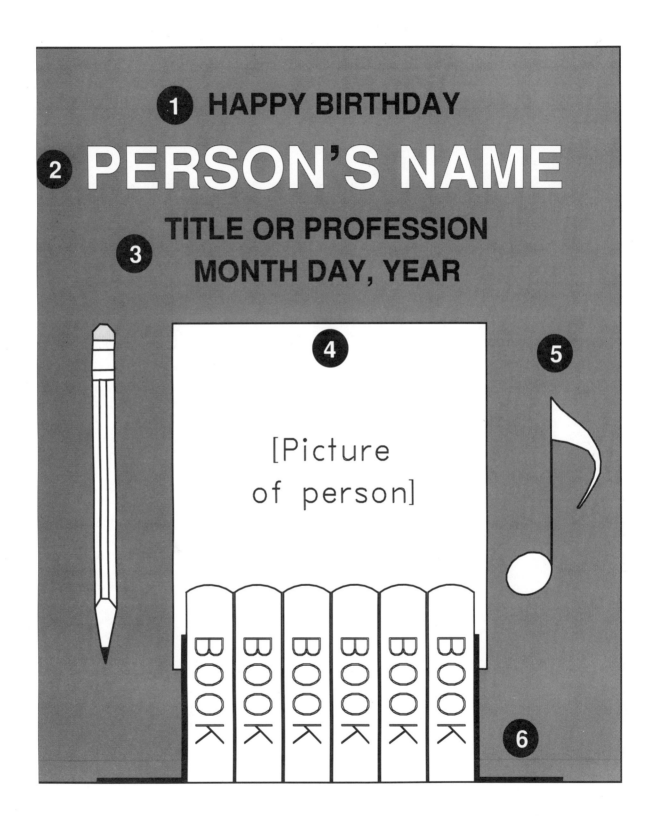

TEMPLATE 4
POSTER: HISTORICAL EVENT

This design can be rearranged to fit a space of virtually any size or shape. The circles are intended to contrast with the other elements (book jackets, pictures, and news clippings), which are typically rectangular. If you wish, substitute other interesting shapes for the circles.

Notes

1. The circles should be made from stiff cardboard. Place cardboard supports underneath to make the circles pop out from the display. The lettering on the circles is best done with paint, felt-tip markers, or stick-on lettering.

2. For greatest impact, describe the event briefly, in headline style, as is done in Appendix D. Notice that the lettering for the event is larger than that on the other two circles; you may want to make it a different color as well.

3. The arrangement of book jackets, magazine articles, and other items shown here is purely arbitrary. Depending on what event your display is commemorating, your arrangement may look very different. For events of more than a century ago, you will have to rely much more on book jackets and pictures than on news clippings. For very recent events, you may have many articles from periodicals and very few books.

   After you have gathered your items, lay them on a table and move them around until you have found an arrangement you like. Fasten them to the display with pushpins, glue, or loops of tape.

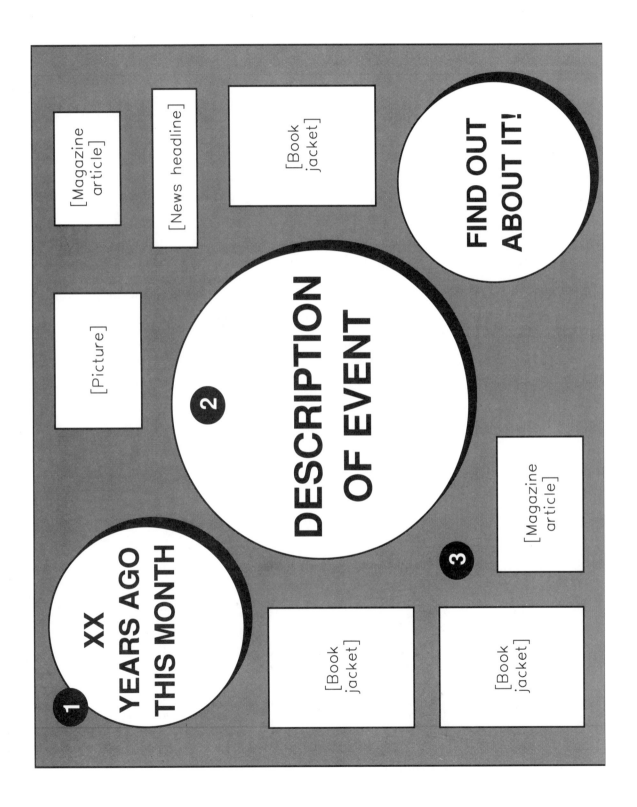

Index